# They're All My Children

# They're All My Children

*Foster Mothering in America*

Danielle F. Wozniak

NEW YORK UNIVERSITY PRESS
*New York and London*

NEW YORK UNIVERSITY PRESS
New York and London

Library of Congress Cataloging-in-Publication Data
Wozniak, Danielle F.
They're all my children : foster mothering in America /
Danielle F. Wozniak.
p. cm.
Includes bibliographical references and index.
ISBN 0–8147–9346–0 (cloth : alk. paper) —
ISBN 0–8147–9347–9 (pbk. : alk. paper)
1. Foster mothers—United States.
2. Foster home care—United States.   I. Title.
HV881 .W68 2001
362.73'3'0973—dc21          2001004428

New York University Press books are printed on acid-free paper,
and their binding materials are chosen for strength and durability.

Manufactured in the United States of America

10 9 8 7 6 5 4 3 2 1

*For my daughters, Jackie, Yajaira, and Eliana*

# Contents

# Acknowledgments

No book is ever the sole endeavor of an author. It takes a host of people working together, supporting an author, to make the vision of a book a reality. I would like to thank those who sustained me through this process and made this work possible. First and foremost I would like to thank the women, men, and children who participated in my research. They welcomed me into their homes and lives and shared with me some of their most intimate experiences and dreams. I was consistently left with an overwhelming sense of gratitude that such women exist and a sense of awe that they are able to persevere.

Second, I would like to thank those who supported me in my professional growth and development. W. Penn Handwerker, Irene Glasser and Robert Dewar believed in this project from the beginning. Their guidance, insight, and scholarship were invaluable. Linda Layne offered insightful editing and commentary and has consistently supported my work. It is she who actively helped me to pursue a publisher and actualize this book. I would also like to thank my social work colleagues at Western Michigan University for their support. I would especially like to thank Linwood Cousins. It is not easy to have work that spans disciplines. While it means that one's scholarship potentially has a wider audience, it just as often means that one feels professionally homeless. It was this latter issue to which my colleagues were sensitive, and my friend Professor Cousins was a fellow traveler. He consistently offered a critique of my work from both an anthropological and a social work perspective and often joined with me in the process of finding an intellectual home.

Third, I would like to thank those in my personal life who made this book possible. I would like to thank Daniel and Helen Wozniak, my parents, who arrived, like the cavalry, to keep my house, tend my gardens, read and edit the terrible punctuation and spelling in my manuscript, and watch my baby while I wrote. Like so many things in my life, I could not have done it without them. I would also like to thank Karen Costello, my au pair extraordinaire, who kept my baby busy and happy and, most of all, kept her from missing her mother so I could write. When the baby was sleeping she also edited text, helped me put together my bibliography, and was a general "Girl Friday" willingly running errands that allowed me to meet my deadlines. Finally, I would like to thank my husband, Jeffrey Bendremer, who also read text, offered his excellent editorial suggestions, helped me weed out most of the Faulknerian sentences, and then worked for many nights into the early morning hours getting the manuscript ready for the publisher. For his support, good nature, and love I am always thankful.

# 1 | Introduction

We are in a car on our way to an interview with a foster mother. I have chosen her name from a random sample of women who foster for the Connecticut Department of Children and Families. The driver of the car is the head of the State Legislative Program Review and Investigations Committee. I have been hired by the committee to conduct ethnographic interviews with foster mothers. He has asked to come with me on an interview. I am also collecting data for this book. The committee wants to find out who foster mothers are and why they foster. They hope to make legislative recommendations for institutional changes in the Department of Children and Families and make improvements in the administration of foster care. I want to know how fostering shapes and changes the ways women think about themselves, about their families, and about children. I want to know how foster mothering is introduced into the landscape of women's lives, how and where it fits, how it changes that terrain, and what those experiences mean. With this information I hope to put the spotlight on the women whose lives will cross mine, women whose lives and parenting experiences have been all but ignored. I am always aware that my motivation is intensely personal.

"Have you ever gotten over it?" he asks. He is driving. He looks at me and then back to the road. The engine of his car seems overly loud.

For a moment I do not know how to answer him. I do not know how much to reveal. Cautiously I say somewhat loudly over the steady roar, "Do you mean . . ." I say, "Is there ever a day that goes by when I don't think of her?" To myself I think the rest of this question. I want to say, "Do you mean is there ever a Christmas when I don't look for dolls for her? Is there ever a time when I don't pass her school and think of her years there? It there ever a moment when I don't see other little girls her age, or young women the age she would be now, and

1

wonder where she is? Is there ever a time when I don't see peas and think of her disdain for them?" But I only say, "No." I shake my head. "I have never gotten over it." I look out the car window, and pictures of her come back to me.

She is in her flesh-colored leotard. She has recently come from ballet. Underneath the dining room table her legs move rapidly up and down to music we cannot hear. She talks about calling her sister tonight at the psychiatric hospital. After dinner she will call, and after the call I will hold her on my lap as she cries because she misses her sister, her mother, her family. Sometimes her sister will talk about their mother's boyfriend, the man who raped them for over a year. Then I will sit in the bathroom with her while she takes a bath because she is afraid of being raped when she is naked. I will read to her in the hope of calming and perhaps distracting her. And then I will put her to bed and stroke her forehead or hold her hand, assuring her that she is safe, that no one can put a ladder up to her window and steal her, as she fears will happen. I will tell her that I will protect her. I will stay with her until she falls asleep. Every day, routine child care is interspersed with considerations, practices, and understandings foreign to most mothers and unnecessary to most daughters. But that is fitting. I am both her mother and not her mother. She is both a child and no longer a child; both my child and not my child. Daily we feel our way through a minefield of uncertainty and pain to build a precarious relationship founded on love and sometimes on trust.

In the candlelight by which we eat dinner I look at her. "She-Ra does not *like* peas," she states decisively when she sees I am looking at her. In case I have not heard her, she repeats, "She-Ra does not *eat* peas." She-Ra is the name of a female deity she once saw on cartoons. She *is* She-Ra she says. She flops her legs wildly underneath her chair. She hums a little tune under her breath. Disdainfully she moves the peas around with her fork. She pulls on one of her braids.

I look at her. I try not to smile. "You should eat your peas. They're good for you." I try to sound matter-of-fact.

She clicks her wrists together over her head twice in a noiseless ritual. She says, "She-Ra-Queen-of-the-Universe does not eat peas."

Only this morning I was in her room as she dressed and watched as she refused to take off her She-Ra-Queen-of-the-Universe undershirt. She stood on her bed, her undershirt tucked firmly into her white cotton underpants, her white ankle socks unfolded and stretched up as high as they would go on her bony legs, a pillowcase cape tucked under her chin in earnest imitation of the She-Ra uniform. "Look, Mother!!!" she said excitedly. She clicked her wrists above her head and sang, "She-Ra-Queeenof-the-Uuu-niverse!" Then she flew across the room, jumping off the bed and diving into my arms, her dark brown braids flying behind her.

"What if I hadn't caught you?" I said breathlessly. She laughed. "She-Ra Queen of the Universe can fly."

Staring at her at dinner I try very hard not to smile. She leans back in her high-back dining room chair and rubs her tummy. She exhales loudly as though proclamations like the ones she is making about peas take a lot of work, and now she is happily exhausted. This is what she calls a "psych" and she watches to see if I have fallen for it. She will get me to believe she has proclaimed a truth, She-Ra does not eat peas, and thus she will not have to eat them.

I look down the long cherry table at my husband. I try not to think that she is the only living thing in our dining room, the only thing that gives my own life meaning, or joy, or happiness. I look at him, pleading for reinforcement. I feel myself wavering and the pea rule disintegrating. For her, consistent rules are important.

"Eat your peas," he says amusedly.

She has an opening. "Sheeeeeee-Ra!!!" she calls again, snapping her wrists together over her head. "She-Ra does not *eat* peas, mister." There is a pause. "Tell *her*." She motions her head in my direction without looking at me.

He laughs. "*You* tell her," he says. I know we have lost.

Her lips pout in an exaggerated imitation of a wounded queen of the universe. She waits. Timing, she has learned from somewhere, is everything.

It is no use. No amount of pleading or sternness will get her to eat her peas. I try. "Three bites," I say.

"Three peas," she barters. She winces and isolates three peas from the small portion on her plate. She plugs her nose, she grabs her milk. She sticks one pea ceremoniously in her mouth. "Uckghghghg," she winces, and chokes. She pushes her chair back from the table with stiff arms. "Oooooooohhhhhh," she shakes her head, then her shoulders, then the rest of her body. "Sheee-Ra!" She pleads for intervention from her deity. She grabs the front of her leotard and pulls down on it, exposing the front of her undershirt. The undershirt is gray. I have been trying to get it from her to wash it. She lets her leotard go with a twang. It snaps over She-Ra. She looks at me pleadingly. These are moments I hate. I have to be firm when, looking at her, I have forgotten why.

"Two more," I say weakly.

She eats two more, each with as much ceremony as the first one. When she is done, after she has had more milk to wash pea three down, she pushes her chair back and jumps into my lap. Her body molds to mine in a tight fit. She pulls her legs up and snuggles underneath my arms and against my chest. I smell her hair, feel its warmth. For a split second she does not move. She is still, thinking. Then she asks, "Am I your child?"

"You are my child," I say. But I know she is asking if I love her. There is a soft warm glow from her dark auburn hair. "I love you more than anything I know," I say slowly, aware of my body melting into hers. "You are my child." I have said this with more intensity than I have meant to. My arms are wrapped tightly around her shoulders and belly. She does not move, she is listening, perhaps to the desperation between the words, perhaps to the sound of my own heart beating. I do not want her to worry about adult things, like the discontent that has firmly lodged itself in my marriage, or the precariousness of her own situation as a ward of the state, or the fact that her new social worker says she should be in a Hispanic home, not a white one, after she has lived with us for over a year. I do not want her to worry about anything. I tell her in nine-year-old language, "And I will love you 'till the cows come home!" I bounce her slightly to distract her.

"And when are the cows coming home?" she asks, placing the inflection on the end of the sentence so the question becomes a command. We call this her attorney voice.

"It's udderly impossible to know!" I say.

She raises her head to look up at me. "Motherrrrrr!" She feigns annoyance.

"I will love you forever," I say, looking squarely at her. "You are my child."

On a warm April morning in 1989, a state social worker brought two little girls to my home. I had known them as their school social worker. They had been removed from their home and placed in temporary foster care when it was learned that their mother's boyfriend regularly beat and raped them. Once detected, their mother and her boyfriend fled, abandoning both children. The girls were then placed in temporary foster care in a home where the mother agreed to take them both. After six months in care, their foster mother asked the state social worker to look for another home for them since both children's behavior was so disruptive. Because I was one of the few people with whom they had a relationship, and because I had maintained an active interest in their welfare, I was asked to be their foster mother. It was to be a short-term placement that would last until the end of June, when a permanent home with their biological family could be found. One evening the social worker arrived with the first child; the next morning she arrived with the other. There were no papers to sign. The social worker left, and my husband and I sat in our living room surrounded by large green garbage bags full of clothes with the two little girls facing us. Each girl clutched the one thing that meant anything to them, the youngest child, a naked doll, her sister, a toothbrush. For a few short moments, the little girls simply looked at us and we looked at them with a hundred unasked questions. How would they fit into our lives? Who were they? Who would they become to us? How long would they stay? Who would we become to them? What would it be like when they left?

This began the construction of a very private part of our lives, the creation of intimate and personal relationships with each other, the foundations of which linked our private lives to much larger public discourses: the nature and construction of motherhood and women's identity, family, kinship, relationships, the properties of childhood, and the care of children. Both girls stayed considerably longer than we expected. The oldest girl, the one most profoundly affected by her experiences in her mother's home, stayed for six months and then entered a psychiatric hospital, eventually being placed in long-term residential care. The younger child stayed for almost three years and then, shortly before being adopted by us, chose to leave in hopes of once again finding her biological family. In a very real sense, however, both children stayed with me forever and became a permanent part of me. I was their mother. And the experience of mothering and the loss of that experience conditioned who I was, who I am, and who I will become. It was the experience of joy and loss and the resulting gift of insight that led me to my research into the experiences of foster mothers and foster mothering in the United States.

It goes without saying that my own experiences as a foster mother shaped my research interests and the questions with which I began this inquiry. It was the impressions and the perspectives gleaned from those experiences that shaped and conditioned the questions I would later ask women and the ways in which I would listen for their responses. My own questions were spun from the memories that insinuated themselves into my daily routines and conditioned how I thought about myself as an individual, as a white middle-class woman, as a mother, as a wife, as a member of a family, and later as an anthropologist and a divorcée. Fostering for me represented what Martha Ward refers to as a series of life "clicks," or those moments when perceptions, thoughts, or perspectives shift forever inside of us. Initially I wanted to know what other mothers experienced, what, if any, "clicks" fostering had created for them. How were these moments experienced? What meanings did they hold and why? Later, I wanted to know where these experiences fit into the landscape of contemporary American society. In particular, how do ways in which we regard women, women's work, motherhood, and kinship condition the ways in which fostering relationships are constructed and defined?

This book is a presentation and analysis of women's personal stories about fostering. Each story is nuanced with people, events, emotions, phrases, and moments women choose to include, omit, emphasize, or leave barely visible in the shadows. Each story, fragment, composition, and intertwining of thoughts and utterances allows a partial and imperfect glimpse of what the full text might be. As George Rosenwald and Richard Ochenberg suggest, "[p]ersonal stories are not merely a way of telling someone (or oneself) about one's life; they are the means by which identities may be fashioned" (1992:1), and, through recounting, refashioned through time. Like my own memories, the stories I heard from the women, men, and children who participated in this study are a part of personal texts of fostering. They were woven through and between themes of personal identity, familial relationships, caregiving, loss, motherhood, poverty, hardship, joy, and womanhood. Each story, each text is infused with personal, gendered, social, and cultural meanings imposed, accepted, contested, created, and contradicted by the storytellers.

When I shared with the women in my study that my interest in foster care emerged from my own experiences as a foster mother, without exception every woman said, "Then you *know*." When I explored this further, "knowing" was translated into experience. Women would say, "Then you know," followed by, "You know what it's *like*." Each time I asked for more information, women talked about what it is like to form caregiving relationships with children that are at once intimate and familiar within a context that is sometimes foreign and confusing, sometimes hostile and frightening.

It became apparent as I participated in the interviews that the ideas and thoughts foster mothers conveyed in their stories were embodied, living dramas enacted through the establishment and reconstitution of personal relationships. Modes of recounting took the form of remembering the individuals with whom their lives had joined and remembering the ways in which their lives and their relationships changed over time. Listeners to the stories became those who could *see* or visualize through their own experiences a foster mother's life *as a text* of personal and public memories recounted on the stage of a deeply intimate theater. I could see this text through my experiences as a foster mother and as a woman, and I was grateful for the opportunity to participate and share with other women in their life stories.

Throughout my research I felt fortunate to be a part of, to watch, to hear, to know, to feel this theater and the life dramas enacted there. I felt very fortunate to bear witness to the ways in which life stories were shaped and conditioned by the sometimes quiet, sometimes passive, sometimes violent comings and goings of children, women, and men through each other's lives within child-fostering relationships. In this book, my aim is to present the life dramas I witnessed and heard about, and to embed those stories within the larger sociocultural, sociohistorical context of "American" life. I would like the reader to be able to see the women whom I met on my journey and to understand their stories as both personal and cultural phenomena.

My own relationship to my foster daughter is conditioned by an enduring and active sense of loss. There is never a day when I do not think of her or when some memory of her does not come back to me, whether it is opening a drawer to find a play-dough heart she made now crumbly and hard with age, or remembering her leaving as I hear other women describe similar losses. Hope Edelman accurately captures that sense of active grief when she says of her mother, "She lives on beneath everything I do. Her presence influenced who I was, and her absence influences who I am. Our lives are shaped as much by those who leave us as they are by those who stay. Loss is our legacy. Insight is our gift. Memory is our guide" (1994:283). While my own story is one of loss, it is but one dimension of a complex and multifaceted story in the text of contemporary state-sponsored foster care. It was the place where I ended my journey as a foster mother and began, as an anthropologist, my journey to understand what fostering and fostering relationships mean to the people who participate in them and in the context of the changing landscape of American culture.

## Redefining Kinship, Identity, and Work: Foster Mothers' Self-Constructions

Within the larger sociocultural context of American family life, women's fostering stories cast light on how we think about and enact intersecting constructs of kinship, identity, and gendered work. As I spoke with women and participated in their relationships with children and spouses, I became acutely aware that with few exceptions foster mothers saw themselves as mothers in relation to the children in their care and saw foster children as permanent, though not always physically present, members of their family.[1] Mothering was consistently based on the ability to share an intimate, affective relationship with children grounded in an ethic of care and a sense of responsibility. Seldom did women differentiate foster from adopted or biological children in terms of relatedness or in terms of the significance of the mother-child relationship. How children came to be a part of the family or how they entered into the mother-child relationship was often irrelevant to the simple fact that they had.

Foster mothers consistently believed that children needed to be claimed, needed to feel they belonged, and needed someone who could recognize and meet their unique demands, desires, and needs. They saw themselves as women who had a special, often innate ability to do this. Motherhood and womanhood were thus essentially linked to each other and to gendered life experiences. Similar to the women in Ellen Lewin's study of lesbian mothers, women who fostered were "heavily influenced by relatively conventional gender expectations centered on women's special vocation for nurturance and altruism" and held motherhood as the critical determinant of their identity (1993:10–11). Thus whether a child was biologically related to a woman, a neighborhood child who needed looking after, or a foster child who had just been removed from her home, foster mothers saw their imperative as mothers and women similarly. As one woman told me, referring to her foster children and a neighborhood child for whom she had recently purchased shoes, "I'm not a *foster* mother. I'm just a mother. And these are my kids."

Every woman in the study said she cared about "children." Within this context, "children" was a social category that made ethnicity irrelevant or, arguably, it *was* an ethnicity. Repeatedly I was told, "I don't care what color child they bring me—black, white, yellow, or purple. If it is a child, then I am its mother." It was not that foster mothers did not see children's ethnicity, it was that its meaning was secondary to the primary concern of providing mothering.[2] While I anticipated the meaning of fostering to be linked to a sense of community survival and the latter to be particularly significant for African American women (see Collins, 1994:45–65), this was not what either African American or Euro-American women emphasized in their discussions about state-sponsored fostering.[3] Both groups defined community vis-à-vis geography: community was the neighborhood, section of the city, or the town in which they lived, the state, and writ large all of America. When children were defined as an ethnic category, or a category that was supra-ethnic, fostering assumed a social importance that linked foster mothers with all of society and linked the work of mothering with the important work of repairing a fractured world.

Through mothering and the work of caregiving, women constructed kinship relations with foster children, and often with children's families of origin, based on claims of belonging. When I asked women, "Who is in your family?" consistently they pointed to rows of pictures hung on the wall or to moments of family life carefully preserved in scrapbooks or imprinted in plaster cast hands. And they talked about their children, those who were both physically present and those long absent, as permanent members of their family. Belonging and family membership were not contingent on an embodied relationship. As children were woven into the fabric of family life and identity, their presence became an indelible part of foster mothers' sense of self. Caring replaced caregiving as a mark of permanence. While the nature of the relationship changed over time and through circumstances (for example if a child returned to her family of origin or went to adoption), the kinship bond endured. As one mother explained about her foster daughter who, after living with her for two years, left to live with her grandparents, "I am her mother. . . . Just because a child leaves doesn't mean our caring stops."

Because foster children belonged in and to the family they had rights equal to those of other family members. They could count on being looked after, cared for, and provided for with the same vigilance as those related by blood or legal ties. When asked when children became a part of her family, one woman replied, "The minute they walk through the door." Most women saw this attitude as an extremely important part of their work as foster mothers and related it to children's ability to survive physically and emotionally. Foster children had experienced the trauma of being removed from families who were unable to care for them. As wards of the state they legally and emotionally belonged to no one in particular; their very existence was often overlooked. Through fostering, women ensured that children who were unwanted or uncared for would survive and flourish by transforming them, if not legally then through claims of belonging, into full family members and into social children. The work of creating a kinship relationship through mothering was, thus, transformative and healing.

These women's beliefs about motherhood and kinship were remarkably similar regardless of social class. Whether very poor or affluent, women constructed extended kin relations based on claims of belonging that included generations of foster children, their offspring, and members of foster children's extended biological families. In addition to foster children, every foster mother appeared to have a network of kin relations based on claims of belonging that she counted on for material and emotional support. While I might have expected more affluent women to supplant kin relations with hired support services or to define the boundaries of their household in a more circumscribed manner, I did not see this.

When these family relationships worked well, they were based on a type of reciprocity. Foster mothers gave the gift of mothering, often to both children and their parents, and received in exchange family membership conferred by the child's family. Foster mothers were recognized as able to provide for children what their parents, at that moment, could not. This attitude was especially true of African American women and was most frequent when the fostering relationship was informal or was one in which the biological mother had some hand in negotiating the placement. The byproduct of these gifts was that children did not have to choose between families for membership, and foster mothers, who had no legitimate claim to children once they left their home, had a vehicle for ongoing contact. Both foster mothers and biological mothers also had a wider net of resources with which to care for their children.

Unfortunately, these extended kin relationships were not only not recognized by the state but were often systemically impeded, since they removed exclusive control of a case from social workers. They also changed the nature of foster care and the meaning of foster mothering. From the state's perspective (expressed in child welfare policy and social worker practice), foster mothers were transitory and interchangeable child care workers who were performing a "job." They exchanged physical and emotional care for money. Fostering existed as commodity relations in which foster mothers, as James Carrier suggests, "are not linked in any enduring way to the people and things that surround them. Instead they are isolated individuals whose identities spring from internal sources and whose relations with others are governed by personal will rather than interpersonal, gift relations" (1993:55–56). As nonmothers and commodified laborers relating to a temporary product, foster mothers were not expected to have an emotional or a kinship bond with foster children or their family of origin. However, by forming enduring kinship relationships with children and when possible with their families, foster mothers preserved their caregiving relationship as a distinctly *familial* relationship and preserved fostering as the work of maintaining children's inalienability in a social context that rejected that construct.

Accepting money from the state in the form of reimbursements was not anathema to mothering. For most women it was welcome and helpful since it enabled them to do their work. This was possible because no woman premised her mothering on a dichotomy between family and work, private and public, the individual and the collective. Foster mothers were mothers. They were also workers whose work occurred within an extended male and female kin network in conjunction and relationship with the state. It was work involving the intentional and continuous process of weaving strangers into family and maintaining that sense of family when and as they left. It was a private and intimate process that took place between each member of a family and all members together. It was also an act that was necessarily public as it instantly situated mother-work within a complex web of state, community, and nonkin social relations.

Just as mothering was an economic activity, children too had a very particular economic worth and function in the household without negating affective relations. As one young boy proudly asked his financially struggling foster mother, "My check comes in every month for us, right?" He was both provider and provided for, sentimental child and economic figure. While most women felt the sting of innuendo from state social workers relative to their motivation for fostering, no woman felt her mothering was commodified or compromised by accepting state reimbursements. Many women said they began fostering for the state because they needed the extra income, but all felt it absurd to think that the need for money made a woman less of a mother.

Juxtaposed with women's definitions of "motherhood" and "family" were those maintained by child welfare agencies and represented in popular culture through the media. These images consistently contradicted foster mothers' constructs of themselves and their work. Through state policies and social worker practices, fostering was defined as a temporary board-and-care arrangement. Foster parents were either temporary families or short-term child care workers, neither of whom had the right to claim a kinship relationship. Foster families saw that they were seen as "different" from "mainstream" American families and integrated difference into their discourse as something both painful and special. Most important, however, difference did not negate foster mothers's sense that they were mothers and that the work of fostering was that of family making. This has been consistently overlooked in the child welfare literature, where difference from nuclear, biological, or legal families has marked foster families as false or temporary families. For example, as Judith Modell states, "Accepting visits from the child's natural parents and, more especially, receiving payment for taking care of a child—make a foster family 'different from' a *real* family in which, presumably, there are no 'other' parents and conduct comes out of love, not for money. Confirming this strangeness, individuals in a foster relationship have been found to experience a 'sense of falseness'" (italics added) (1994:46).

Traditionally alternative families gained legitimacy, and thereby avoided being stigmatized as "different," by reproducing "natural" family relations, i.e., kinship premised on biogenetic or legal relationships (Schneider, 1980:21–27). For example, Judith Modell submits that adoptive families gained legitimacy by appropriating the template of "family," "by making the constructed relationship as much like the biological as possible" (1994:2). Helena Ragone suggests that the rhetoric of gift giving used in surrogate relations "reflects the enduring quality of the blood tie, a relationship that can not be severed in American kinship ideology" (1999:72).

In their quest for legitimacy, foster parents reproduced "natural" parent-child relations in some fundamental ways. For example, women placed heavy emphasis on the fact that their relationships with foster children were "just like" those with their blood children. And similar to blood relations, once a kinship tie had been established, it was permanent. But fostering also forged new constructs of family and new family forms, challenging the notion that *real* mother-child relationships are necessarily dyadic, that *real* family membership is fixed rather than fluid, that *real* families are based on a cohort of children moving from minority to majority with one set of parents. Perhaps most important, fostering challenges the idea that mothering and wage labor are necessarily separate entities. These transformations of American kinship occur, as Christine Ward Gailey reminds us, in a "political and cultural climate that reifies kinship as bloodline . . . and integrates biological determinism into the concept of human nature" (1995:3). And thus the price of transformation was high.

Women were constantly faced with the daily exigencies and ramifications of cultural disjuncture and delegitimacy. As Hoecklin suggests about the welfare system, foster care is also "connected to other institutions, ideas, and discourses. It represents, justifies, and reproduces broader social ideas about social persons and appropriate social relations. The identities it gives and the structural conditions it creates materially and socially penalize those not conforming to the model of the family with which policy is conceived" (1998:92–93). On an abstract level, this meant foster mothers were excluded from the discourse on foster care and, when included at all, were included as the object rather than the subject of study. On a practical level disjuncture between foster mothers and the foster care system was staggering, since ultimately the state had enormous power over foster mothers, their lives, and their vocations. Many foster mothers talked about the fear they had of losing their licenses or of being "punished" by having children they cared about and loved precipitously removed from their homes if they did not conform to agency practices or angered a social worker. Many women spoke of their reimbursement checks being delayed, of not being given any children, or of being further excluded from any information or decision-making exchanges.

For social workers, disjuncture between foster mothers and the system fed a sense of futility and hopelessness about their work. They frequently talked about the agency's need to weed out "bad foster mothers" and to try to recruit better ones. "Better" almost always had social class, ethnic, and educational connotations; "good" foster mothers resembled social workers. They were white, middle class, and had some education, and therefore could be trusted to follow, rather than subvert, agency rules and to work cooperatively with social workers. Perhaps the most significant consequence of disjuncture was that it created a closed system for social workers in which new information was fed through a preexisting ideological lens. This made it difficult for social workers to understand or incorporate into practice the ways in which important context variables contributed to foster mothers' construction of meaning. That is to say, when evaluating foster mothers' behavior or motives, social workers seldom assumed an emic perspective in which they attempted to see what foster mothers saw or to understand the way women saw it (Douglas, 1973:28). Instead foster mothers' responses, descriptions, and actions were generally evaluated from social workers' own frame of reference, which tautologically supported their perspectives.

To some degree this tautology was normalized through the foster care literature's objectification of foster mothers and the positioning of social service workers as the only legitimate "experts" and facilitators of fosterage. This translated into agency policy in such a way as to further normalize an exclusive conception of kinship, which ultimately served to preserve a systemic status quo predicated on very specific constructs of motherhood, family, and work.

As a result, the meaning of women's fostering assumed the quality of resistance. Home and family became the center for dissent contesting not just particular social workers' evaluations of a case or their treatment plans but state-imposed constructs of motherhood and kinship articulated in policy and embodied in practice. In the face of unequal power relations with the state that were both threatening and frightening, women's narratives and the way they lived them were intentionally designed to be what James C. Scott calls hidden transcripts. This refers to the protective "realm of relative discursive freedom outside the earshot of power-holders," which is "the privileged site for nonhegemonic, contrapuntal, dissident, subversive, discourse" (1990:25). It is these discourses that I heard most frequently when I stood in kitchens, family rooms, and backyards with women as they tended their children. They were expressed at times in tones of frustration, anger, and bitterness as well as with a calm sense of their own worth and abilities stemming from the importance of mothering work. It is these discourses I have tried, with foster mothers' approval and support, to convey in this book. By calling attention to the radical nature of kinship and mother-work through fostering, I hope to broaden that privileged space where they and their families live.

# 2

## Portrait of a Foster Mother (1)
### *"They're All My Children, They're All My Family"*

### *Reconstructing Motherhood, Past and Present*

She meets me at the door. Her hands are dotted with white paint, and she is wearing an oversized man's shirt. She has a paintbrush in her hand, and she seems somewhat embarrassed. I realize that she has forgotten our appointment. I offer to come back, but she ushers me into the downstairs family room while she runs upstairs to put the paintbrush down and to check her youngest foster daughter. Mrs. Hansen has dark circles beneath her eyes, a gentle manner, and a soft, melodic voice. She is married and lives in a suburb of a large eastern city. Her house is a split-level raised ranch in a quiet, racially integrated, though primarily African American neighborhood. The house is comfortable and immaculately clean.

She has two grown children, a daughter who is a social worker and a son who is in college majoring in special education. She has four foster children: Catherine, twenty-one, has been with her for a year. She is blind and mentally retarded. Cassandra is almost fifteen and has been with her for two years. Mrs. Hansen is Cassandra's legal guardian. Cassandra is also mentally retarded. She does not walk and is self-abusive. She also is sometimes abusive to those around her, hitting if she feels threatened. There are two younger children. Bertie is five and has lived with the Hansens for just over a year. She has lived in five foster homes since entering foster care at the age of two. She was sexually abused by her mother's boyfriend. Sarah is a baby, Mrs. Hansen says. She is two and was born addicted to crack cocaine. As a result, she is in constant motion, sleeping sometimes only two or three hours a night, and is always eating. Mrs. Hansen explains that this is because she was born with an addiction and a craving that cannot be satisfied.

This chapter presents the life history of Mrs. Hansen, an African American woman in her mid-fifties who met with me on three separate occasions to talk about her life and her experiences with fostering. (See Appendix for more details about life history interviews.) Mrs. Hansen's experiences and perspectives are unique. But in what she included when she talked about herself and fostering, she was similar to the majority of women who participated in this study. Six themes emerged as important in her discussion of fostering and were shared by almost all of the other foster mothers. They are (1) the importance of motherhood and caregiving through affective relationships with foster children; (2) women's healing and transformative work with children through the foster-mother/foster-child relationship; (3) the creation of enduring kinship relationships with foster children through affective claims of belonging; (4) the importance of women's embodied knowledge relative to the work of fostering and mothering; (5) the experience of loss and bereavement; and (6) the way in which fostering relationships and women's sense of motherhood is conditioned by conflicts with the state. These themes will be explored in subsequent chapters through the collective experiences of all study participants and in this chapter through the eyes and voice of Mrs. Hansen.

In a soft southern drawl, Mrs. Hansen explains that she was painting the ceiling of her kitchen because she, like Sarah, cannot sit still. "I have always done. I have always worked very hard. I don't need very much sleep. I just can't stop. I don't stop!" She says that she could have asked her husband to do the painting, and when he comes home he will ask why she did not let him do it. But she says it is hard to depend on someone else, hard to trust them to do the job well. "He will say, 'Why didn't you just wait and let me do it?' It is just that I am so used to doing it myself, you know. . . . I have been alone this long and have always taken care of myself, you know? And even if he does it, I would probably go over it."

As we begin to talk about foster care and about the life experiences that have led Mrs. Hansen to become a foster mother, she describes herself as a not very emotional person; she has survived a hard life, she says, by becoming someone who is not easily overwhelmed by sorrow or death, someone who is not easily touched. Yet evident in her words is the way in which personal sacrifice signifies both love and kinship.

I am not the affectionate-type person, but [my husband and children] know that I love them because, I mean, there is nothing on this earth that I wouldn't do. I will sacrifice things for myself to make sure that they have. So they know that, but I was never taught [affection]. To me that was not a part of life. You clean them up and you bathe them. You make sure that they are fed, and you don't have time to do anything else. You really didn't. There wasn't time for that. And it makes you a hard person. . . . I remember the first time I actually held my daughter, actually really hugged her is when she was getting ready to go to [college]. . . . Yeah, because I didn't have that as a kid. I just taught them to be strong, and hugging and kissing is wimpy, you know.

But this self-proclaimed hardness exists in juxtaposition with another self she also describes. It is a self woven through the decision to become a foster mother. It is a text of loss and recovery, of transformed motherhood and transforming mother-child relationships.

My mom used to live with me. I took care of her. And then one day I found her dead in her room. It was hard, 'cause that was my mom, but . . . she was very sick. . . . After my mom had passed away I watched this movie, one night. It was about 1:00 in the morning, and it was about this Down's syndrome kid that his parents didn't want him because he was so sick and I cried so much through the movie and they gave a phone number at the end of the movie. They were saying there are so many children like this, and they have no one to take care of them, and I called that 1-800 number, and that is how I got involved.

And when I brought Rachel home, my husband said I don't think you are going to be able to deal with her. . . . She was sixteen and she wouldn't keep on her clothes. . . . There were things she *could* do, but she never had anyone to really make her do them. And she would, she trashed her room the first day she was here. She had a heart problem, and she was not to get excited or nothing like that. I said, well, just let me work with her for about a month and see what happens. And it took me about six weeks and then Rachel and I—mmm [she pauses and looks away]. I loved her *so* much—even when I think about it now it makes me sort of [she loses control of her voice, and tears come to her eyes; she pauses but does not cry].

I really loved Rachel. And they told me that she would probably die. And she died ten months after I had her. But she achieved everything they said she wouldn't. By the time Rachel died, she was going to school like—*before* she was only going to school like maybe three days out of the month, four days out of the month. But by the time she died, she was going to school every day. And she was taking these tests; she had to go and have her blood thinned. And *before* [she came to live with me], it would take the whole day to do it. And by the time she died, we would go at 10:00, by 11:30 we were back home. . . . She only crawled [before she came here], and before she died she was chasing me all over the house. It was not that she couldn't do it. No one had taken the time. You have to take the time 'cause—I truly believe this—there is nothing that no one can't achieve.

. . . I think my life is more complete now. A lot changed with them [foster children]. 'Cause it's like when I got Rachel, Rachel needed me so much, and the only way I was going to be able to give it to her is that she let me into her world. And I was not going to get into her world being the person that I was raised up to be. So I had to sort of like, you know, be more affectionate with her, you know, be a *lot* more.

Mrs. Hansen's fostering story is about the changes that occurred within her that enabled her to love Rachel in a way she had not loved anyone else before. It is about the transformations that occurred in Rachel that enabled her to move, talk, and think in a way she had never done before. Through the story, Mrs. Hansen describes both her own and her foster daughter's ability to experience their worlds in such a new and different way as to make the world itself different and themselves transformed within that world. For Mrs. Hansen, the decision to foster was consistent with her self-definition as a caregiver. But fostering required her to redefine mothering and thereby redefine herself in relation to mothering work and children. Thus, the decision to foster and the meaning fostering holds not only had an immediate, immanent relevance but assumed relevance relative to her personal history as well.

Mrs. Hansen was born in South Carolina. She was the oldest girl in a family of six children. Her grandparents were sharecroppers on a cotton farm. She, her siblings, and parents lived with her grandparents and worked the fields. Her earliest memories are of backbreaking labor and of the way in which grinding poverty conditioned her childhood and her relationship to the adults in her life. "You had to work. You had to work. It is not like you go to work and goof off. You worked. Oh yeah, because . . . I mean they expected so much cotton you picked in a day when you picked it. We never saw the money as kids. I am sure they must have given it to our parents, but I never saw it." Her life changed when she was ten years old. Her mother and father were on the verge of divorce, and her mother could not afford to support the entire family alone. Mrs. Hansen and two siblings were sent to live with a relative.

> I came to Connecticut when I was ten years old. I had an aunt that brought myself and my older brother and my sister . . . here to live with her. [M]y father was not home a lot, and it was a lot for my mom to take care of all of us. And she allowed the three oldest ones to come to Connecticut. And she followed within a year and a half herself with my other three younger siblings.
>
> My mom was not able to give us the love that she would like to, but we knew by the way she took care of us that she loved us. Because there were so many of us she had to work two jobs to do that. I had to take care of my [brothers and sisters]. . . . I was like the mom for them . . . and I was only a child myself. . . .
>
> I dropped out of school in the ninth grade when I came here because I thought it was bad there, but it was worse coming here without my mom. It was hard [to leave my mom], it was hard, very hard. But living in the South on a farm you are used to . . . things not being exactly the way you want it and being [from] a large family and my mother and father was in the verge of a divorce. So, it toughens you. It makes you a tough person even as a child. [I was not] able to have the things that a child should have.

Mrs. Hansen missed her mother desperately. And while her aunt took care of her and fed her well, she describes the anguish of feeling orphaned, of feeling like an outsider, a stranger in her new household.

> I came here, I came to live with an aunt, and I guess she did what she felt was right, but . . . I was more like house servant. I did a lot of work in the house . . . it was hard because we were without my mom . . . and we were in a strange place. Coming from the south the kids teased us. Oh God, it was horrible. Yeah, it really was. I've always felt like I was an outcast. I am sure she loved me. I don't know. This is hard to say. I never felt that I belonged.

From the moment she arrived in Connecticut until the moment her mother came to reunite the family, she was dispossessed, out of place, and lonely. It was a feeling that, rather than going away when her mother joined her, remained with her and conditioned her sense of self. She was, and to some degree has always remained, a stranger in a strange land—has always remained the girl who was teased, rejected, isolated, unloved, and emotionally homeless. She was also a black girl in a society dominated by whites, a reality that conditioned her relationship to her mother and her life choices. For Mrs. Hansen and her mother, mothering was embedded within an economic relationship of domestic and paid labor inextricably linked to the struggle for survival. The language of love was the children's knowledge that their mother's long hours away from home and her backbreaking labor ensured their survival and offered the hope that their lives might somehow be easier, their life chances somehow better. Later, Mrs. Hansen's responsibility to do her part to ensure their survival would impel her to quit school and go to work.

> I worked in tobacco and . . . it was horrible. It was hot work . . . and you had almost like a production and they expected you to do a certain amount, and the men that they had over you were almost like slave drivers . . . you were always under the gun. And because of that, sometime, now I am a nervous-type person due to my childhood, I am sure. . . . I worked at the Forge [when I was] fourteen years old, fifteen years old. By that time I had left my aunt's house 'cause . . . my mom had come here, and I left my aunt when I was about fifteen, I think, and I went back to live with my mom. We all lived in a two-room apartment . . . and we all packed in there. I did domestic work, and then I dropped out of school when I was sixteen. . . . I hated it.

Later, the same legacy of mothering was passed from Mrs. Hansen to her daughter. The price of survival was all-consuming work that exacted from both mother and daughter opportunities for a relationship based on the luxury of physical closeness and embodied presence. Mrs. Hansen's relationship with her mother, like her relationship to her daughter, was inextricably linked to the drudgery required of both mothers and daughters to ensure that the family could eat and pay the rent. The language of love once again was translated through idioms of commodified labor.

> [I met my husband] through family. But it didn't last. And I had two children. I worked two jobs for more than fifteen years. I worked as a nurse's aide for the Visiting Nurse Association [during the day], and then I worked at a convalescent home from 11:00 at night until 7:00 in the morning. When I would get off from there, I would go home, get my kids dressed, send them off to school, and be at my other job by 8:15, and I worked there until 4:00. . . . My daughter at that time was ten years old. She is a carbon copy of me. She's a very hardworking person because at ten she ran my house. She really did. She ran my house, and I hated it.

Because . . . she was not allowed to be a child either. She really wasn't, you know. It was hard. Believe me when I tell you. It was hard. My son wrote an essay for his last year of school, and I read it, and he was saying that my mom was a very strong woman, but she was not there in body [when I was] growing up. It was true. I mean he knew I loved him, and I was trying to give him the things I never had as a child and overlooking the things that I really didn't have as a child, and that was a childhood. I just wanted to be sure they had a comfortable life.

So it was hard. Believe me when I tell you. It was very hard, very hard. Raising two kids, I didn't want to go on welfare. I went on it for about a year, and it took all of my pride. [So] . . . I took a lot away from my children not being home with them. I did. I took a lot away from them.

Mrs. Hansen's decision to foster, and her commitment to an embodied mother-child relationship, is a story about emotional transformations as much as it is about missed opportunities restored. The state contributes financially to each child's care, and Mrs. Hansen and her husband both work. Because of her relative financial security, her relationship to her foster daughters is not conditioned by the constant worry of economic survival; the choice she faced in her relationship to Rachel was not that of drudge labor requiring long absences from home or starvation. The context for mothering was changed and redefined in Mrs. Hansen's life. This required her to transform herself through the relationship into someone she had never been before.

I can give them [foster children] what I couldn't even give my own children. And I often think about that, and, even as an adult, my son tells me that now. He says, "Oh boy, Mom, when we were kids you would never allow that."

And I am sure my husband noticed a softening [in me] because I am not as hard with him. And even my son notices. He says, "Wow!" You know, because he would say, you never cry . . . because before, I mean, that was a sign of weakness, but yeah, now I will let them see me cry. I let them know that I am hurt, and I am sure by that they know that I have mellowed out. I am surprised too! Even I notice myself that I do things that I am surprised at myself—like being easy.

In some ways I am happy the way I am because it is a protection. And in some ways I'm not, because people wonder about me. You know, some people feel that I am cold 'cause this is my world, right here, you know . . . taking care of the children. I enjoy them. I truly enjoy them because they need me, and I need to be needed, and they need me, and that is why I can be so [loving and affectionate] with them.

## Transformations and Embodied Relations

Themes of change, transformation, healing, and affective and embodied relationships were central to most women's stories about their fostering experiences and the meaning of those experiences in their lives. Like Mrs. Hansen, women spoke of transformations they had observed and experienced through relationships with foster children and sometimes with the foster children's biological families. Like Mrs. Hansen, women also spoke about significant life changes that occurred for children, or for themselves, or both. Each story of transformation contained elements that conditioned the transformation: hard work, sacrifice, often instinctive perceptiveness, always desperate struggle.

The result of transformative relationships was almost always healing: accomplishments achieved against the odds, insights into someone or something they had not had before, changes in long-standing patterns of behavior. The subtext of these stories was that relationships formed with children based on love and caring are powerful vehicles through which monumental changes *can* occur. That is to say, the possibility for transformation exists for foster mothers within their relationships at all times whether or not it happens. These transformations are rarely temporally delimited. Those that occur for one brief moment only are as significant as those that are lasting. Those that never occur do not diminish the possibility and the hope that they may.

Part of mothering work is to be a part of the relationship in such a way as to effect change. Part of a mothering identity is to be an empathic healer or to be the conduit through which healing may occur. Mrs. Hansen's descriptions of her foster daughters reflect the painstaking processes of change and transformation that occur through an embodied relationship. Through her descriptions, it is also possible to see the knowledge, dedication, perseverance, and hope with which she approached each mothering relationship.

> I've had Cassandra for two years. And Cassandra is abusive. She will hit Bertie, she will hit anyone who she feels is invading her territory, and her territory is that bookshelf. And . . . if she has something, and you want it, you cannot walk over to Cassandra. You have to sit there and talk to her and convince her that it's her idea to give it over even though it doesn't belong to her. It could be Bertie's doll or anything. If not, she will kill you for it. She used to have tantrums like that at least two or three times a day. Now it's down to one, and when she's going to have her menstrua-

tion I know just to try to keep her calm, and other than that she doesn't have outbreaks. . . . She has calmed down a lot.

### About Bertie, she said

It's hard [because] Bertie is very jealous, very, very jealous. And if Cassandra or Catherine's mom or dad comes to visit, then she will say, "Oh, I don't have anyone. I wish I was blind." I say, "Why would you want that?" Then, she says, "Everybody would love me." And Catherine doesn't walk, and she will say, "Well, I wish I couldn't walk." Why? "Because then you'll love me." Then she says, "I wish I was Sarah. Because Sarah's a baby."

She's never content. And if I get up in the morning and I pick out an outfit, maybe something that she's worn maybe twice, well, we have a problem there. Because every day she wants something new on. It has to be new. Every morning practically we battle about that. And she will tantrum if she don't get her way. Oh, she would tear the place up. She would really tear it up. She would go in that room and demolish it. Throw things, bang her head, hit. Up until about, I would say, three months ago they were really bad. . . . And they have subsided down to now where she is screaming a little, but it is not unbearable.

### About Sarah, she said,

The youngest one was born addicted to crack cocaine. . . . She is active—overactive. Because of her being addicted, she runs all the time. I mean all the time. She's up all during the night. I have to lock her bedroom door because . . . she has opened the refrigerator and she has climbed up to the top shelf in the refrigerator. I have to lock the cabinets because she's going in. She's looking for food. She's hungry all the time, and she has such a craving. And we have to literally put her in her chair, her high chair, where she can't get out, and make her sit to eat. And she's been up since five this morning. She will never sit and play with a toy. She's all over the place. She is everywhere. At all times either myself or my husband have to always be where she is because she cannot be alone.

As with Mrs. Hansen, a sense of mothering as an identity often emanated from pain that women identified in their own lives. This pain came from an awareness that they had in some way been stigmatized, objectified, or made invisible. The labels women spoke of were often intersected by discourses of ethnicity and social class. These texts were always about a time and place when women felt excluded from something: a loving family, an image of childhood, a peer group, a relationship, or a way of life. These were also texts in which women's own lives and life choices contested or contradicted dominant discourses of gender, work, or family. In telling their stories, women emphasized their sense of powerlessness, frustration, sadness, injustice, and sometimes outrage.

> I never really had a childhood. I've always been an adult. I hated the fact that I was not allowed to be like a normal person, a normal kid. I never went to parties. I never went to dances. I hated it. I always had to work. I have always worked. I have supported myself really since I was sixteen .
> . . . I always let [my children know] that I had it this way, you don't have to because I am here to fight for you. Unfortunately, there was no one there for me. I never felt that there was, even when I was with my mom. I knew she loved us, but she worked two jobs so how could she. . . . That is why these children are my life. . . . If you come here 365 days of the year, you will see that these children are my life, and that is why I fight so hard for them.

In many ways the circumstances of fostering reproduced these hallmark life experiences. For example, women spoke of the pejorative labels attached to being a foster mother. But the women who offered their stories were keenly aware that the context had changed, and so the content and, potentially, the outcome of the stories had also changed. One got the sense from listening to many women's recounting that there were painful events they as children had experienced with a sense of impotence. For those who had these experiences, there was little they could do to change their life circumstances but endure the pain, remember it, and learn from it. What women learned was that they could survive and through survival transform their pain into a testament of personal strength. Foster-mothering stories became active, transformative dramas in which women recounted their pain through empathic recognition of children's pain and worked toward a transformation in children's lives that simultaneously affirmed their own sense of survival.

> I knew, especially coming from the South. I knew how whites were, and I just accepted it as a way of life. Even today I don't allow it to bother me. I can't afford to because I am who I am, and I am what I am, and I can't change it, and even if I could, I wouldn't want to. There are some things that you can change in life, and if you can change them, you do. If you can't, you learn to live with them. And that is what I did. I was put

through too much of that as a kid. I cannot allow what people think whether I am black or whatever color [to] bother me. . . . So if whites and blacks are here and if you allow me to take an inch, that is all he [the white man] is going to give me, then I will take the inch and do what I can with it. Even if he don't allow me to multiply, then I will work that inch until I can't work it anymore. You have to love yourself, and you have got to think good of yourself no matter what anyone else thinks. And if you can instill that in your head and let it be your guide. . . . Life can be beautiful, and life can be miserable, and it is what you make of it. Nobody else can make it for you. . . . You know, I can make it whatever I wanted it to be in my mind. No one can take your mind away from you unless you allow them to, and I strongly believe that, and if you can condition your mind, there is nothing in life that you can't achieve. You may not reach the top, but you can get so close to it that you won't even know that you didn't get to it. And that is what I tell Bertie. Regardless of what has happened to you, Bertie, in your life, you are important to you, and no one can take that away from you. Don't worry about what people think of you, 'cause everybody is not going to like you. And so what!

Through their interventions, women hoped to spare foster children the suffering they had endured. In effect, foster mothering became a reenactment of a personal history through which women, remembering and recounting their own suffering, became guides for children who were negotiating very similar subjectivities. This hope enabled women to have the emotional strength to deal with enormous hardship in their relationships with children.

Bertie has been around so much and she's been exposed to so much. But I am very, very strict with her. What's no today is no tomorrow. That's the only way you do it. You've got to be very consistent. The other foster moms were afraid of her . . . because she used to lie, and because of that they were afraid that she was going to fabricate a lie and [cause a Department of Children and Families investigation]. But I let her know I was not afraid of her. She's been shifted back and forth from home to home. I think I remember four or five. I'm not sure.

And see, she could resent the fact that her mom is not here. I try to put myself in her place. How would I feel at four years old not being with my mom? And how would I, maybe that's what makes me keep her. Somebody has to, 'cause she will go through the system until she is eighteen years old, and then you've really got a problem. And now you don't have a six-year-old anymore, [you have an adult].

### Fostering Identities, Fostering Kinship

As with Mrs. Hansen, mothering for most women was premised on the ability to see past socially imposed labels (e.g., "retarded," "abused child," "sick child," "handicapped child," "hopeless child") or symptoms (e.g., compulsive, hyperactive, rigid) and construct relationships with children premised on intimate knowledge and recognition of the human being. Through this transcendence, women healed an element of the injustice (stereotyping and labeling) they had experienced in their own lives. Because foster mothering was intimate and personal, it was always and necessarily conveyed in the language of emotion.

Identity discourses were also intersected by themes of power and powerlessness. Bertie had been sexually assaulted when she was two years old. Sarah was born addicted to crack cocaine. Mrs. Hansen became her aunt's maid at the age of ten and lost her childhood. These were clearly understood as wounding events over which one had no control. But Mrs. Hansen's message to herself and her children was that, while you cannot affect or control external events, you can create yourself and control who you are and who you become. To most women, this knowledge was power. It was the power of authorship and creation in the face of hopelessness and powerlessness. It was a personal legacy they shared with their children. It was this hope that conditioned most emotionally intimate fostering relationships. Of her foster children, Mrs. Hansen said,

> They are starting off with a lot against them. But people can cause things to happen in your life, and you can cause that negative to become positive. It may not change in a physical sense, but you can change it here [your mind]. . . . Unfortunately, Bertie has been made an adult, and she will never be a kid again. . . . Only once in a while [does she even play], and even if she is playing she is playing things that you would never even dream. . . . It's sad. If I could achieve anything between now and before she becomes at least eight years old, I would love for her to be a little girl.

As women recognized a child's struggle and formed a relationship based on caregiving and the hope of transformation, they also forged a relationship of kinship and spoke of the ways in which foster children belonged to them and their family. The intimate and personal knowledge women gathered about their foster children facilitated their mothering work. Children were incorporated affectively into women's lives through claims of belonging, and into a foster-mothering discourse through the assertion of personal recognition and mothering knowledge.

[Bertie] was sexually abused. And she will move her body on this [pole in the basement], and I asked her what are you doing? And she told me, practicing for when she gets married. She is five. She is a grown-up trapped in a kid's body. She is very, very mature for her age. She acts up sexually if a man comes here. She's all over him . . . she'll sit, straddle them, facing them, and she's kissing them all on the neck and right in the face. . . . She is very hard to handle, but she has calmed down a lot since she has been here. . . . She's been shifted around from home to home since she was two years old. She's been in four or five homes.

I can see why the other foster mothers didn't want her, but I feel I will not give up on her. . . . I get enough to keep on going. No, I can't [give up on her]. If I did that, it [her problems] would just keep on going. Someone has to say okay I will go through it, whatever it takes, whatever she needs. And I tell her that all the time. I say, "Bertie, I am determined that you are going to be a nice young lady." I says, "I am determined that you are going to grow up to be proud of yourself, never mind what I think of you, proud of yourself." Oh yeah, she is very mouthy. And she will try me all the time, but I don't give up. I don't let up on her. And see, *I know her.*

She has to find a place. When she first came to me she used to keep everything in a paper bag. And I still find her resorting back to that once in a while. And the minute she did something that she thought would make me angry she would say, "Well, let me get my bags packed," 'cause she just know that I am going to send her away. I says, "No, I am not going to send you away. . . . This is your home. . . ." Most of the time she calls me auntie. . . . Once she called me mom, and I said, "I'm not your mom and I don't think your mom would like [you calling me mom]." She asks me, she says, "Do a mom put you in bed at night?" She says, "Do a mom dress you in the morning? Do a mom give you the food?" And I said, "Yes." Then she said, "Well, I guess you're my mom."

Through their daily interactions foster mothers took "state children" and created a space for them to be "children," while simultaneously creating a space for themselves as "foster mothers" to be their mothers. Through the creation of a protected space, women mothered based on both agency and power and forged bonds of kinship that were intimate and mutually reconstitutive. "Rachel was our kid," Mrs. Hansen said. "Rachel was our baby. They are all my children. They are my family." Of her son, Mrs. Hansen said, "Oh, God, he loves Catherine so much. He will call long distance to talk to them on the phone. I said, 'Wait a minute!' And when I go to enroll him in school, you would think he would be ashamed of them. 'Cause I take them all with me. And he's not."

Descriptions of kinship through fostering never excluded the child's biological kin. In many cases, kinship and kinship titles like "mother" and the care/responsibilities associated with the title were shared collaboratively between a child's family of origin and the foster family. Biological and foster families were, in these cases, united rather than separated. In other cases, the shared relationship was acknowledged but never integrated into the foster family's daily life. When asked whether or not Bertie and Sarah's mother was a part of her family, Mrs. Hansen described a foster-mother/biological-mother relationship riddled with complexity and ongoing negotiation common to women's fostering experiences.

> Yeah, they [the girls' family] are. I feel that she [Bertie and Sarah's mother] is—but she doesn't feel that way, and I can understand that because I am like a threat to her, and I am doing something that I won't say she *couldn't do,* but she wasn't able to do. And her children, especially Sarah, looks up to me as their mom. And that's hard. She used to come here a lot. Department of Children and Families stopped her because she used to promise to come and she wouldn't show up, and then it would cause problems.

Shared claims of belonging between the foster and biological family often meant that it was incumbent on foster mothers to manage a delicate balance between sharing kinship bonds and making sure foster children were physically safe. Even though some women held the biological mother responsible for the child's trauma, and this was especially true for younger children, most foster mothers regarded her with a mixture of sympathy, empathy, and frustration. Most saw in the biological mother not a monster but someone who also needed care and mothering. Some mothers wanted no contact with children's biological mothers; others were willing to work with them, to teach them mothering, and to include them in family activities.

> If I adopt Bertie and Sarah, if their mom wants to, she will be part of my family. Now I have to rephrase that. I don't know. It depends on her, her attitude. And if she cleans herself up—her life[1]—she is welcome to see

her children. I would even allow her to stay here occasionally. They are her children. But I have to protect them, you know, and if she is doing good, yeah, why not? I want them to know who they are and where they come from. I don't want to take that away from them. But I feel if that is a threat to them, then I won't allow it. . . .

I think that their mom just had a lot of things happen within her life as a child, I am sure, growing up as a teenager. I don't know, but I just assume that she did, and she just hasn't found her place in life, and she is not, to me, not secure. And her daughter, Bertie, is just like her. And I don't think a person like that will be good to teach [Bertie differently] unless she can overcome those fears herself. She will never be able to do anything for [Bertie] as far as making her a rounded out person. . . . But I am not angry at her. I feel that could be my daughter. That could be my daughter that had a bad life. I don't think that people are just born bad or born wanting to have children and not take care of them. Something had to trigger it. No, I don't feel angry at her. I feel angry when she promises [Bertie] and don't keep it. You can make a promise sometime and not keep it, but not constantly. . . . I mean I lose so much ground when her mother calls. See that makes her feel she is going to be going home so she feels she doesn't have to listen to me. You see, and then she starts acting out. We can accomplish so much, and one phone call can tear it all down. . . . [But their mother,] she is like a child herself. No, I can't say I am angry at her. 'Cause it could have been my kid, anyone could fall into that [drugs]. We can say where we been, but we can't say where we're going.

Claims of belonging and reconstitution also had implications for family structure, dynamics, and kinship names. Mrs. Hansen's foster children all called her auntie and claimed her as their mother. Like Mrs. Hansen, foster families rarely experienced their family developmental life cycle as linear. Seldom did a familial cohort of children grow to adulthood and leave home, signaling the end of the live-in parent-child caregiving relationship for the parents, since children of all ages joined foster parents of all ages. Because "family" was not limited to biological reproduction or to legal kinship status (i.e., adoption), seldom did a woman's age signal an end to active mother-child caregiving relationships with young children. Mrs. Hansen had raised Sarah from infancy and had raised Bertie since she was four years old. She was trying to adopt these children in order to secure their permanence. As a result, she might well continue mothering young children well into her sixties and seventies, when she might simultaneously become a biological grandmother.

In Mrs. Hansen's home, the walls of the family room were adorned with family photos and individual pictures of children. She spoke of a number of children she had raised who either had left her or had died. These children were all a part of her current family, and she often referred to them in the present tense. This practice was common to foster mothers. Foster families were able to emotionally accommodate physical changes, such as children coming and leaving, because belonging was not contingent on continuous physical presence. Instead, membership was premised on the foster-parent/foster-child relationship. Children who had long since physically departed a foster home were often still considered part of the family. This included, when possible, maintaining contact through telephone calls, letters, or shared reminiscing. Children's physical presence was almost always maintained through photographs, scrapbooks, and drawings. These were displayed prominently in most women's houses and adorned bookcases, walls, and table tops. Most women defined their families as extended kin networks rather than nuclear families even when there were no foster children physically present. In this way the foster-parent/foster-child relationship became an enduring component of a woman's individual identity and of family identity.

## Mothering Identity, Kinship, and the State

The presence of the state in foster mother's lives also conditioned women's sense of identity and their ability to maintain mothering relationships. In a very real sense, foster mothers and their foster children lacked the authority to control their own fate. For many women this meant living with the constant threat of loss. For many children, this uncertainty meant that it was never quite safe to accept the offered feeling of familial membership and really belong.

> The problem is that the first child I got was Down's syndrome. And I was connected with DMR [Department of Mental Retardation]. . . . And then I got involved with the Department of Children and Families—well, that's the problem, because I have two children from Department of Mental Retardation and two children from Department of Children and Families, and their licenses conflict with each other. They do not allow, they do not want me to hold licenses from two different agencies, which I can't see for the life of me. What on earth does that have to do with

children who need a home and don't have anyone to take them? . . . I wouldn't trade anything in the world for these kids. Nothing. And this is why I fight so hard for them . . . . I've gone through hell with them now. You know, I could not—I can't [her voice wavered and she fought back tears]. . . . It's going to be so hard to give them up if I have to. I suppose if I have to, I will. But I don't want to. Even just thinking about it makes me upset. . . . I have such a problem with DCF, I thought they were supposed to visit like every two weeks or so. I have not seen or heard from a social worker in almost five weeks. And I have been calling, and I don't get an answer.

At the time of this interview Mrs. Hansen was in danger of losing her family. She fostered for two separate state agencies, and, according to her, there is a policy that prohibits foster mothers from holding licenses from more than one agency at a time. To Mrs. Hansen, Catherine, Cassandra, Bertie, and Sarah were her children. As she cared for them, loved them, fed them, and endured their rages she waited to see if they would be taken from her or if she would be asked to choose which children to give up. While she defined herself as a mother in relation to her foster children and defined her children as family in relation to her, her experiences with the Department of Children and Families and other social service personnel dramatically contested these definitions of kinship and personal identity.

Implicit in the department's definition of foster care (i.e., foster care is a substitute family life experience) is the belief that foster care and the relationship that foster parents form with foster children is transitional and thus temporary. This construction of foster mothering is communicated to social workers through agency policy and to foster mothers through their interactions with social workers. The practical implications of these constructions were that women often felt embattled in their relationships with social service personnel and felt that their relationships with children were denigrated or trivialized. Many foster mothers also felt that their expertise was invalidated and were discouraged about sustaining their work over an extended period of time.

Mrs. Hansen had a mother-child relationship with her foster children because of who she was, how she saw herself, and how she saw herself in relation to children who needed her. In other words, she formed relationships with them because she could not *not* do so. Yet, like all of the women in the study, she formed permanent kinship bonds within the context of relationships defined through the state as impermanent and transient. Thus a part of mothering was the constant battle to assert her right and need to hold onto her foster children and, through holding on, to maintain the kinship relationship of mother that she had carefully established. She also fought for her children's right to be held onto by her and their right to claim her as family.

The often painful struggle to have one's self-defined identity recognized, valued, and legitimated in practice was a hallmark experience of fostering for these women. Foster mothering was effected through the tension between foster mothers' definitions of fostering and motherhood and state policies and practices that contested this construction. This tension was felt by women in varying degrees, but no woman was unaware of it or unaffected by it. The pressure was further exacerbated by the fact that social workers defined a "good" foster mother as one who could relate to children as a "mother" and who could love and care for a child as though it were "her own" but let the child go immediately and completely when asked to by the state.

In spite of this, women still added foster children to their families and formed close and intimate relationships with them. But loss and bereavement also became a hallmark of fostering. This was especially true if women felt that the child was going to live in a less suitable place than the foster home. As in Mrs. Hansen's situation, the anticipation of loss and the sense of powerlessness to influence their children's fate became a loss in itself: a loss of power through state appropriation of their parental responsibility.

> They are all my children. And I could lose them. It's a possibility that they could take the DMR children away. And I have had Cassandra for so long now, I mean, you know. And I will [fight this]. Because I mean I put my whole heart into taking care of my children. And Cassandra's guardian gave me guardianship of her but DMR does not allow you to be a guardian of a child because they say it is a conflict of interest. Who would have more interest in a kid than the person taking care of her?

## Conclusion: Contested Motherhood

Softly, she ushers me out of the house, and I realize that everything she does is with a soft deliberateness, a gentle forcefulness: her voice, her stories, her interactions with the children, her memories of her own childhood. The house has been quiet during our talk, and I know that after I am gone she will investigate the quiet and make sure that each family member is functioning within the carefully negotiated grooves they recognize in each other as normal and routine. Bertie will soon step off the bus from school, and Sarah will no longer be pacified in her high chair. Cassandra has been calling for Mrs. Hansen during our talk because she wants to go to bed. But sleeping during the middle of the day is not good for her, and she will have to be kept up and amused. Mr. Hansen will pick Catherine up from the DMR day treatment center, and after dinner Mrs. Hansen will get the children ready for the night as she gets herself ready for her job as a private duty nurse's aide.

As she goes about the daily family routines she and her foster children have built their lives around and through, she carries with her the knowledge of another and simultaneous reality and the burden of impending grief. She is aware that the way she thinks of herself and her foster children is very different from the way she is defined by the state, and sometimes by her neighbors, and the children's teachers. They are her family and not her family. And she is aware of the power others have to impose their definitions of mothering, family, and fostering on her and on her world.

While Mrs. Hansen's story is about her experiences and the meaning she has given critical life events, it is also a story about the politics of motherhood shared by most women in this study. As Evelyn Nakano Glenn points out, "Mothering is often romanticized as a labor of love, [thus] issues of power are often deemed irrelevant or made invisible. Yet . . . mothering takes place in social contexts that include unequal power relations between men and women, between dominant and subordinate racial groups, between colonized and colonizer" (1994:17).

Clearly unequal power relations with the state are a hallmark feature of women's fostering experiences. It is these power relations that condition how motherhood, family, and work are defined and ultimately determine how they are enacted by foster parents. Foster motherhood is lived through this tension. It is an experience marked by state policies and procedures that, to some degree, reproduce gender, class, and ethnic hegemony. Yet, women's fostering stories do not so easily fit into dichotomized power relations characterized by the powerful and the powerless. Women's fostering stories are about their labor *and* their love. They are stories about women's power and agency to define and enact particular visions of identity and gender and to have those constructions socially recognized and valued. *And* they are stories about women's pain, disappointment, and struggles to define themselves through relationships premised on assumptions of gender and generation that contradict the state's.

While the social relations of fostering encompass oppression/resistance patterns, they also create new patterns of interaction and social change. Unfortunately, for the women, children, families, and social workers involved in the daily struggle to care for children who can no longer live with their families of origin, these processes of change are often experienced as painful, disappointing, and exploitative. For foster mothers, subjugated motherhood is often an intricate part of this pain. At the same time, however, the experience of foster motherhood and resultant fostering stories are an important factor in the reshaping of gender ideologies that ultimately redefine motherhood, kinship, and work.

# 3

## Mothers and Workers
### *Becoming a Foster Mother*

Oh, sure, yes, there are days when I go, whoa, I should get a job,
it would be easier than this! I think raising kids is work, but I
wouldn't call it a job.
—Sarah Perkins, a married Euro-American woman
in her late forties

### *Mothering and the Decision to Foster*

Like Mrs. Hansen's most women's decision to foster emerged from a simultaneous vision of themselves as mothers, caregivers, and social actors with significant knowledge and ability to contribute toward soci-
etal change. It also emerged from a concomitant vision of themselves as
mothers and workers whose lives revolved around home and children,
and whose life work was associated with intersecting public, political,
and economic realms.

Foster mothers tended to link their mothering abilities to essential
cultural experiences. Empathic knowing and an ethic of care were imprinted on and through a gendered body that served as a lens through
which the social world was negotiated.[1] As one foster mother in a focus
group told me, and others echoed their agreement, a foster mother "really has to have it in her heart if they want to do it. It can't just be
something you do because if you don't have it in your heart, it won't
work." Another woman put it this way: "No one just decides to be a
foster mother. It is something that is in you already. You do it because
there is an emotional attachment to motherhood."

In general, women's reasons for fostering fell into five overlapping
and inclusive categories: (1) altruism and social and moral responsibility, (2) family tradition, (3) social action, (4) the desire to increase the

size of one's family, and (5) the need or desire for income or employment. In addition, several themes about self and community were consistently woven through women's discussions: (1) physical space as a metaphor for emotional availability, (2) being chosen rather than choosing to foster, and (3) informal fostering as a pathway to formal fostering. Seldom did foster mothers cite one or even two discrete reasons for fostering. Rather, when talking about their journey into foster care, they consistently wove many or all of these reasons as well as several of these themes through their discourse. The following comments about how and why women got started in fostering represent the range of themes expressed in the larger sample.

> Where I work at the railroad, once there was some kids that come in—one kid about seven years old came in. His mom had put him out, okay, from the projects, which I work right across from, the Church Street projects. The mother had put him out. And he stayed in there for like a couple of days. And I wanted to take him and bring him home. But it was like, I knew there would be trouble if I tried. And finally, I decided we needed to talk to the policeman about it. And a policeman went over there. And I don't know what they ever did with that child. We never could find out what happened to the kid. But we did find out what happened [i.e., find out why he was sleeping in the train station]. The mother had left the little sister for the boy to watch, and I guess they went outside or something, and she put the little boy out. And that's what got me really going to help these kids. (Clara White, a single African American woman in her late fifties)

> Well, I was baby-sitting just friends and kids, and I was working at Pratt and Whitney, and I got laid off, and I went back in the workforce. It was probably at the time when there wasn't very many jobs left. So I went into a temp, and from temp I knew an attorney and she was there, [saying] "Why don't you become a foster mother?" And I was like, "A foster mother?! I just about killed myself raising my own kids." She said, "No. You'll be good. You will like it." [I said,] "Oh, I will think about it." So after doing temp for a while, and I said, okay, I am just doing temporary assignments, maybe I should look into that. So I looked into it. . . . I went to classes, and became a foster mother. (Beatrice Rollins, a single African American woman in her late fifties)

> Because my husband and I, not to toot our own horn, but we think we're pretty good parents. . . . For kids who need good parents—I mean, you look at the world today, and there's so many kids out there who just, if

they had a better start or a better, you know, someone else that could help them along the way . . . [would make it.] (Sophia DiMaggio, a married Euro-American woman in her middle thirties)

She [my wife] had been baby-sitting for years and doing family day care and stuff in upstate New York. . . . She likes the challenge. She likes the kids, and we've got to have kids around. She'd rather be here than out working, so this is her job. (Stan Ferguson, a Euro-American married man in his middle fifties)

In all honesty, I didn't decide to become one, I knew someone who was a foster mother and . . . she took three siblings in, and she asked me if I knew somebody in the area because they couldn't find a home for this one particular girl. And I decided that I would take her. . . . I mean I do it because I really want to, I really have a love for children, and I want to see children succeed and give them a chance to succeed. I truly do, from the bottom of my heart. (Belinda Evans, a married Euro-American woman in her early fifties)

Well, we wanted to help a little girl, and she—we're pastors, and we wanted to help this child. . . . We wanted to give the kids a foundation, all right. We know a man that was in the system as a child. For three months he was in a Christian home. He said it changed his life. You know, he was in foster care for ten years. But that three months in that home made his life. He always remembered that there was a better way to go, and now he's a minister of the Gospel. And I would think about that, and I'd think, now if I don't have a child but for a few weeks or a few months, we'll just love them and we'll pray over them, and send them on. (Martha Conrad, a married Euro-American woman in her late fifties)

## Altruism and Social and Moral Responsibility

Central to almost all women's reasons for fostering was the desire to "help" or change things for individual children and their families. While both social workers and foster mothers articulated this desire, the meaning of it and the position of the self relative to those being helped was significantly different for the two groups. For social workers, helping was a personal commitment delimited by professional responsibility. Their work was supported and sustained through a socially legitimated bureaucracy that defined their daily actions through a carefully articulated hierarchy. Foster mothers consistently saw helping in terms of an intimate relationship through which all necessary things emerged—healing, material resources, kinship, individual and social transformation. While mothering held a definite connotation of strength, power, and agency, it was seldom if ever power over another. Instead the mother-child relationship was defined as collaborative, its balance of power subject to change through time, circumstances, and need. Foster mothers prized the mothering knowledge they brought to the relationship but did not see knowledge as power, since through a relationship knowledge was frequently negotiated, modified, and always collaborative.

Through their relationships, women also empathically felt children's needs and recognized their own obligation to assume the responsibility of children's care regardless of the hardship it represented. The obligation to respond was moral. Once one saw, experienced, or intuited another's need, there was no turning back. Diana Bubeck captures this sentiment of a caregiver's empathy: "[F]eeling with the other arouses in us 'the feeling I must do something.' When we see the other's reality as a possibility for us, we must act to eliminate the intolerable, to reduce the pain, to fill the need, to actualize the dream" (1995:155). Whatever joys, burdens, or hardships came with fostering, they were accepted; while they were a part of the story, they were never a part of the choice. And as a consequence of their acceptance, children with numerous physical or emotional problems were integrated into a woman's life. As this mother suggested,

> My mother took in our cousins and there were three of those. So, we—I became acquainted with having other children in the home. Also, I thought it was a very good way for me to do something for my community. You know, some people volunteer for the ambulance service or, you know, do things in the hospital, but I thought it was more of an impact to do something for families, so that's what I did. . . . I wanted my—I didn't want, ever, ever want a child to say "I was in foster care and nobody cared." So I just tried to not let that happen. (Ann Howle, a married Euro-American woman in her late forties)

The knowledge and expertise women brought to fostering were necessarily gleaned from their own life experience. It was not uncommon for women to relate experiences from their own childhood and family to their reasons for fostering. This was often combined with the belief that children represented the future of society and therefore must be well cared for and protected. Exemplifying these sentiments were two foster mothers who had been foster children through DCF. One woman was raised in a home with her sister for eight years before eventually returning to live with her father. She remembered her foster mother with affection and was grateful for the care she received. Her experiences impressed upon her, in a deeply personal way, that there were other children like her who needed a home, needed to belong to someone, needed a mother.

The other woman who had been a foster child had a poor experience. She was treated as a maid and baby-sitter by her foster families. If she complained about her treatment, she was moved to another home. Based on insights gained from her experiences, she viewed fostering as a way of righting a wrong, of providing other children with what she knew they needed.

### Fostering as a Family Tradition and as Social Action

Other women placed their ability to recognize children in need, and their decision to respond, within a historical legacy passed down from their grandmothers and mothers or through close family friends. It was an embodied experience woman located in their hearts, heads, and hands. As one foster mother explained,

> It's always been in me. I've always been a person with children. I came from a large family that my father died when I was a ten-year-old. My mother raised me. We had a stepparent. And I always feel like this, I look at *how* the kids grow up.
>
> My mother did it, my grandmother did it. My grandmother raised fifty foster kids; she'd just take them in. The kids would be—she don't care. She just take them in. My mother did the same thing. Somebody come, they got no place, she just take them in. It was just something that was in my heart, within me. . . . I'm doing it because I love children, and I felt like they need somebody to take care of them, and that was my reason for doing it. Other than that, I would never have—I mean, I wouldn't have even taken her, even though she was my grandchild. (Mrs. Michaels, a single African American foster mother in her early sixties)

Through mothering one could ensure that the upcoming generation received the care, skills, and knowledge they would need in order to face the world with a solid sense of self. It was a woman's response to social and community survival. Through mothering, one altered the life trajectory of others, changed their opportunities, and conditioned who they would become.

> Friends of ours had done it for years. My husband always lived as a child with foster brothers and sisters. So he mentioned that he wanted to do it. And we had decided that when our youngest was school age, we would look into it. And we had neighbors move in, no mom, very busy dad, and the eight-year-old was just left home constantly alone. So we unofficially fostered him. I mean, he actually lived with us for seven days a week. I took him to school, shopping, I got him ready for school, play, the whole bit. We did everything. And he was just a wonderful little boy, and he fit well into our family, and it's just something naturally we did. So after they moved out of the area, my husband said to me one evening, we ought to look into foster care. (Ellen McKnight, a married Euro-American woman in her mid-thirties)

Those women who had contact with fostering through sisters, aunts, grandmothers, or parents had a sense of family that extended beyond nuclear family relations and a sensitivity to children's needs for a home. Exemplifying this sentiment were the Gordons, a Euro-American couple both in their early forties, who described their commitment to fostering as a way of repaying a debt incurred through the care given to them by stepparents. Mrs. Gordon stated, "Well, our stepdaughter lives with us, so I'm a stepparent. I was raised by stepparents. Tom was raised by stepparents. So it was like, not a big issue being raised by other people. So it was kind of like, let's do it for someone else. You know?" Her husband said, "We both have extended and step families. So it was no big deal. It was give-back time."

The ability to welcome children into one's family and into a relationship was an important part not only of being a mother but of being mothered and thus was a skill learned through emulation. As this mother suggested,

> I came from such a dysfunctional family. . . . [My husband] was from this mother, father, long-term married, loving family with five kids. They [did] really well together, well cared for, well-nurtured family. And I fit right into it. I saw the difference of a dysfunctional family and a loving family, who could take in anybody and give them the same love that they gave to their own children. Wonderful, wonderful. She [mother-in-law] was like my mother. I called her "mom." Her and I had such a wonderful relationship and we were really very, very close. She treated me in some ways maybe a little better than her own. . . . She showed me how parents

could love not only their own children but other people's children equally, and provide them with equally as good a home. (Lillian Rosebud, a married Native American woman in her mid-forties)

The decision to foster was also a decision to become an agent of interpersonal and social change. What women did with and for children mattered, it "made a difference." Through this difference, mothering became a part of the legacy both women and children passed on to future generations. It also linked them with all other mothers.

> I think a child needs a sense of security. I think that's very important. You just—you take them into your home and they are your child while they're here and they have all the rights and entitlements of your other children. We've done babies. We know they're not going to remember us. But if we do our job well, they'll remember things like never breaking that love, that, you know, just as a continuance of love. And I think that's really important. (Ann Howle, a married Euro-American woman in her late forties)

While women related their relationships with children to social action, children were always the subject of mothering, and women's position relative to children was consistently that of caregiver. In foster mothers' view, this attitude made them unlike social workers, who set about to change society through their casework, premised on authoritative knowledge. Foster mothers never lost sight of children in the abstract goal of social repair. Most women felt social workers could not see the person of the child, which was contingent on a caring relationship. They could intervene only with "case information" or "theoretical knowledge" rather than the embodied knowledge foster mothers valued.

> I had a very rough childhood, and I think that's why I do what I do is because I want to give a kid a chance to not have to live like that. [Q.: Did somebody give you a chance?] No. That's why—no. And that's why I feel as strongly as I do. (Belinda Evans, a married Euro-American woman in her early fifties)

> I had done this before. . . . It was not a foster care. I just took them on because two of the children had left [their parents] and they could not go back home. So I says, well let me try and just see. Maybe I can love them enough so when they go back that love will keep them and hold onto it until they'll be big enough to do something for themselves. They will always know in their minds someone loves me. So this is one of the

reasons. (Monica Stevenson, a single African American woman in her early sixties)

Almost all foster mothers had some experience with informal fostering (Stack, 1979:62–89), other-mothering (Collins, 1994:44–66), or caring for children through child lending relationships (see Lange and Rodman, 1990; Ennew, 1982; Brockman, 1987; Stack, 1979) prior to fostering for the state. They spoke about their informal fostering relationships both in terms of community survival and as a familial legacy. Informal fostering has long been an important part of African American women's histories. It has ensured individual, familial, and ethnic-community survival and development and has offered women a place of prestige and importance within local communities (Collins, 1994: 50–55). Relative to African American women, Carol Stack suggests, "The black community has long recognized the problems and difficulties that all mothers in poverty share. Shared parental responsibilities among kin has been the response" (1979:62). This commonly involved fostering children out to those who were not biological kin, thereby increasing the number of people who could "assume appropriate behaviors ideally associated with parental and grand parental roles" (63). This pattern was true for those African American women in my sample who fostered informally prior to being licensed by the state. I also found evidence of this survival and social action strategy among poor Euro-American women, though it was most frequently limited to those who fostered children related by blood.

Of those who fostered informally, most women decided to become licensed for financial reasons. Licensing allowed women to continue caregiving while assuring them of a reimbursement rate that defrayed child-rearing expenses and made sure that they would have children to foster on a regular basis. As one foster mother suggested, "It was a way to have a big family and all the fun of a big family without having the financial burdens of a big family because they [the state] paid their board and care."

## Physical Space and Adding to One's Family

Other women spoke about having the "physical space" within their homes to accommodate additional children. The availability of physical space was often a metaphor or a symbol of emotional availability.

But discussions of space were also a way in which continuity between the larger community and mothering was expressed and maintained. Women's homes, and the room to keep and raise children, situated the work of mothering and intimate relationships within the context of social action and community survival. Physical space, and women's decisions to use the space for fostering, became a form of "sexual geography" (Reiter, 1975:256), but not one in which women felt oppressed, confined, or limited from resources, but one through which they could express a powerful sense of agency and connection. As these women commented:

> It was just something we always thought about. We rented—at one point we rented a remodeled barn, and it had five bedrooms, and we had only two children. So we thought, put it to use. And that was when we applied. . . . I just wanted my kids, too, to grow up caring about people. And I thought that was a good way to get them to, to start early on. (Sandy Pescatori, a married Euro-American woman in her late thirties)

> I think all that you read in the paper, all that you hear on TV and the media, you know, you want to do as much as you can for as many as you can, because they depend on us, you know. And I'm glad that we can do it and that we have the space, that we have the experience [parenting]. . . . [And] there are some selfish [reasons]: the slightest bit of improvement or growth or the absence of a behavior that was inappropriate is really thrilling. (Sylvia Pollins, a married Euro-American woman in her early fifties)

> Well, I had seen a commercial, they were asking for foster parents for children. And we had just bought this big old place up in East Killingly, and we had so many extra rooms. So we decided to go into foster care. (Fredrica DaSilva, a married Euro-American woman in her late fifties)

Several women spoke of wanting to have a family or to add to their families and of not being able to. For example, women spoke of losing children to miscarriages or of not being able to get pregnant a second or third time. Since foster children were regarded as family members, fostering became a way of doing this. Others spoke of how "God" or "nature" had dealt them a particular hand, implying a certain degree of powerlessness to remedy their reproductive limitations. Paradoxically, while women felt control over their family was diminished through involvement with the state, fostering was a way of exercising control over family size and membership that eluded women through reproduction. As a result, the decision to foster was articulated in terms of relief, gratitude, empowerment, and a sense of agency. By choosing to be foster mothers, they effectively changed the hand they had been dealt.

### Being Chosen to Foster

At times, the decision to foster was expressed in a discourse in which women emphasized their being chosen rather than their choosing to foster. Their decision was generally prompted by knowledge of a particular child and her/his situation, or by a previous relationship with a child. Several women spoke of becoming aware of, and being moved by, a particular child's situation and getting licensed in order to care for him/her. Others spoke of being approached by a social worker who told them of a particular child and asked them if they would take her or him in. These parents generally held a special license enabling them to foster only those children. Most of these parents, however, later pursued a regular license allowing them to accept other children into their homes.

The subtext of stories in which women were chosen was that as women and mothers, they possessed recognizable gifts of caregiving and empathy that had been acknowledged by people in their community. Despite the culturally devalued social status of full-time mothers (i.e., women who do not "work") and of foster mothers in general, these women found mothering a source of prestige and power. It meant that they were special and what they did with and for children was important, since their talents had been confirmed through public affirmation. Euro-American women tended to talk about the ways in which they had been approached by someone in authority, such as a DCF social worker, or someone from the local school, or a minister to foster a child. Thus, "community" tended to mean someone whose recognition conferred a degree of social legitimation and prestige.

In contrast, African American women, as Patricia Hill Collins suggests, tended to "receive respect and recognition within their local communities for innovative and practical approaches not only to mothering their own 'blood' children, but also to being other-mothers to the children in their extended family networks and those in the community overall" (1994:56). This was clearly evidenced by the way in which neighborhood families called on foster mothers for emotional support in times of crisis, for childrearing advice, for material support, for parenting advice, and for childrearing assistance (see Chapter 5 for a case illustration). These foster mothers gave their assistance to those who asked with the clear intention of making a difficult life, or particular life challenges, easier.

## Mothers and Workers

Woven within women's descriptions of mothering and the act of establishing an intimate relationship were idioms of work. "Work" referred to the reimbursement received for fostering or the tasks required of women when caring for children. It also referred to the way in which the reimbursements enhanced a woman's financial position. In this respect, fostering was like a job. It emerged from informal fostering or from a woman's experiences providing child care in exchange for money. For example, many women began as day care providers or baby-sitters and saw fostering as an extension of this work with the added benefit of having more input in children's lives. Several women said fostering was like a job because it enabled them to contribute to the family income without participating in wage labor they might not enjoy or labor that had little social value. For example, one woman with two young children said, "If I didn't do this [fostering], I might be working at McDonald's."

Others acknowledged that they possessed few marketable skills other than caring for children and did not want to do anything but mother. Fostering was consistent with their needs, interests, and abilities and was a way to supplement their income through a cottage industry. For married women whose husbands were employed outside the home, fostering was a second family income that allowed them to stay home and care for their own children as well as foster children.

> I'm home and helping my husband run the business, and yet to me I'm still working for myself, because I'm a foster mother, I'm doing what I want to do which is taking care of kids. I'm running my husband's business while I'm here at home doing the things I have to do, and I have to agree, I feel that younger children need a mother at home in the house so when they get off that school bus, mom's home to listen to their problems and supervise and care for them. And that's what I'm able to do. Foster care gives me that ability to stay home and work. Because to me

foster parenting is working in the home. (Lillian Rosebud, a married Native American women in her mid-forties)

While fostering always included some thought and discussion about the economic aspects of motherhood (i.e., the need for money, the cost of raising children, of maintaining a household, or of simply surviving), no woman thought of mothering as wage labor in the following respect: no woman looked at foster mothering with cool dispassion or thought it possible to maintain emotional distance from children. Neither did any woman talk about fostering or foster children as a business, though many foster mothers said they knew of, or had heard of, someone who did. Thus for the women I spoke with, fostering was necessarily work that involved creating and maintaining affectionate relationships and required an emotional investment. The reimbursement was incongruous neither to their mothering work nor to the emotional relationship established with children. Many women said things like, "This is not a job, this is my life."

In a discussion about what a foster mother is, one woman combined the language of a mother with the language of a worker who provides an important "service" to children. The "service" she was referring to is mothering, that is, loving, nurturing, and empathically caring for children. Even though an aspect of this work may be time limited, this mother suggested that it is critical to totally commit yourself emotionally to children.

> Mother. If you look at yourself as a temporary mother, although you know it's a temporary situation, I don't think you can provide the proper kind of service to the kids, because children deal with emotions and they are very susceptible to picking up on things that maybe you don't think about. But if you hold back from them in any way, they can sense that. If you really want . . . to be good to the kids and provide them with all the love and attention they need, you have to put all the other feelings aside and just let yourself completely fall in love with a kid basically. . . . That's what you have to be willing to deal with. You have to be willing to take [the pain that comes from separating after you have fallen in love]. (Lillian Rosebud, a married Native American women in her mid-forties)

Another foster mother, while discussing how and why she began fostering, suggested that mother, foster mother, adoptive mother, and worker are necessarily inclusive identities. Her decision to foster emanated from her need for money and her affinity and experience caring for children. She was a woman with a family, and she was a worker who needed to contribute to her family's support. Economic survival was an important part of her life story.

> It's a long story. I moved from Atlanta, Georgia, to here. It was hard for me to find a job at that time. I had a eighth-grade education, no skills, nothing but domestic work. That's all I knew how to do. So I decided, well, I heard it on TV, please open your hearts to children. I decided that I could do this for some money. I would get paid. But little did I know it was $69 a month. That's all they offered me. So I went to it [to apply], but I told them no. But when they sent the references to the people where I had worked and private homes where I had took care of their children, they came back and asked me over and over, the state did, to reconsider. So I still said, no, because it wasn't enough to help us, you know. [Then] they brought these two little twin babies and let me see them. When I saw those babies, I just had to have them. But we were not allowed to adopt them then. So we waited until they were six years old, but every time they would take them out for visitations for somebody to adopt them, they wanted one, not both. They didn't want two babies. They were just looking for one. But I prayed and cried, don't let them take my babies. So eventually they became six years old and the law changed and we adopted them. From then on, I got into it— and there was another brother and sister, and continued it all the way through [for thirty years and fifty-four children]. (Norma Peel, a married African American woman in her seventies)

Because she approached her work through her love of children, her story also points to the emotional exploitation women who become licensed frequently encounter. Most women, like Mrs. Peel, had experience caring for more children than they were comfortable with, for longer periods of time than they wanted to, more frequently than they wanted to, and often when they could not financially afford it. This contributed to the public (and DCF) perception that women "stacked up" children in order to make money.

Since women defined their mothering as work, as an important service and responsibility, receiving money from the state logically followed. While many women stated that the money they got from fostering "supplemented" or "helped" their family income, others observed that reimbursement rates for foster children were too low to adequately cover all of their expenses. Differences in the way women responded to questions about state reimbursements generally were based on their socioeconomic status. Those women who lived in poverty or just above the poverty level viewed the money they earned from fostering as helpful. It was steady, predictable, consistent, and a supplement to their incomes that afforded them opportunities they would otherwise not have had. While foster children were treated like biological children, mothers were clear that neither biological nor foster children had opportunities for "extras" (camp, art lessons, dance lessons, class rings) or luxuries (new versus secondhand or hand-me-down clothes) women might have wished for.

For these women, state reimbursements meant that they could do certain things (care for children, pay the rent or mortgage) or have certain things (a washing machine or a larger car) that they could not otherwise afford. As foster children became a part of women's families, money earmarked for taking care of them was reasonably spent on activities or household expenses that assisted the entire family. Most women said that their state reimbursement checks were placed in a general checking account used for household management and daily expenses. In this way, money from the state actually gave women autonomy, since the state did not stipulate what the money should purchase or exactly how a child should be taken care of. If the child was part of the family, and the head of the household deemed it good for the family to remain in a certain house or apartment, then it was good for the foster child. State reimbursements could be used in good conscience for mortgage or rent payments.

Those women whose incomes placed them in the middle class complained either that the reimbursements added nothing to their household incomes or that foster children cost them money. In these families, women said they treated their foster children identically to biological children in terms of the amount of money spent on their care. These households tended to be very aware of the children's appearances. Foster mothers complained that their foster children often needed new clothes when they arrived, and it was foster mothers who had to pay for them since a lump sum clothing voucher was a one-time occurrence and reimbursement checks often took at least a month to begin.[2] They also wanted and often paid for their foster children to participate in extracurricular activities (such as camp, dance, music, or art lessons, hockey, etc.), and family vacations.

When talking about the reimbursement rate as a salary, or as money they received for child care and thus money that made them "professionals," all women said the compensation was not enough considering their expertise and the time and energy required for raising foster children.[3] In fact, when talking about this aspect of child rearing, most women expressed a sense of exploitation. As several women commented, being a foster mother, like being a mother, was a full-time job spanning twenty-four hours a day, seven days a week. Several asked, "Where else could you find someone with expertise and knowledge to do this kind of job?" But although they often complained of being financially exploited, their sense of exploitation emerged primarily when they felt that the services they provided for children were undervalued, marginalized, or overlooked. That is, women were able to tolerate what they perceived as financial exploitation until it was paired with being emotionally and professionally unappreciated. Efforts by the state to show foster mothers appreciation, such as annual appreciation luncheons or special awards, were mentioned by some women as evidence that their services were not completely undervalued. But women overwhelmingly talked about their daily interactions with social workers and with agency policy as evidence of their devalued status.

## State Reimbursements and Tainted Mothering

Foster mothers were clearly comfortable with their dual identity as mothers and workers, but it often provoked tension, ambivalence, and mistrust in state social workers. Unfortunately these sentiments are not new and have plagued the foster care system for over a hundred years. In 1874 this commentator suggested, "The principal weakness of the boarding-out system lies in the fact that it is founded on two opposite principles. The first is confidence in the benevolence of human nature. The second, is distrust of its selfishness and dishonesty. The former is expressed in the affectionate title of foster parent, and the latter in the elaborate supervision by which his conduct is watched and reported on to the Guardians" (in Zelizer, 1985:206).

This ambivalence on the part of social workers emanates from confusion about foster mothers' identities and work. As temporary child care workers, foster mothers are considered untrained paraprofessionals who are subordinate to social workers. Because they are "workers" (economic figures), they could not possibly engage in affectionate, caring, familial relationships with children. They are economic figures whose short-term caregiving services are purchased, and so they cannot really be mothers. According to foster mothers, social workers often thought of foster care as little more than a convenient holding place for children. Seldom did they regard foster care as a "home" with the connotation of permanence, love, and affection. They often placed foster mothers in a classificatory limbo, treating them as nonmothers and as nonworkers. Social workers often expressed mistrust through a discourse of delegitimation in which foster mothers' money-spending decisions were suspect. The derisive phrase "in it for the money" was repeated fairly consistently by social workers, as though the economic need experienced by most foster mothers negated an affective relationship with children.

Social workers tended to believe that the money women got from the state should be spent directly on foster children. And most expressed the view, consistent with policy, that women should be economically self-sufficient without state reimbursement. Money from the state was rightfully money for the foster children and so was seen as the child's money. Social workers expected foster mothers simply to act as mediators or agents. They should receive the check and either turn the money over to the child (this was true if the child was a teenager), or spend the money directly on younger children. Social workers looked with suspicion at women who did not demonstrate this spending pattern. According to most foster mothers, social workers questioned women's decisions about how money was being spent and voiced mistrust to foster mothers who could not be trusted to "have the child's best interest" at heart.

Thus more than being seen as nonmothers, they were automatically seen as bad mothers. Most women understood the stereotypes through which they were being defined but felt they were powerless to correct or change them, since agency/foster-mother power relations allowed for no direct dialogue, only innuendo built into casework services and relationships. Many women felt that social workers used visits to ascertain how foster parents were failing, based on the assumption of bad mothering. For example, caseworkers' relationships with foster children were, from women's perspectives, often premised on the assumption that foster mothers could not be trusted to tell the truth or to treat children well. They had to be monitored, supervised, and checked. Rather than loving mothers or dedicated caregivers, they were perceived as a potential threat to foster children. Foster children were seen as potential victims of yet more "bad mothering."

These dynamics were most often enacted during social workers' visits. Commonly, social workers took children to get ice cream or went to McDonald's to ascertain if they were happy in foster care and were being treated well. They also used that opportunity to share information about the disposition of the child's case. This was necessarily a one-sided inquiry, and women expressed fear that children would exaggerate, or would not tell the truth, or would express anger at foster mothers by telling the social worker lies about the care they were receiving. It also meant that a lot of the information foster mothers received about case plans came from the children themselves rather than social workers, since, as many women pointed out, social workers had limited time to spend on a visit and perceived themselves to be exclusively the child's social worker. It also meant that foster mothers had no say when children received certain news about their situation.

Those foster mothers who complained about social workers' interactions with children said that social workers tended to undercut women's parental authority by asking questions about foster mothers' rules and parenting behaviors. As one foster mother cautioned her adolescent daughter when the social worker was coming to take the girl to McDonald's, "Don't sell me out for a hamburger!" Other women complained about how social workers dropped in unannounced. As one mother stated, her foster children's social worker kept coming by at dinnertime. "It was so clear that she came over at dinnertime to see what I was feeding the kids. You know we don't eat steak, but we eat OK."

Social workers who visited foster children often complained to foster mothers if the child's clothes were dirty, mismatched, or not new. Many social workers felt that, since the foster family was being given money for the child's care, the child should be wearing new or matching clothes all of the time. What was important to social workers was that a child should not *look* like a stereotypical image of a foster child, one who had few material resources, or one whose clothes signified poverty and temporary, thus nonfamilial, care.

Foster mothers' responses to this were twofold, and ironically they were just as concerned with the appearance of "difference." First, they asserted that children were being integrated into their households and should dress in the same manner as the rest of the family. Second, foster mothers expressed irritation with social workers who complained that children or their clothes were dirty when they were playing. Dirt was a "normal" and expected part of childhood. Social workers who came infrequently for short visits were likely to see foster children at play or just having come from play and therefore disheveled and dirty. Women did not feel it was right to make children "clean up" for the social worker's visit. This cleanup, in combination with the visit, was regarded as a pointless ritual that unhappily signaled a foster child's "difference" from other children in the family or from the family as a whole.

Another example of social workers' mistrust of foster mothers' use of "state money" was their suspicion of women who bought new cars or large household items such as washing machines. Social workers attributed a woman's ability to purchase these items to the money she received from fostering and felt this was not a legitimate way to spend "the state's" or "the child's" money. Social workers saw such a purchase as a decision that took money away from the rightful recipient, the foster child. Foster mothers were relegated to "bad mother" status because they essentially stole from a child. Foster mothers attributed their decision to buy a new car or a washing machine to increased household need. For example, most women found that with an increased number of children, one car was no longer sufficient to hold the whole family, or an old unreliable car was no longer adequate since foster children had to be transported to appointments on a regular basis. Faced with the decision to take two or three burdensome trips to the same location or to spend reimbursement money on a new car most foster mothers felt the expenditure was justifiable and appropriate. This also applied to washing machines or dryers. Women claimed their laundry loads increased sometimes four or fivefold with foster children. A new washer and dryer enabled them to deal with the increased strain on their household more effectively since trips to the laundromat with a number of children were as impractical as they were difficult.

Poor women were especially suspect in social workers' eyes. According to social workers, they were always asking about or demanding money from the state. Social workers inferred that they were only interested in money, a sign of their inability to provide good care. In the cases I witnessed, the lack of an economic safety net, combined with the desire and need to provide for children, prompted these women to discuss money with social workers. When children were placed, many women saw that they needed new clothes, shoes, toys, haircuts, or school supplies. While middle-class women had the resources to purchase these items and wait until the reimbursement check arrived, poor women simply could not always adequately provide for a child without the state's immediate help. Some inquired about the reimbursement and asked that processing be speeded up or asked for immediate assistance for needed clothing. Frustrated with the state's unresponsiveness and desperate for money to care for children, some threatened to have the child removed if support was not forthcoming. This was shrewd, since new placements were often harder to come by than clothing vouchers. It was also justifiable because most women regarded the state as the economic supporter of foster children. Women labored to provide emotional and physical care for foster children; the state's responsibility was to support children financially. When the state was negligent (and it often was, either by not sending checks or by sending checks late), then the message was that the relationship was in jeopardy. Short of threatening children's removal, another solution was to stockpile secondhand clothes. But such stockpiles too were regarded as suspicious by social workers, who felt they must mean that foster mothers were pocketing reimbursement checks and making a profit on children.

Women who worked outside the home and had a reliable and adequate source of income did not necessarily see the state's reimbursements as a good thing. These women were glad they did not have to rely exclusively on the state for financial support since to do so could ultimately restrict their freedom and could place them in a situation where they could be degraded by state social workers. As many suggested, if fostering was their only source of income, they would have no recourse but to tolerate interactions they found abusive. They often regarded the state as a potentially controlling force that could try to limit or unfairly direct their activities and would humiliate them through imposed dependence. These women were much more likely than those who had no other source of income or a meager source of income to express indignation at the way in which they were treated by state social workers. While few women felt they had any recourse to correct a perceived injustice (either in the way they had been treated or in the way case decisions about foster children had been made), women who perceived that they had financial security outside of the state's reimbursements felt they could at least terminate their relationship with the state. These women often said, "I don't need this. I could quit." On the basis of my sample, it is highly unlikely that many women would terminate that relationship, but the perceived ability to do so was important. Women who were not dependent on the state financially also felt they had the ability to take restorative breaks from fostering for a few months or a year.

In response to mistrust and delegitimation, foster mothers were sensitive about money, preferring not to talk about it, especially with those whom they did not trust. In casual conversations about fostering, they often minimized their need for income or the importance of reimbursements to their household. The idea that work, mothering, and income were compatible and necessarily related was important, but it was also a self-conscious part of a fostering discourse. Thus almost every woman maintained a dual vision in which she saw herself as a worker who earned a living at mothering and was also aware that socially this identity was problematic if not impossible.

> DCF thinks they're steering you some money. They think you're not in it for anything except to get the money. I really don't think that they understand that our hearts are right there. I can't say in all cases because I do know some foster parents that do it that way. But in 80 percent of the cases, you know, our hearts are right there. And I don't think that they understand that when they're shifting a child out of your home, it's not only the child suffering. It's us suffering. It's the biological parents [suffering] because their contacts have now been broken.[4] Everybody suffers. It's a no-win situation. But the agency's attitude is "You have to learn to deal with it. It shouldn't bother the child. It shouldn't bother you." [But] you can't just be standoffish. You just can't ignore that child. . . . We were told that they were "foster children." That means emotionally we should be cut off from them because they can come and go. . . . So be standoffish. Don't get attached. Don't fall in love. [But] it just doesn't work that way. (Eleanor Gordon, a married Euro-American woman in her early forties)

## Fostering for the State

> An angry Black social worker says of a grieving white woman whose Black foster child was taken away after three years: "She had no right to love that child. It was just a job." (Katz Rothman, 1994:139)

They see you as a caretaker. The whole agency sees you as a temporary caretaker. You're being paid to take care of that kid, feed 'em and clothe 'em and that's as far as it goes. You're not supposed to love 'em, not supposed to get attached to 'em. If you get attached to the child and try to advocate on the child's behalf, the department will step in and take that child out of there because they're afraid of going up against you . . . the whole Department runs that way from the top to the bottom. (Lillian Rosebud, a Native American foster mother in her mid-forties)

Shaping women's experiences of fostering were state policies and social worker practices that regulated the formal operations of foster care. Foster mothers were all aware to some degree of these policies and experienced the way they were translated into practice on a daily basis. Thus these policies, and the assumptions upon which they were based, formed the backdrop against which the social relations of fostering were negotiated. The way they were translated into practice often formed the basis of definitional disjuncture and foster mother discontent.

The following sections provide an examination of the Connecticut Department of Children and Families policies women both referred to and experienced once they decided to become licensed by the state. While each state had particular policies and practices, the overall policy structure was remarkably similar nationwide. Often what varied the most from state to state were the names assigned to the positions social workers held within child-protective agencies or the names of specific programs; the services themselves did not vary significantly.

The Department of Children and Families (DCF) was guided in its interventions by the belief that "a child's growth and development is best served in his or her own family" (LPRIC, 1995:3). "Family" meant exclusively kinship determined through blood or legal relationships. The agency's primary role was the "protection" of children from family abuse and neglect. In Connecticut, as in many states, the goal of child protection existed concomitantly with an agency goal of "family preservation" and "family reunification."

Policy clearly stated that while the state would intervene to protect a child from abuse or neglect, the first goal of intervention was to maintain the child within her or his family and to "preserve" the integrity of the family. This was done through casework and counseling services, as well as ongoing services through DCF to monitor families and the safety of children. If a child had to be removed because her or his safety was compromised, the goal was to place her in a temporary living situation that most closely resembled the family from which she was removed, to work toward ameliorating the conditions that led to her removal, and to move toward her return.

The assumption upon which these goals were premised was that abuse was for the most part temporary in nature and situationally induced. Through time and effort, these conditions could be reversed, making it possible for the child to return home. Family interaction was assumed to fall within a prescribed range of behaviors that could be upset through environmental or situational stresses. Correcting these "stresses" allowed the family to "return to" a previous level of functioning. Thus, child abuse could be stopped by removing the conditions that caused it, and it was possible to identify these conditions. Another assumption upon which this policy was based was that a family is incomplete without all of its birth members.

Unfortunately, policies based on these assumptions of "family" often missed important cultural and ethnological differences in the meaning of kinship. Policies based on these assumptions about the nature of abuse were obsolete and could not account for the complicated and often intransigent problems faced by many families identified by DCF. As the Legislative Program Review and Investigations Committee noted in 1991, "Many of the problems that affect a client simply lie outside of the control of the department such as unemployment, drug and alcohol abuse, school dropouts, poverty, lack of housing, and teenage pregnancy. The department is called upon to treat only the symptoms of child abuse and neglect. It must choose between its role as an enforcement agency and a social service agency" (LPRIC, 1991:1).

Based on these definitions, goals of child protection and family reunification often conflicted. Child protection policies asserted that the child was the primary focus of agency intervention (the "client") and that services should be provided to ensure his/her safety. The goal of "family reunification," a goal premised on the agency's philosophy of locating familial affiliation with the child's birth or affinal kin, stressed that *should* a child need to be removed from his home, case management services should clearly focus on his return to his biological family of origin. This policy meant that the focus of casework intervention shifted from the child to the parents, thus making them "the client."

The agency's idea of foster care as a temporary "place" to put children when they were removed from their homes, and the shift in focus from the child to the birth parents, created poor working relationships between DCF and foster parents. As the Legislative Program Review and Investigations Committee noted in their most recent report on foster care, "[F]oster parents are not viewed by DCF as *families raising children* but rather as *providers of room and board,* which has resulted in an adversarial working relationship between DCF and foster parents. Most of the concerns in this area result from the department's narrow view of family reunification, which is limited to full custody of the child by the birth parent(s) and closure of the child protection case" (LPRIC, 1995:6).

In general, the agency attempted to manage these two competing goals by emphasizing each at different points in the casework process (LPRIC, 1995:5). When social workers were investigating a complaint of abuse or neglect, child protection was stressed. If the social worker had any doubts about the child's safety, or any question about a family's ability to parent, the child was removed from the home and placed in foster care. Once a child had been placed, "family reunification" was emphasized, and caseworker intervention focused on returning him to his family of origin. Foster care was seen as a severe familial disruption or "disconnection" that could threaten ongoing familial relationships (see Maluccio, Warsh, and Pine, 1993:6).

Prior to 1995, whenever children were removed from their birth homes, aggressive casework action was implemented to return them to their parents as soon as possible by providing casework services to the parents. Subsequent events in Connecticut had a dramatic impact on the way in which these two policies were managed. A legislative report noted, "In early 1995 a series of events resulting in the deaths of several children whose families had been involved with DCF caused the department to shift its policy focus to child protection from family preservation and reunification" (LPRIC, 1995:6). As a result primarily of the "Baby Emily case," in which an infant in a family known to DCF was raped and murdered, DCF implemented a more aggressive investigation and risk assessment process for all cases. The result was that more children were removed from their homes and there were greater demands on foster care resources, severely overcrowding many homes and greatly straining casework services.

Quoting from a report on the investigation of the Baby Emily case, the LPRIC investigating foster care stated that while returning children to their homes and closing cases may be "the ideal for every child and family . . . DCF must recognize that in some cases complete reunification is not in the child's best interests. In these cases it must be clear 'that protection implies the need of a child for a sense of permanence and stability, and this may require that, in some cases, parental rights must be terminated' or other forms of contact arranged, such as family visiting that affirms the child's status in the birth family" (LPRIC, 1995:6). At the time I conducted my interviews social workers were instructed to err on the side of children's safety, though the department had not amended its policies with regard to "family reunification" or the meaning and definition of this term. Essentially the LPRIC concluded that treatment plans limited primarily to removal of children with the goal of working toward their return were no longer adequate to protect their safety in the face of chronic problems experienced by their parents.

Removals of children from their homes were based on lengthy risk-assessment guidelines. DCF had guidelines for both emergency and planned removals. Once the decision had been made to place a child in foster care, social workers had to find a home. The "most desirable" placements were considered to be, first, relatives' homes, and second, "a foster family of similar ethnic background and living nearby [the natural parents] so as to allow visitation by the natural parents" (LPRIC, 1991:57).

However, this was not always possible given large caseloads and an inadequate number of foster families. Placements were generally based on availability. While recruiting foster families continues to be an important effort for DCF, more foster families have been lost than have been replaced. Recruiting foster families has become "progressively more difficult as the type of children needing foster care changes to include violent behavioral problems, substance abuse, fetal alcohol syndrome and "crack babies," AIDS and HIV positive children, and children with severe emotional or psychological problems" (LPRIC, 1991:57–58).

## Foster Parent Licensing

Once a woman decided to foster, she contacted the Department of Children and Families to be licensed. During the initial telephone inquiry, a foster care social worker asked several questions about the caller, her spouse, and her family. These questions included her age, address, ethnicity, and occupation, the age and sex of her biological children, and the age and sex of children she preferred to foster. Inquirers were then invited to an "open house" at a regional office of the Department of Children and Families. Open houses were educational meetings designed to give information to potential foster parents and to give social workers an opportunity to informally assess a couple's "appropriateness" for fostering. At the end of the open house, couples deemed appropriate were sent home with a formal assessment tool, a questionnaire designed to determine their temperament and parenting styles. They were asked to fill out the questionnaire and return it to the licensing department.

In two-parent families, both husband and wife were required to attend the open house and, once deemed appropriate potential foster parents, to attend a series of educational classes covering topics like how to parent sexually abused children and how to help children deal with loss. Classes ran for about six weeks for one evening a week, and no child care was provided. They were often team taught by a social worker and a licensed foster mother. Concurrent to attending classes, prospective foster parents were visited twice by social workers, who continued to assess parents' "appropriateness" by interviewing all family members separately and together about their relationships, interactions, and parenting styles, as well as the family's financial status. In order to be licensed, families had to have a source of income other than money from fostering.

Social workers defined "appropriate" or "good" foster parents as those who could provide a home in which children would be loved and as those who had the ability to put children's needs first. Most also mentioned the ability to be flexible, to work with the Department of Children and Families and to accommodate requests from social workers, without complaint, even when those requests required extraordinary effort on the part of foster mothers.

Approximately six weeks after initially contacting the Department of Children and Families, a foster family could receive children. One person in the household was licensed. Usually this was the foster mother. It was to this person that Title XIX medical cards for foster children and monthly reimbursement checks were sent, correspondence was addressed, and telephone calls regarding children's health, welfare, and treatment plans were made. Several foster fathers commented that they resented this arrangement since they assumed an active parenting role and developed as much expertise in dealing with children as their wives. But all felt they could do nothing about it and were resigned to remain "invisible" to the state.

Women were licensed according to the number of beds their households could provide. According to regulations, a foster home "is defined as a private family home caring for not more than five children, except: (1) when local ordinances specify a lesser number; (2) no more than two children under two may be cared for, including foster and biological children; or (3) no more than three non-ambulatory children incapable of self-preservation can be served" (LPRIC, 1995:27).[5]

Families were licensed for the age and type of children they were willing to foster. For example, a woman might be licensed to take infants, and thus theoretically would not be given a teenager from one family and an infant from another to foster (though several parents took teenage girls who either had a baby or were expecting one).[6] At some point during the licensing process, foster parents were also asked to specify the kind of fostering they wished to provide. This might be exclusively short-term or emergency placements, where theoretically a child would be placed overnight or for no longer than two weeks, or long-term placements, where a child might potentially stay for several years. Families could also specify their preference to be considered an "adoptive risk home," that is, to accept foster children whose ability to stay with their family of origin was tenuous. Generally in these situations the state was in the process of, or considering, terminating the biological parent's rights. Children would then be available for adoption and could be adopted by their foster family. However, after an extended stay in foster care there was a chance they could be returned to their families of origin, should the family prove to be capable and desirous of once again caring for their children.

Depending on the type of foster care, foster parents were reimbursed $567 a month in regular foster care for a child who was between the ages of birth and five years old, $586 for a child between the ages of six and eleven, and $637 for a child who was twelve years old or older. This rate structure was based on standards recommended by the U.S. Department of Agriculture and represented 100 percent of the USDA standard. DCF also gave foster parents a $300 clothing allowance per child at the time a child *first* entered foster care in order to provide the child with seasonal clothing.[7] Relatives providing foster care were certified rather than licensed. This meant that they were not required to complete a training program. It also meant that children were placed for forty-five days if a "home visit is conducted, a basic assessment is completed, and a criminal history check of all adults living in the home is done" (LPRIC, 1995:3). The reimbursement rate for relatives was the same as for regular foster care except if the family already received Aid to Families with Dependent Children (AFDC) in which case the Department of Children and Families considered the child's needs provided for and did not reimburse the foster parents.[8] Both regular and relative foster parents had to renew their license/certificate annually.

Foster parents could also be licensed for therapeutic foster care, in which they cared for children with severe behavioral and psychological problems, or medically fragile care, in which they fostered children with chronic and debilitating diseases like AIDS. These foster families were given additional training and provided with additional support services. The reimbursement rate for both types of care was $1,200 per month per child.

Once a foster parent became licensed, they entered into a relationship with the state that was somewhat ambiguous: foster parents provided daily care to children, but it was the state that was legally the child's guardian and that made all decisions about the child's welfare. While women who foster were parents to the children in their care, they were also employees of the state and were required to allow the state into their personal and daily lives on demand. As per policy, foster parents were required to report to the Department of Children and Families any changes in their household, such as births, deaths, criminal arrests, changes in marital status, or moves. DCF determined if the changes in some way compromised the parents' ability to continue fostering. If a foster parent was deemed out of compliance with state regulations, she was given thirty days to correct the problem, at which time her license could be revoked.

Similarly, if there were allegations of abuse and neglect of a child placed in a foster home, DCF had procedures for investigating. This generally involved a series of lengthy and comprehensive interviews, during which time a "hold" was placed on the foster parent's license. This meant that no new children were placed in the home, and potentially, though not always, all foster children were removed. If the allegations were unfounded, the case was closed. If they were founded, DCF might recommend a spectrum of interventions, from revocation of a license to counseling or additional training depending on the nature and severity of the abuse. Most women dreaded allegations of abuse and felt vulnerable during investigations, since there were policy measures protecting foster children but none protecting foster parents.

# 4

## "I'm Their Mother"

### Fostering, Motherhood, and the Construction of Kinship

I'm their mother and when one hurts, I hurt. . . . I can't tell no difference, and sometimes, like I said, I forget about it until somebody or something reminds me.

—Norma Peel, a married African American woman
in her seventies

### Mrs. Michaels's Family

I have finally found her apartment. She lives in a long low row of public housing embedded in a tangled block of winding one-way streets. The streets ring a large teaching hospital offering services to the poor families in the surrounding neighborhoods. Later I will eat in an empty luncheonette near her apartment and watch a news report of a daytime shooting in her neighborhood. The shooting is attributed to gang activity. It is not an uncommon event.

I am late, but she does not seem to notice. Instead, Mrs. Michaels, an African American woman in her early sixties, ushers me into her apartment. She fosters her grandchild, Mary-Margaret, who is six. She has fostered Mary-Margaret since she was an infant and was removed by the state from her mother.

I repeat what I have explained to her over the telephone. I am not a social worker, and I do not work for the Department of Children and Families. I once again explain the research I am doing. She says she is glad to talk with me. I turn the tape recorder on. Like most women in the study, she is not shy about the tape recorder. On the contrary, she speaks clearly, often leaning toward the recorder to make sure it is on, to make sure what she has said has been recorded, perhaps to make sure what she says may finally be heard by someone. She begins her fostering story by answering my question, How did you become a foster mother?

[Mary-Margaret] was five weeks old and the mother didn't give her the best care. She [the baby] had problems with her eyes and stuff, so they put her in the hospital and the mother called and told me that DCF has got involved and they was going to take the baby and she didn't want them to take her. She wanted me to have the baby. So then I talked to a couple of social workers. They came up to the house and we talked, and then some more of them came out and we talked and then did an inspection of the house. And, anyway, she [a social worker] asked me, you know, if I was interested and I told her I [was.] I said I'm the mother of eleven children and none of them—I raised them by myself, they was never in a foster home. I was sick for a couple of years off and on, but I still kept my kids intact. I kept them at home. And I just said, no, not one of my grandchildren would ever be raised in a foster home. I want her.

I've had her ever since. And you know, we had to keep going back and forth to court, back and forth to court. So you know, they give the mother a chance to pull herself together. Well, the father, which is my son, we never had no problem with him. He has very, you know, he'll come see her, he'll call and check on her and everything. But it was just that the mother was, you know, she was on drugs and everything, so she was kind of like out there and really, you know, can't get it together. So then you know, we start going back to court and hope she [the mother] would show up and she didn't. So, finally, they took away her parental rights. My son signed his away. He said as long as he know that the child was with me, he would sign his parental rights away, no problem, because he know she would be taken care of. . . . And finally, at one time they didn't know where the mother was at or nothing, they couldn't keep up with her. So I told them, I said, I've had her [Mary-Margaret] now for a couple of years, and I know things ain't going to change [with her mother], and you done take away her parental rights and everything, I want to adopt her. And they said fine. So we went through all the stuff with everybody coming in. And you know it was okay. [Mary-Margaret was adopted by Mrs. Michaels.]

It is midmorning in early August. Mary-Margaret is upstairs sleeping. We are sitting on the couch in Mrs. Michaels's living room. The small sliding glass living room window is disguised with ornate fabric drapes. The fabric is bright and bold. There are matching slipcovers on the couches and chairs. Behind the sofa is a bookshelf full of dolls, all wearing hand-sewn African clothes and headpieces. Dried flowers and bright ostrich feathers rest in large glass vases on the floor. Mrs. Michaels has made the drapes and the slipcovers, and she makes the dolls. One of her daughters recently got married. Mrs. Michaels sewed the wedding dress and all the bridesmaids' dresses and made the bouquets. She is in the process of doing the same for another daughter. Mrs. Michaels explains that Mary-Margaret is still asleep because everyone was up until 2:00 A.M. the night before, preparing for the upcoming wedding.

Unlike many women in this study, Mrs. Michaels did not intentionally seek the Department of Children and Families to become a foster mother. Fostering Mary-Margaret through DCF fell to her through circumstances of family commitment and obligation. Initially, Mrs. Michaels thought of fostering as temporary, lasting only until Mary-Margaret's parents could resume their responsibilities. Once it became evident that neither parent could care for the child, Mrs. Michaels took steps to adopt her.

> Well, I know the mother wasn't going to get it together, and she [Mary-Margaret] was in my home ever since [that time]. This was like the only home she knows. So I feel like [she should be adopted] in order for her to be stabilized in a home where she can say, "Well, this is my home." And I always taught her that she had a mother, she had a father, you got to know what their name was and everything. And I said, "I want you to know you can call me anything you want to call me, but I'm your grandmother, you have a mother and you have a father." I let her know that from day one growing up, and I started talking to her as a baby, you know, "I'm grandma, you've got a mommy," and I tell her what her mommy's name is and what her daddy's name is. You know . . . but then when I see things wasn't going to change, then I say, well, if I'm going to have her, I want to keep her.

Adoption is important to Mrs. Michaels for several reasons. Young children need a secure, steady home. They need a place where they know beyond a shadow of a doubt they belong. They need a parent who can protect them and provide them with a consistent caregiving relationship. The only way Mrs. Michaels could ensure that Mary-Margaret would have what she needed was to change Mary-Margaret's relationship with the state and end their involvement. As a ward of the state, Mary-Margaret was at the mercy of a fairly unpredictable state bureaucracy, which controlled her ability to stay with her grandmother.

Whether and where she "belonged" was determined by the sympathies of social workers Mrs. Michaels did not trust. Mrs. Michaels also needed to secure Mary-Margaret's belonging for herself, since she loved the child and did not want to risk losing her.

Even though Mrs. Michaels forms a mothering relationship with Mary-Margaret and adopts her, she is careful not to usurp Mary-Margaret's parents' place. "Mother" is a shared kinship position, and Mrs. Michaels takes pains to explain to Mary-Margaret where, how, and to whom she belongs in the Michaels family. Mrs. Michaels's approach to the baby's mother and her son is a nonjudgmental one. Their inability to care for Mary-Margaret presents a family problem rather than a tragic mistake or a failing.

The doorbell rings, and as Mrs. Michaels gets up to answer it, I turn off the tape recorder. There is a small dark girl in shorts and bare feet at the door. "Mama wants to know if I need stitches for this," she says, holding her bloody thumb near Mrs. Michaels's face. Mrs. Michaels takes a quick look at it. "You do," she says plainly. "You really do. Tell her to take you now to the emergency room. They're gonna stitch it up and it will be fine. But you have to have them. Go tell your mama right now." The girl, forlorn, acknowledges the command and disappears. I ask Mrs. Michaels about the girl. She looks at me as though there is little to tell. Her mother had a question about whether or not her child needed stitches. I ask if many mothers in the neighborhood consult her when there is a health or parenting question. Yes, she says. How does she know what to tell them? Why do they come to her? Because, she says, she is a mother, and they count on her to know the answers. They count on her expertise and experience. She looks out for the neighborhood children, she helps their mothers care for and raise them. I ask if she is a mother to more than her own blood kin. Yes, she says. She has always raised and cared for children who are not legally or biologically related to her. She has always been a mother to those around her.

> I love children, I love children. I've raised children in my home that was not mine. During the run of my lifetime with children, I think there were about fifteen or twenty children that went through my home. I didn't adopt them or nothing like that, but it's just that they didn't want to stay home. Their mother drank, their father drank, they was abusive parents and stuff. They would leave their homes sometimes in the middle of the night and say, "Can we stay? Can we stay?" I mean back then, people didn't report things to the authorities like they do now. So I would just

say, fine. And sometimes I would call the parents and say, "Look, your son is over here. Are you looking for him?" [They would say,] "No, we know where they're at and they're happy over there. Let him stay." You know, they just confident, "let them stay." And I said, "All right, no problem." And two of the fellows stay in my house until they got grown. They went in the service and everything. One lived in California but he won't miss a birthday. He would phone from California for my birthday. And you know, they all of them call me mom. One of them—some of them will come by here every week to see me. "How you doing, mom?" You know, I just, yeah, that's how I am with children. Because I told them like this, they didn't ask to come here, but somebody has to look after them. Whether it's their biological parent, whether it's an aunt, or uncle, or somebody, somebody has to take care of the kid.

One reason Mrs. Michaels fosters Mary-Margaret is that the child is "family," and it is important to keep family "intact." The subtext expressed by many women who cared for relatives—either grandchildren or nieces and nephews—was that family cares for family in spite of the potential hardships that edict presents. Mrs. Michaels's decision was initially made in consultation with her adult children, all of whom met with their mother to talk about who would be the best parent for the baby. But the decision to foster Mary-Margaret was not based solely on the fact that the baby was a blood relative.

For foster mothers, blood relationship is a *part* of the idea of "family." But "kinship" and "family" are defined primarily through *need*, through a woman's ability to recognize need, and based on that recognition, to form an intimate and caregiving relationship with a child. This definition enabled women—in fact compelled them—to become "mothers" to children. Motherhood is not defined through kinship but defines kinship through a relationship.

## "Any Child Could Be My Child": Defining Motherhood

For most women, the ability to love children, the act of giving, the acceptance of sacrifice, and the ability to recognize and respond to children's needs signified motherhood. Children's needs were uniformly believed to be the need to be loved, to belong, and to be cared for. The way in which women met these needs varied according to a child's age, developmental stage, abilities, and emotional state. It also varied with the individual personality of both the foster child and foster mother and the length of a child's stay in a particular foster home. What did not vary was that the ability to form caregiving relationships with children was valued as important and life-giving work. As this mother suggested,

> I see myself as a mom . . . a mother . . . who nurtures her children, does the responsibilities of a mom, carpooling, schlepping them around, washing their clothes, cooking for them, cleaning their room. "Mom, can you sew this button on my blouse?" Those are duties that come with being a mom, a housewife, a domestic engineer. My mother took care of me for how many years? I don't consider it caretaking. . . . Caregiver, love giver. I suppose you could use that term. Mothering is something that I love doing. . . . My mother said it's like you have a calling. She said you should open up a home, or whatever. . . . I'd say I probably have the calling for it because everybody that I talk to said they don't know how I could have done it this many years with the kids I've had. (Linda Vanderbrink, a married Euro-American woman in her late forties)

Some women acknowledged that the fostering relationship may be temporally limited in ways biological mothering might not be. Some spoke of the ways in which caregiving work differed from the mothering they experienced with their biological children. However, no woman felt that these differences negated her motherhood or necessarily conditioned the nature or intensity of the mothering relationship. Fostering was mothering. It was not a substitute for mothering, nor was it something other than mothering even though women's *experiences* with the two were quite distinctive.

> I feel that any child could be my child. I mean, they're all, you know, I think just caring for someone and being there and living with somebody, the bond is so strong that, to me, there is no difference between being born, biological or blood or anything. There's no difference to me, that's why I can say Tony and Issey will be my children for life and I would not treat them any different than someone that was born [to me]. (Claudette Samuels, a married Euro-American woman in her mid-forties)

> [T]hey are part of the family. . . . I don't make no difference in the kids you know. (Jerry-Ann Matthew, a married African American woman in her late thirties )

Deemphasizing difference also had to do with how foster mothers saw children's needs. As wards of the state, foster children were excluded from the nuclear family ideal articulated in popular discourses of American kinship. They were stripped of one of the essential elements that make "children" in American society, i.e., belonging to parents and family in which care and dependency needs are met. As "nonchildren" or as "temporary children" in a temporary relationship, foster children lost the singularization generally reserved in Western culture for human beings (Kopytoff, 1986:64) and assumed the quality of a commodity—a possession, a "case" that could be shifted from one location, one owner, to another. Foster mothers saw this status as damaging to children's emotional health and physically dangerous since it had implications for how they could be treated.

> It was like they were "placed." Thank you we placed them, fuck you! That's what it was like. Excuse my French. But that's what it was like. It was like okay, we got three kids placed, fuck it let's move on to the next. There has to be a lot more. They're gonna lose a lot of children that have great potential. . . . Once they're placed nobody really gives a damn. (Deleah Smith, a married African American woman in her late forties)

Inclusion in a familial relationship in which foster children were entitled to the same care and resources as other members signified the child's transformation from a "foster child," a transient visitor and an item of trade, into a singularized human being and family member. Through this transformation women also changed themselves into "real" mothers and thus moved from the liminality of foster parenting to the socially accepted domain of mothering.

> This isn't a stable, this is a home, and these kids are treated—when they come to our home you don't have to call us mommy and daddy but we are the mom and dad here. And you are a part of the family, you're not an outsider. Everything that I can give you that I think you need or every normal little child needs or wants, we try to give the kids. We never ostracized or separated any of the children from our little circle. Everybody is part of the whole. (Celestine Gordon, a married Euro-American woman in her early forties)

When asked what a foster mother was and did, one foster mother responded in a way consistent with most other women's replies—a foster mother is a mother. Contained within her comments about what a mother is or should be are two important differences between mothering and foster mothering. Fostering entails a process of watching and learning that mothering may not, since foster mothers often must piece together a child's past in a historical vacuum. In the absence of a shared past or of historically concrete information, foster mothers work hard to understand what a child has experienced and, based on those experiences, what a child will need from the mother/child relationship. Because mothers learn from children what they need, children rather than women define the healing process. Another difference is the way in which a child's past traumas are woven into and through the mother/child relationship and the empathy with which foster mothers receive their children's pain. This is the nexus of the relationship. It conditions how, and in what ways, a woman may relate to a child.

> Very difficult question. You know, it's almost impossible to answer. . . . When you have your own children, it's a much more natural process. You get [through fostering] an infant that needs to be mothered and needs to be nurtured and loved and have their needs met and know somebody's going to be there for them. You get an emotionally disturbed teenager who needs a friend and somebody to just say it's going to be okay. It's different for every—every child you get into your home is totally different. Totally different. This nine-year-old that I got yesterday is very standoffish. She doesn't want somebody to hold her. She wants to know, "I'm going to be okay, nobody's going to hurt me."
>
> So what should a mother be, depends on what the child needs. Your own kids, that's all just a very natural progression, very, very natural. You go from holding your toddler's hand and wiping their noses to giving your teenager five hours' unattended [time]. And it happens gradually and it's easier. The first few months [with a foster child] is always very, very, very hard, you know. I mean, it's stressful. I didn't sleep last night. This poor nine-year-old cried herself to sleep. I mean, I stayed with her, I rubbed her back. You know, she's been ripped out of her home, even if it wasn't the home you or I would choose for her, that was her home. That's the bottom line.
>
> Now she's dealing with the fact that she can't be with her mother either, which is a double blow—plus, she's been sexually abused, you know. And now she's in a strange home, and she did fine up until bedtime and then she cried. And she's nine years old and she has every reason to cry. But you don't think I slept well last night wondering if she was okay. You know. I mean, I couldn't even go to work this morning, even though she knows who was going to be with her and all of that, I couldn't go to work without waking her up and making sure she was okay. You know, I didn't want her to leave and not find me there and think that, you know, nobody cared. (Ellen McKnight, a married Euro-American woman in her mid thirties).

A very few women, however, noted that one always had to be aware of the inevitable ending with foster children. Therefore, they held a small part of themselves in reserve.

> There probably aren't a lot of differences. Being a foster mom is kind of easier because if they get sick, you take out your little medical card and take them to the doctor. You don't have to check your wallet and make sure you have enough money and is the insurance going to cover this or that. As far as loving the kids, I think there's no difference between my biological and my adopted. I think with foster children you kind of hold back a tiny piece of yourself so that you're not completely shattered when they leave. You know? It's like you love them 98 percent, but 2 percent is you and you just can't give it all. (Elicia Wagner, a married Euro-American foster mother in her mid-forties)

## Real Mothers, Real Families

Many women expressed discomfort with the term "foster," believing that it connoted a temporary, fake, or pseudo mother and, reflexively, referred to a nonfamilial relationship with children. This connotation was considered by women to be a misinterpretation of their work, and it was perceived as a potential threat to foster children. "State children" lived in the opposite of their "real" families—they lived in foster homes. They had no claim to kinship, an inferior claim to parental affection, and a subordinate claim to material goods. Foster mothers were also aware that through these designations foster children were signs of failed nuclear family ideals. Children were "state" children because their "real" parents, echoing the words of a nineteenth-century social worker, "didn't love them in the right way" (Zelizer, 1985:72) and failed to meet state-specified parenting standards. As products of failed families, foster children themselves were tainted. They were culturally constructed through policy and practice as damaged, failed, or nonchildren and could legitimately be excluded from resources.

> I don't see myself as a foster mother. Because I don't believe there is anything such as a foster mother. Because I look at the animal world and if they can adopt—if a dog can adopt a cat and he knows that he is not a cat, then I have to say to myself as a foster mother, I am just a mother that had to step into a situation where there was no mother. "Foster" to me means "substitute," and I am not a substitute. I am the real thing. I

am all that you've got when you are here. When you leave this situation . . . and go back to your mother, okay.

Being a foster mother to me is to try to instill in them that, no matter what the situation, that they are loved, and that they are important, and that we are striving for the same goals that we want them to get right back into the home environment and a good, loving situation. . . . You just try to do your best and do whatever you can do for them while they are here and to make them feel as much a part of your situation as they would feel if they were in a good family structure. (Beatrice Rollins, a single African American woman in her late fifties)

[A foster mother] should be a mother. A child comes into your house, and you are a mother to a child. He [foster father] was a father to George. . . . You know, that was his dad for a year. You can't get away from that. (Cindy Rogers, a married Euro-American woman in her middle thirties)

Women went to great lengths to contest constructions in which foster children were somehow different from, i.e., less than, biologically related children. Norma Peel, a mother who had been fostering for over thirty years, described a situation in which her child was relegated to the inferior status of "state child." This is something Mrs. Peel actively contested and redefined.

When I get them, I tell them that God loves you so He put you where I could take care of you. I just teach them that you know, try to treat them all as if they were mine. Sometimes I forget in mind that they're not mine until somebody reminds me that, hey, this is a foster child. We had a problem with one girl in glasses, she became a teenager and needed glasses. She wouldn't wear them because the state said only "X" amount of dollars paid for this type of glasses and the children laughed at her, made fun of her. So she didn't wear them. So we went out and put out money and bought her some glasses so she would wear them. So we tried to keep them just like any other child. I asked them, "What do you have?" to the eye doctor. He said, "These are all we have for state children." I said, "What do you have for normal children? We don't have state children. We have children."

Women also objected to a connotation of impermanence, since the relationships they developed with children were always on some level permanent, important, and meaningful. Whether or not the child stayed in a particular foster home, the relationship endured for foster mothers. Children's permanence came from the life events, impressions, and memories shared between foster children and the foster family. Every woman felt changed by a child's presence in her life. As those changes were incorporated into a woman's sense of self, each child was an important strand of her identity, each memory an important element of an identity text. Of her foster daughter, Arabelle (who after two years left to join her maternal grandparents), Sarah Perkins, a married Euro-American woman in her late forties, said, "Right now, Arabelle is still my family. You know, I'm still her mom and I hope she always calls me mom. It doesn't have to be the same mom that her other mom was. And I'd like her to do that because I think I still am. And if she came up against hard times, I would still be her mom."

A child's physical absence did not mitigate a woman's sense that a child belonged to her kin group. Belonging was instead conditioned by a reconstitution of the relationship over both time and physical distance. Children were *part of* foster mothers, incorporated into their bodies, psyches, and memories through the events and crises of daily life, and became a permanent part of who they were and how they related to the world. Linda Layne (1999:167–214) describes similar findings for women who sustained a pregnancy loss. Motherhood resulted in a changed status even when the relationship to the fetus/child was fleeting. Thus active constructions of motherhood were not contingent on the physical presence of the child or an ongoing embodied relationship. Motherhood was instead a change in selfhood actualized through ongoing *caring* even when *caregiving* was no longer possible.

Al and Betty Hobbs, a Euro-American couple in their late fifties, have fostered for over five years. They primarily foster infants. The waist-high wainscoting in their kitchen is lined with pictures of the babies they have fostered. Their refrigerator door is covered with letters, pictures, and holiday cards, some written in adult script, some in childish scrawl. They estimate that they have fostered more than nineteen children for periods of time ranging from days to years. They keep in contact with as many of their foster children and foster children's biological or adoptive parents as they can. The following excerpt, in which they point to the pictures on the wall and tell something about several of the children, illustrates the way in which their foster children have become a permanent part of their lives and have been incorporated into the story of who they are. It is interesting to note the way in which husband and wife build on each other's statements to tell the story. Together and separately they are caregivers, foster parents, parents. Children's presence, both emotionally through their memory and physically through pictures and letters, remains an active part of their daily lives.

> *Mr. Hobbs* [pointing to the first picture]: The children like you see on the wall. We've had some lovely experiences. The first one you see on the right there, she came up to visit us last Sunday. She's five. And that was our first child.
>
> *Mrs. Hobbs:* And she was four days old when we got her from the hospital.
>
> *Mr. Hobbs:* Yes. And the second one, she was adopted by a single mom. We haven't heard from her. But most of them . . .
>
> *Mrs. Hobbs:* We get a letter at least.
>
> *Mr. Hobbs:* We went through open heart surgery with her [he points to the next picture]. When we got her, she was Downs and she had a bad heart. And we went through Yale–New Haven with her with open heart surgery. And she was adopted and she's out in Wisconsin. And we hear from them . . .
>
> *Mrs. Hobbs:* They send us [letters]—you know, two or three time a week.
>
> *Mr. Hobbs:* That's some of the benefits of being a foster parent. You got all these little fellas go out in the world and then you hear from them back. That means a lot. It means the child has had a chance, and it's developing properly. And that's what it's all about.
>
> *Mrs. Hobbs:* Well, the last letter I got from her parents, you know, she apologized for not writing sooner. And I'm "You don't have to apologize; you don't even have to keep in touch with us if you don't want to."
>
> *Mr. Hobbs:* It's a benefit to see how the children are developing. [They take out a scrapbook full of pictures. Among them are pictures of the baby they are talking about, taken at the time of her heart surgery.]
>
> *Mrs. Hobbs:* I have the picture here, right here, what she looked like. Now the social worker up at the hospital said, "I don't think *you* [as foster parents] can take pictures like that." And I said, "It's for her life book. She's up for adoption. I'd like something for her life book." And I feel she's going to ask questions about the scar . . . want to know. And what better way to show her than by pictures, this is what you went through. . . . And then mommy

can tell her stuff like that. And I just figured, you know, just to show her how she was so tiny, six weeks old, just laying on that great big bed with all these tubes and needles and everything else sticking out of her.

Mr. Hobbs: And that was quite a two weeks.

Mrs. Hobbs: You know, they told us before we went in to see her that "Everything was fine. She's doing real good. She came through it fine. She's down at ICU. Her heart rate is beautiful. But you're going to see a lot of tubes and needles. And the nurse there will explain everything to you. Everything has a purpose, don't get shocked."

Mr. Hobbs: And they knew we were foster parents.

Mrs. Hobbs: They couldn't get over that we were there every day. They'd say, "Are you sure you're her foster parents?" [We'd say,] Yes. [They'd say,] "Why are you here every day?" [I would say,] "Because it's our child. That's why we're here every day."

Another way in which foster parents created *real* families was by creating a protected space through which family relationships could be normalized and the social stigmas that characterize fostering relationships removed. While domestic space was used to express continuity (that is, home was seen as part of the larger community, economy, and politics), women also spoke of their homes as safe havens for children. This meant that they also thought of home and their work as separate from the larger community. Many women perceived the familial and social world from which children came (abusive or neglectful families) and in which they survived (as wards of the state) as dangerous. Thus the need to establish a protective space was imperative. Initially this boundary excluded children's biological family and was not altered until foster mothers were sure the family (mother, father, grandmother, aunts) would not pose a physical threat to children. It almost always excluded social workers and the state.

The need for this boundary made foster mothers guardians of the home and meant that they had to be vigilant gatekeepers. It also meant that part of the role of a foster mother was to protect and maintain a dual boundary, one that was inclusive of those who were perceived as helpful, and one that was exclusive of those who were a threat. The latter particularly included those who could neither see the personhood of foster mothers and foster children nor understand the importance of the affective foster-mother/child kinship relationship. This further suggests the importance fostering relationships held for women. They were vehicles through which children were not only protected from harm but also defined as "real" rather than "state" children and claimed as family members. As Shirley Ardener suggests, "One may be tempted to argue that when the line between the hostile environment and the favorable one is drawn close to the front door, the importance of the home and the status of the woman inside, as its symbol and guardian, become correspondingly greater" (1981:19). This presents an interesting contrast to women's constructions by the state as nonmothers and interchangeable child care workers. Through the creation of protective boundaries, women create a space in which they, and what they do as foster mothers, are important and valued even while they are devalued by the state.

## Other Mothers, Grandmothers, and the Problem of Adoption

There were a very few exceptions to the characterization of fostering as "mothering." The exceptions appeared in two women who were both in their late sixties and early seventies. However, among the older women in the sample (between the ages of 60 and 75, n = 9), these were the only two who described their relationship to foster children as other than "mother." One woman, a Euro-American woman in her middle sixties, described herself as a "grandmother" and as a "stepping stone." She stated that she always knew she wanted to foster but had intentionally waited until her own children were grown and living out of her home. For her, fostering was a temporary stepping stone for children who had no place to live and who were going either back to their parents or on to adoption. She stated that she related to them much like a grandmother in that she knew she was not the permanent or primary caregiver.

Another woman, an African American in her early seventies, whose fostering career spanned more than thirty years, stated that initially she had looked at herself as a mother and had adopted many of her foster children. As she got older and became a grandmother, she said that she began to see herself as a grandmother in relation to her foster children and relate to them much the same way. She explained that when she cared for her grandchildren, she told herself that they would eventually be going back to their parents; when she cared for her foster children, she also reminded herself that they, too, would be going back to their parents.

When asked what a foster mother *did*, both of these women talked about the same foster-mothering tasks as those who considered themselves mothers. In both cases, I asked the women if they had ever considered adopting any of their foster children, that is, becoming legal parents to them. The first woman said that there had been one child, a girl who had lived with her for a year. The girl was emotionally troubled, and the foster-mother/foster-child relationship was quite turbulent. At the end of the first year, when DCF began to make permanent plans for the child's future, the girl asked if she could stay with her foster parents and be adopted. The foster mother said no, and told the child that their home was a temporary home, that they were a stepping stone. Their purpose was to get her ready for her permanent family and a permanent home. The child was later adopted by a schoolteacher in the community.

The second foster mother laughed when I asked her this question. She stated that her husband had made her promise that they would not adopt any more children. She said that it was his contention that since they were both in their seventies they should be thinking of a retirement that did not involve the care of young children. She stated that they currently had in their care two young children who had lived with them for over six years. They were considering adopting them because they simply could not imagine life without them, since they had been a part of the family for so long. She said that her husband was softening on his "no adoption" stance since he was quite close to one of the children, a young boy, who periodically approached his foster father saying, "Pop, we gotta talk," presumably about his adoption.

This latter case points to a problem experienced by many foster parents but most visible within African American families. While children's cases must be reviewed periodically by the Department of Children and Families and permanent plans made for them within six months to one year of placement, the department is often unable to meet these requirements, and children are frequently left in foster homes on a long-term basis. After a child has lived with a family for a considerable length of time, the family is approached by the state social worker and given a choice: either adopt the child or have the child adopted by someone else. This approach by the agency is not a volitional act to "trick" foster parents into adopting children but a manifestation of high caseloads and difficulty disposing of cases in a timely manner. It also reflects a department emphasis (by necessity rather than by choice) on triage and crisis intervention.

The director of the state foster parents' association (a Euro-American woman who adopted two children) acknowledged that this is a problem potentially faced by nearly all foster parents, especially those who take long-term placements. From her perspective it appeared to be "emotional blackmail." Once a child becomes part of the family, it is almost impossible for foster parents to willingly give the child up. A sense of belonging is intensified through limited contact with the agency. That is, the agency may place children with foster parents and then have little or no regular contact with them other than an occasional phone call to confirm the children's whereabouts. Foster parents raise the children "as their own," incorporate them emotionally into their family, and when they hear nothing from the state, assume that the child is a permanent addition.

Several women talked about the importance of "keeping after" the state, of calling them regularly to find out what plans the state was making for the child's future. Social workers often interpreted this behavior as "pushiness" or a reluctance on foster parents' part to assume their full responsibilities, which may include long-term care.

That this pattern was most evident among African American women leads me to believe two possible factors are involved. First, there was consistent evidence of differential treatment between African American and Euro-American women by DCF. For example, it was African American women who consistently spoke of not receiving reimbursements, regular visits from social workers, or medical or health-related services for children. I suggest that this is attributable in part to institutional racism and stereotyped ideas of African American women perpetuated through social worker practice rather than policy. Second, there seemed to be a reluctance on the part of older African American women to contact DCF. Many of these women did not know who in DCF to contact in order to receive services or ask questions. To many women, the department seemed to be a confusing and unfriendly tangle of workers, supervisors, and departments that was anything but accessible. In addition, the agency's role was associated solely with "trouble." That is, there was no need to contact the agency if there was no problem, if the child was not unhappy, not a severe behavior problem, and if reimbursement checks were arriving on a regular basis. In these cases many African American foster mothers assumed they were doing what they were "supposed to do" by caring for and mothering the child. Based on these factors, children were simply left in foster care and became a part of women's families by default.

On the other hand, some women dealt with potential loss by asking whether they could adopt children, especially those who had lived with the family for several years. Adoption was a very complicated subject for women and a difficult one for a researcher to understand. There seemed to be no consistent policies governing adoption of foster children by foster parents. Two variables seemed to condition the decision to allow foster parents to adopt. One was geographic region. In some regions of the state, foster parents adopted children and had no difficulty doing so. In other regions, foster parents in similar circumstances were unable to adopt. The other conditioning variable seemed to be the ethnicity and age of the child. Older children were easier for foster parents to adopt, especially if they had lived with the foster family for a significant period of time. African American children appeared easier to adopt by African American foster parents. Ease of adoption was also conditioned by time. Many foster parents said that when they first began to foster (in the 1970s or 1980s), they were automatically told that they would not be considered for adoption. Parents more recently licensed were told they might. Still others were told that they had to be specially licensed to be "adoptive risk" homes. It is also possible, in the situations in which I was told families could not adopt, that there were extenuating circumstances involving the child's biological families or even the foster family themselves. If there were, foster parents did not know about them. While there may have been a pattern to the state's adoption decisions, it was not one foster mothers were privy to.

From foster mothers' perspectives, whether a woman should adopt the children in her care was a complicated often ambivalence-ridden decision. One seventy-five-year-old foster mother began fostering with the knowledge that these children "belonged" to someone else and would not be able to remain with her physically forever. But as she continued to love, care for, and treat them as her own, her ability to see them as someone else's children diminished. After adopting seven children, she had to face the painful reality that at seventy-five years old she could no longer continue to adopt young children, since she was afraid she would not be able to care for them or raise them to adulthood.

I fell in love with them and then when you fall in love, [you don't want them to leave]. I fall in love with them and then they set it up for adoption. I do have first choice if I want to adopt. And so that's the way I adopted them. I got to the seventh and then I said to myself, okay, this is enough now because I'm getting older, you know. . . . When I first started I just said, I knew they wasn't mine, I knew they wasn't mine. But it looked like to me in here they was my children. In my heart, they was my children or right now when they're with me they're still my children, but now I think like this, well this child has got to go. And so part of me say, let go. And then part of me say, hang on, if you know what I mean. But there will come a time for the child to go and you will get attached to them now. You will get attached to the child. It's hard, but I've learned to deal with it. But oh, I felt they was my children, yes. Knowing that they didn't come to stay, but you get that little, wait a minute, this is my child and I treat all of them just the same. (Myra Anderson, a married seventy-five-year-old African American woman)

Another mother suggested the decision to adopt is conditioned not only by the foster parent's age but by other factors such as the child's ethnicity and the number of children a woman has already adopted.

Tatyiana would be six. She was biracial. We had her for over a year and I still send her Christmas and birthday cards, and the adoptive parents live in South Carolina and this is one of the few that we really . . . we adopted three of the foster children and we really considered adopting again and—we tried to take into consideration our age and the fact that most of our children were grown and we were going to do this again. And she was biracial, did we want to have to deal with all of the issues that went around that? I mean, our youngest daughter is Hispanic so that wasn't an issue for us, but we knew that by taking a biracial child it may be an issue for other people. So it was really a tough decision to make to not keep her. Now, when I see that my daughter is eleven and we finally have the freedom, finally after thirty-two years, I am glad we didn't adopt her. But still there's this part of me that wonders if I did the right thing. Its tough. (Sarah Rill, a married Euro-American woman in her late fifties)

Other foster parents spoke of their responsibility to think of what was best for foster children. While they spoke of their love for children, many also spoke of their belief that the best thing for a child was to return home to his or her biological family. Or in cases where a woman's family was already quite large, many felt a child should be adopted by someone with a smaller family and more time and attention to offer the child. For those women who continued to foster through their late sixties and seventies, adopting young children was a concern because of the care they required. They also worried they would die and leave the child an orphan. Even when foster parents were given the option to adopt some children, the decision was difficult since women fostered many children at a time and were faced with the possibility of having to choose which children to adopt and which to let go. This often created significant tension within women's families and within women themselves.

> I remember when Kaitlyn was probably three and, you know, and Jessie went into adoption. But it was handled really well. They visited a lot and we took her to visit and everything. But it moved into adoption. And Kaitlyn was so angry with me. She wouldn't talk to me when Jessie left. She said I gave Jessie away. And I had loved Jessie. Oh, it's so hard. It was very hard that time. (Jessica Langston, a married Euro-American woman in her mid-thirties)

Or as this mother suggested, they had to face the painful reality that their resources were finite and they could not always give particular children what they needed. Even when foster mothers said it was their own decision not to adopt, this did not diminish a sense of loss and bereavement.

> [The state] pressured me to adopt her. And I had her for eighteen months, and then I fought for this little girl. The mother was a paranoid schizophrenic who smelled like beer or booze when she came for visits, and was dirty. They should have terminated [her parental rights] and let that baby go to adoption. I had to consider the whole picture. I have my own children and one adopted child, plus I take care of our parents. I couldn't adopt another. After eighteen months I pushed to have this little girl placed in an adoptive risk home. You know, I wished it could have worked out, I would have loved to keep her. . . . It's real hard when you have a little tiny baby clinging to you. [She started to cry.] And I had my son's feelings to deal with. He knew he was adopted, and he was always asking questions like, "Why can't we adopt her? Why can't we keep her? We have an extra room. Why are you crying?" and him thinking maybe, you know, we don't want him. . . . A worker called right after [the child] left. I was crying and told her, "I can't talk now." The worker asked, "Why are you crying?" I told her, "I know I had to give her up, but I have a *right* to cry too." (Linda Vanderbrink, a married Euro-American woman in her late forties)

Further, since adoption policies and children's family situations seemed to be quite variable, there was no predicting which children a family would be allowed to adopt. As the Gordons (a Euro-American couple in their early forties) explained,

> *Mrs. Gordon:* He's been with us for two years. He was eight weeks old when we got him.
>
> *Mr. Gordon:* And, you know, we're going through trying to adopt him now. And that's been a year-and-a-half battle.
>
> *Mrs. Gordon:* It was the agency had selected another family that had been on a waiting list for a long period of time. So regardless of how many months we had him, he had to go to this other family.
>
> *Mr. Gordon:* He was with us for about nine months . . . they were working for reunification. And in the back of our mind it was if the reunification doesn't work, we would like to adopt him.
>
> *Mrs. Gordon:* But his worker came out one day and said he'd be leaving in a week. He was going out for adoption. We said we'd like to adopt him, and she said no. As soon as she left we went hysterical.

Many parents considered adoption because without it they would lose all contact with their foster children. While foster parents often looked at the biological family as a part of their kin group and were happy to share children, state policy and practice made this difficult at best. Contact between foster and biological families was often discouraged, sometimes prohibited after a "placement" was "terminated."[1] Foster parents were reminded that their conceptions of "family" and "belonging" were inconsistent with those of the state. They were thus held hostage in a zero-sum game. Either they made the decision to adopt and legally incorporate children into the family, or they relinquished all claims to, and future contact with, children. Unless foster parents could on their own establish a relationship with children's biological or adoptive parents, it was unlikely that they would ever see the children again or even know how they were fairing.

In order to combat this situation, many foster parents tried to establish a relationship with the adoptive parents. Even when adoption was not a viable option, this contact provided them with the peace of mind they as parents needed. As one foster mother commented,

> Years ago when we first started doing foster care, we never met the adoptive parents. The social worker would come and get the baby and

bring it to the office for a visit maybe once or twice and come and get the baby and it was gone. At least now, its done better. You know, the adoptive family comes to your home and you get to meet them. And I think its planned a bit better. There are more visits. Like when Tatyiana went to adoption, the . . . adoptive parents they visited for a month. We took her to their home . . . and spent a day in their home . . . so she was able to be in their home for a day. (Sarah Rill, a Euro-American woman in her late fifties)

When asked if this was done for the foster mother's sake or for the child's sake, the mother responded, "For the child!" and then acknowledged that *she* had been the one to arrange the visits between the adoptive parents and her foster child, because she as a mother needed to make sure the child would be safe and well taken care of.

# 5

## Managing Difference, Coping with Delegitimation

*Foster Mothers as Nonmothers*

We took kids in our house. We never had any problem. Anything we have, we have because me and my husband work hard for it. DCF doesn't give us absolutely nothing. What DCF gives us I buy the clothes for the kids. By the time you buy food and clothes and transportation and vacation, because we take the kids on vacation, and these people can't believe we take the kids on vacation. And I'm saying out of the country. Because I have to go through hell to get their birth certificate, all over the nation to get their birth certificate. But we do because they're part of our family. And we do. We're going down south. We're going down to a funeral, to my husband's mother's funeral. Instead of leaving the kids, we rent a van, we pack them up and we take them with us. And I call [the social worker] and tell her. "Oh," [she says,] "you took the kids down to the funeral?" "Yeah," [I say,] "that's their grandmother who passed away. That's the only grandmother they know."
—Lydia Simmons, a married African American woman
in her middle thirties

### Difference and Nonmotherhood

While foster mothers consistently defined themselves as mothers and worked to make foster children members of their kin group, their vision of motherhood and family was constantly articulated and enacted in the face of social relations that contradicted, doubted, or delegitimized it. Thus women's self-constructions always included a vision of themselves refracted through a contradictory gaze. This necessitated actively managing social relations and negotiating ambiguity both publicly and within their intimate relations with children.

Foster mothers routinely received questions about their fostering from acquaintances, strangers, or friends, like "Why do you foster?" and "What is it like to foster?" On one level, women recognized that questions about fostering were ways in which people sought information. On another, women understood that these questions marked their difference. In most cases "difference" carried a negative connotation. For example, these questions often implied that one's motive for fostering could not possibly be simply the love of children. This was probably best captured in the most frequently asked question *I* received when talking about my research with foster mothers: "Aren't most of them in it for the money?" or "What is the *real* reason they foster?" Even when messages or constructs about foster mothers were positive or neutral (as in many popular representations where foster mothers were depicted as temporary mothers, as women who were substitutes for "real" mothers, or as good-hearted women doing a public service), foster mothers still felt that they and their families were misrepresented.

While both Euro-American and African American women reported overt and subtle feedback from people with whom they were acquainted, by and large Euro-American women reported that the feedback was negative.[1] This was particularly evident with acquaintances and strangers and most overt in public places such as grocery stores, churches, department stores, doctors' offices and hospitals. African American women said they either received support from members within the community (either their church, social club, or neighborhood) or were almost impervious to the stares and hostile looks they received outside their community. These women reported feeling a sense of approval in most of their close social relationships; they were doing something beneficial for particular children or, if the child was also African American, for African Americans in general. New children were easily integrated into African American woman's social relationships, and women were often provided with resources like diapers, baby clothes, caregiving assistance, and advice. Churches were especially welcoming and made efforts to quickly get children involved. Many African American women spoke about how their churches offered material support (especially from women's organizations or simply from concerned women acting in concert) to foster mothers. Feelings of support, however, were not reported as women got further from social relations with the other African Americans they knew and related to on a regular basis. As one woman pointedly said, "Of course we're stared at—but we're used to it. If we come in there with a whole bunch of kids, they expect that from us. We're all on welfare!"

Euro-American women (and men) who went to church or entered department stores with numerous same-aged and often racially different children in tow spoke about being stared at, whispered about, or confronted with questions or comments. The signaling of difference (disapproval) indicated to Euro-American foster mothers that they were violating a cultural norm of motherhood and family. Assumptions of difference were largely based on social constructions of "family" defined through blood or legal relationships and on images of a family life cycle as chronological and linear. Women who nurtured and raised children, relinquished them on command, and took money for it fit historical stereotypes of the mercenary baby farmer and of the evil mother who was willing to prostitute her mothering nature for profit (Zelizer, 1985:180).

This latter point is important, since all foster mothers were aware of the stigma associated with fostering and accepting "state money." Most (especially poor and working-class) women had had their motives for fostering questioned and felt that they were often regarded with the same suspicion and hostility as "welfare mothers"—women who are unwilling to earn an "honest" dollar and who exploited taxpayers by sponging off the state (Jewell, 1993:97–98). Euro-American foster mothers expressed anger at the prejudice they experienced and indignation at the way others' perceptions of fostering contradicted their own. As one woman reported, when she took her three foster children (all of whom came from different families and were of different ethnic origins) and three biological children into the grocery to use her WIC coupons (given to foster mothers who care for infants but also commonly associated with AFDC benefits, thus, with poor women), the clerk at the checkout was so rude that, incensed, the foster mother proclaimed, "Look, these are my foster children. I work hard taking care of children. I'm *doing* something for our community."

Thus fostering represents what Erving Goffman (1986:5–42) refers to as a social stigma, and women felt compelled to "manage" their social identity relative to nonfostering adults. Women's response was either to make their identity as foster mothers known in an attempt to manage the tension generated from their "differentness," or to hide their identity in an attempt to manage the amount and way in which information was shared. In the former, fostering was publicly declared through actions or through a direct confrontation. As in the above example in the supermarket, fostering was represented as mothering, public service, or a combination of both. Fostering was mothering that ultimately benefited the community and society. The end result was to privilege a maternal ethic of other-centered, self-sacrificial caregiving work (Bubeck, 1995:9–14), in such a way as to position those who fostered as *better* than those who did not. In other words, foster mothers intentionally transformed the stigma associated with fostering to a social marker of their superiority to nonfostering mothers, thus essentially critiquing "normal" families as lacking, inferior, or potentially self-centered.

When women attempted to hide their foster mother status to minimize stigma, they experienced fostering as a spoiled identity, or as a "discrepancy between an individual's virtual and actual identity . . . [so that] he [*sic*] stands a discredited person facing an unaccepting world" (Goffman, 1986:19). Women attempted to manage a spoiled identity through "passing." As one African American mother said, "If we went someplace I wouldn't say this is my foster child. So people wouldn't, you know, ask a lot of questions." And as one Euro-American mother stated, "When I introduce Talia, I introduce her as my daughter. She can introduce me as her foster mother when and if she wants, but I call her my daughter." Passing was facilitated for both women and children by verbal signifiers (children called their foster mothers "mother," "mom," or "mommy") and by visible interaction patterns that signified familial relations, such as mutual affection, caregiving, and dependence. "Passing" was difficult in situations where identity signifiers were revealed—for example where children's medical cards issued by the state had to be shown or it had to be divulged that children had different last names from their foster mothers. In these situations, foster mothers continued to maintain as much ambiguity as possible about the relationship, maintaining the possibility or illusion of familial relations (such as a stepparent relationship, adoption, or extended family relation). One mother's response when she was "found out" by a neighbor was to maintain the appearance of "normal family" by concealing the identities of her foster children and by deemphasizing the relevance of a distinction.

> When I moved to this place all the children I had was either adopted or foster, but after they are in this home for a while they start resembling my

husband, my other children, they start looking alike. There was a neighbor who went [to] my mailbox and took out the mail and saw that they had different last names. Said to me, "I can't tell which is the foster and which is yours. Which ones are they?" She didn't even know I had state children, but then she figured it out. I said, "Which ones do you think?" "Well," she said, "I don't know." "Well," I said, "then I won't tell you." So we left it like that. They all were mine. (Norma Peel, a married African American woman in her seventies)

Many foster parents talked about "forgetting" that foster children were not their "own" (or intentionally not thinking about foster children as anything but their children) and thereby developing a way of "fitting in" with a referent group or with a "collective we" (Leach, 1967:34)(that is, families with exclusively biological children). Most also talked about jarring experiences that "reminded" them they were in fact being perceived as Other. This meant that they had to question where in fact they did fit in and to maintain a reflexive awareness of others' perceptions.

This questioning caused an angst that could not be ignored. For example, Mr. Hobbs (a working-class Euro-American man in his late fifties) related a story in which he went to K-Mart with his two-year-old foster daughter on his shoulders to buy some tools. He and his wife had fostered the child since infancy and thought of her as their "own." However, at the store Mr. Hobbs was confronted with a scornful and accusatory question, "Is that *your* baby?" from one checkout clerk while others looked on. This he attributed to the fact that his foster daughter was a very dark-skinned African American girl. Because people with whom he identified perceived his relationship to his foster daughter as different, he perceived it as such. Moments of "forgetting" were juxtaposed with a tension in social interactions.

Another message Euro-American women received was that accepting responsibility for "someone else's" children was detrimental to "your own" and was an example of "bad" mothering. For example, many foster parents reported taking their foster children on family vacations and receiving incredulous comments from friends, acquaintances, even DCF social workers. Other foster parents spoke of paying out of pocket for their foster children's expenses. Since most families had few "extra" resources, these expenses required a family sacrifice. For parents, this sacrifice signified that foster children were full family members. They did not get the hand-me-downs, the "leftovers," or the "extras." The sacrifice, however, often met with disapproval. As one mother experienced it, people often commented that fostering was in fact damaging her "own" children, since she was depriving them of a "normal" family and of precious material and emotional resources.

> I think when you are part of a group of eight kids, you learn to help others. You just learn that. That's natural. It's amazing. People will say to me, how can you do that to your own kids? What am I doing to my own kids? You know, they're learning that there's others not as fortunate. What am I doing exactly to my own kids? And when people say that to me, [and I ask them that,] they just shut up, they don't know what to say once you ask them that question. What am I doing to my own kids? But it's amazing the people that think that, it's just horrible that you're in foster care. How could you do that to your own kids? (Ellen McKnight, a married Euro-American woman in her mid-thirties)

While these encounters were troubling and were resented, they did not pose a threat to the foster-mother/foster-child relationship. Because they were voluntary associations, women could generally move away from them or avoid them. For example, several Euro-American and African American women spoke of changing churches when they did not feel that they or their children were welcomed or supported.

In consequence, women developed a wariness of nonfostering relationships until they could be tested. At the same time, most families actively developed close relationships with family and friends who *were* supportive and who *were* able to share their understanding of foster mothering. This often meant that social relations taken for granted by biological mothers had to undergo an evaluative stage for foster mothers. Of course, the necessity for this process again marked foster mothers as "different" both publicly and to themselves, since nonfostering women seldom had to be so careful or guarded.

## Foster Mothers and the State: Difference and Delegitimation

While foster mothers sought to reduce the sense of impermanence and abandonment children felt by rooting them in a family through mothering and claims of belonging, their efforts were consistently undermined by agency policy that defined fostering as nonfamilial and foster children as *different* from women's biological children. Foster mothers' interactions with state workers led them to believe that, as liminal mothers or temporary workers, they were not expected to develop close affective relationships with foster children, nor were they accredited with special skills or competence. Therefore "difference" was consistently experienced as a delegitimation of who they were and of the meaning they attributed to mothering work.

When asked how they thought the state saw them, most women responded negatively.[2]

> Trash. I don't think they have no respect for foster parents. And I'm not talking about everybody at DCF. . . . But I think a lot of them either get harden on the system or they drop out because they can't cut it. . . . The whole thing is, their attitude is that you're foster parents and you toe the mark, and do what I tell you to do. And if we tell you to march, you march, and don't go getting any ideas of your own. (Martha Conrad, a married Euro-American woman in her early fifties)

> You have no rights. You're a glorified baby-sitter is what everybody's been saying, and it's true. Their [the state's] first thought is don't get too involved when you take in a child. (Marjorie Johnson, a married Euro-American woman in her late fifties)

> That I was doing a job and my job was terminated [when a child left]. It was ended and it was over and so that's the end of it. I don't need to deal with her anymore, as though it was no more than that, you know? (Sarah Perkins, a married Euro-American woman in her late forties)

> You know, we are a facility. You've got to keep that in mind, because they're going to keep reminding you. You're not a human being, you're a facility. (Louise Montaro, a married Euro-American woman in her middle forties)

> Not good at all, not good at all. I'm just there and you do this and do that, do what we want and that's it. . . . You know I didn't have a voice, no kind of a voice. (Jerry-Ann Matthew, a married African American woman in her late thirties)

> I don't think they [saw me]. I think they just looked at me as another person to take on their kids. I think they don't look at foster parents as being people. They look at them as being places to put bodies. . . . Even from things you see on TV with the news, it's like it's just a business to place kids. And there's no personality in it. There's no nothing. I mean like when I got these kids they never came to see if these kids had a bed to sleep in. (Deleah Smith, a married African American woman in her late forties)

Since foster children were, according to state definition, temporary residents in temporary family settings, it followed that foster mothers were only temporary caregivers performing a service in which they cared for children's needs until a "real" family could be found. As one mother said, "They told us when we applied that it was a job and not to get overly attached to the children, that they weren't placed with us for adoption." Consistently foster mothers said they were seen by social workers as "only" foster mothers, hired nonskilled caretakers who were performing mechanical tasks devoid of feeling or passion in which their knowledge and expertise were invalid. As nonmothers or temporary workers, they had but one obligation, and that was to follow agency commands and direction. It was painful for them to consider themselves important family members to foster children and yet be treated by the state as hired hands or little more than taxi drivers.

Now they want me to go to Danbury on the thirtieth . . . . They didn't ask me. I had nothing to do with it, but they insisted I come and be there and they set up Trina for 3:00 and Ricky for 5:00 [to have a psychiatric evaluation]. So that's a long day. And my other children will be out of school. So what do you do? . . . You don't have a hand [in it]. That's the way they got it set up. They might ask you questions, but they got the rules set. I don't feel that it's right. I feel like they should have asked me, is this a good date for you? Can we make appointments at such and such a time? And explain to me why you making this appointment and what is it to do [with]. I have to guess that this is the reason, I feel like they should tell me: "We are trying to terminate the mother rights. We want to find out if the kid is doing better there than it was with the mother or is it doing better with its father or brothers and sisters in the other places." I feel like I should have been told something. (Norma Peel, a married African American woman in her seventies)

The way foster mothers were constructed through policy and practice impacted every aspect of their and their children's daily routines. Foster mothers were excluded from decisions made by social service personnel (i.e., decisions "professionals" or "experts" might make) and divested of the most routine child care decisions made within the home and family (i.e., decisions mothers or intimate caregivers would make). For example, while monthly meetings were held by the Department of Children and Families to discuss the treatment plans made by the social worker for a child and his/her family, the foster mother had no input into decisions made there, like how long a child should be in foster care, how many times a child should visit his/her family, where a visit should take place, where a child should go after foster care, or what kind of emotional, psychological, or medical services or evaluations a child in care might need. The same was true of all school-based meetings. While foster parents could attend school conferences, they could not grant permission for a child to participate in a program, have particular scholastic or psychological evaluations, or exit a program.

They were also prevented, as a matter of policy, from making even routine child care decisions, such as when or if a child should receive a haircut, spend the night at a friend's house, or accompany his or her class on a field trip. They were not able to authorize routine or emergency medical treatment or sign a report card. Instead, they had to refer all questions and inquiries to the child's caseworker, who was often unavailable, or who, because of a high turnover at the agency, barely knew the child or the foster mother. Practically, this often meant that children could not go on school outings if the social worker was unavailable or had not signed a permission slip, they could not accept invitations from friends to spend the night, nor could they be taken with other children in the family for a haircut unless the foster mother had been able to secure permission prior to the outing. Somewhat more devastating, it also meant that *when* children left a particular home or *where* they went was something foster mothers were told rather than a decision to which they contributed. Most women experienced policies and practices that valued social workers' authority and knowledge over theirs as insulting and as a sign of a usurious relationship. As one mother suggested, "We're good enough for them to drop kids off with us when they need a home, but not good enough to make decisions when we know what is best."

While women found ways of coping with misinterpretation, none felt they had input into redefining for social workers or for DCF what they did. This meant that definitions of foster care policy and practice were unidirectional and hierarchical, coming from the state to foster parents. Knowledge or expertise relative to children's needs or futures was limited to those within the "official domain."

Unlike social workers, foster mothers based their claims to expertise not on formalized and authoritative knowledge about a "case" but instead on knowledge emerging from an intimate and personal relationship. Unfortunately, since they were not "professionals" and their "official training" was limited, they were not only excluded from decision making but defined as unknowledgeable. As Brigette Jordan suggests, "The power of authoritative knowledge is not that it is correct but that it counts" (1993:153). When foster mothers challenged social workers, most found that practice supported by policy firmly anchored them in an inferior and excluded position. As this mother related,

> There are so many times that we know what's [best]—what would work and wouldn't work. DCF does not like foster parents to know more than they do. They don't like [it when you tell them something]. I had a little girl, and then I got her five-year-old brother for about eleven days before I had to have him moved. And that was my first placement—was these two children. So it was devastating for me to call them and say, "I can't handle this." About six months later, they were looking to move the little girl [to join her brother]. DCF felt these children should be together, 'cause if they were going to get adopted, they were going to get adopted together, so they should be together now.
>
> So I called up DCF and I said, you know, they do not get along [the brother and sister]. They do not even like each other. I really don't see the need to do this to this child [move the child in the middle of the school year and after she had been with this mother for over six months]. [The worker said,] "Now I'm going to have you talk to the supervisor, because she is doing the treatment plan, which is due [tomorrow]." And the supervisor said to me, "We know more about these children than you'll ever know. We have books and books on these children. There are things that happened in these children's life that you'll never know. And we know it all." And I said, "Oh, yeah? Who's their third-grade teacher? What's the little girl's middle name? Tell me you know it all!" She actually said that to me. "We know more about these children than you'll ever know." But they know nothing about the day-to-day lives of those children. I was very angry. Why do we bother to do this? You know, why do we bother to do this? (Ellen McKnight, a married Euro-American woman in her mid-thirties)

Most women were hesitant to challenge social workers directly, since it would not bring about the desired results and would only antagonize the social worker, perhaps inviting retaliation. Challenging the state directly also meant they would be reminded of their devalued status and their ultimate powerlessness relative to foster children's lives and futures. They would also be reminded that the interstice of protective family relationships they created was an illusion.

Her mother could have had four babies and been in jail for sexual abuse for those three and this one she's come clean. . . . You say, gee, is this a good idea for this kid to go home, because mom was in jail, serving time for sexually abusing a fifteen-year-old? Not her own kids but what's going to happen when her own kids are fifteen years old? . . . You know it's a bad situation. This is never going to work. She don't remember where she left her TCBY yogurt, she's going to remember where she left her kid? I'm saying, wait a minute, this baby is going to go back home? This mother is never going to change. She's paranoid schizophrenic, she's got seventeen different personalities, which I've heard three. I heard three of them at a visit, and I'm saying no, I'm sorry, this is not a good situation. But it's not for me to decide. (Linda Vanderbrink, a married Euro-American woman in her late forties)

## Delegitimation, Power, and Control

Foster mothers also experienced the delegitimation of their mothering through withheld information. Consistently, information about a child's history or family was defined as "confidential" by social workers. This was information that only professionals, i.e., social workers or other members of the health care community, or "family," i.e., the child's biological parents or relatives, could access. This excluded foster mothers, since they were accorded neither professional nor kin status. Information ranging from children's family life, the trauma that prompted their removal and placement into care, or any medical condition the child might have was routinely withheld from foster mothers.

Many women felt that information was withheld because social workers did not want foster mothers to refuse the placement. If a foster mother was not told about a child's traumatic history and severe emotional problems, then she would agree to take the child. Most foster mothers complained about the risks this practice posed to the child and to the foster family. Several women spoke of having children who were asthmatics, or who had seizure disorders, delivered to them with no medication and no information about the preexisting condition, only to find out when the child had a medically compromising episode. Others complained that the lack of communication from social workers impaired their ability to protect the child or their family from potentially communicable diseases. All talked about feeling manipulated and used. As this mother suggested,

[W]hen you get the child, it's like getting a child with nothing. No background, no nothing. Most of the time they won't tell you. They will say, well, we was called early in the morning or late in the evening, please take this child. Parents are unknown most of the time, but sometimes they might know the parents and have their names or know where they are or how come. We don't have a medical record on the child most of the time, they don't give us one. And we have to end up taking it to the doctor to kind of find out. 'Cause it got scary 'cause the child might be an AIDS baby of any kind and the state will not tell you. I don't care what they say, they will not tell you. We went to a meeting once and had heard them say, I don't recall his name, that if it was [HIV positive] they wouldn't tell. If they told people, they wouldn't have nobody to take these children. (Norma Peel, a married African American woman in her seventies)

Other women felt that their ability to understand children's complex emotional needs was compromised through withheld information. For example, one foster mother spoke of receiving two little boys with no information about why they entered care. Each night as she bathed them, she noted that their behavior changed. She thought their behavior could be attributable to anxiety, sadness, distractibility, fatigue, or a fear of water. She also wondered if these children were simply predisposed to crankiness in the evening. She found out some weeks later, from children who had been in the boys' class at school, that when they lived with their mother both boys had been sexually abused by her. The abuse had taken place during routine caregiving, like bathing and dressing. The foster mother was furious with the social worker who had withheld the information because it was "confidential" and had needlessly caused the two boys to be anxious and perhaps traumatized further. The foster mother stated that she would have handled bath times very differently had she known that this was an area of emotional trauma for the children. She, like many women, also felt that social workers were willing to use children in an effort to devalue foster mothers and maintain exclusive control over "the case."

In response most women felt lied to, manipulated, and patronized. They felt that their abilities to mother and to take responsibility for children had been misjudged and their mothering work severely hampered. As another mother related,

[W]hen they brought . . . both of the sisters to my house, that is all they told me [that the mom had problems and was going with an older man].

Then one day, they [the two girls] were outside to the playground. . . . And the younger sister came in and I said, "Where is your sister?" [She said,] "She is in the playground." So I said, "Tell her it is time for lunch." She went back out and [then came back in and] said, "She is not in the playground." [I said,] "What do you mean, she is not in the playground? Okay, I will come outside and see." So I came outside and she wasn't there. So I was looking around, and I was asking the neighbors, did you see a little girl looking like so and so, and they said, "Yes, she went over that way." Okay. She was sitting on the highway. The highway might have been about maybe 150 to 200 yards away from the house. And you had to go up a—like a little hill like. She was sitting on the [guard] rail.

So I go up and I call her and I said, "Why are you there?" and she said, "I was just looking at the traffic." And I said, "Why are you looking at the traffic? You can see it from way over there." And she said, "Well, I was wondering how it would feel to just kill myself." She said, "Because you know, I am not clean." She started telling me what the boyfriend had did to her. And this is my first knowledge of this, right [that the child had been raped by the mother's boyfriend].

And so I call the social worker back. I said, "I keep telling you all, do not bring me kids that you haven't given me a full background on, that I don't know what is happening." Because suppose—just suppose, I had been down the bottom of the hill screaming and hollering and saying, "What are you doing up there?" and you know, just frantic instead of walking up to her and talking to her and seeing what was wrong and then hugging her and bringing her back down. Just suppose it had been the opposite? I said [to the social worker,] "I could have caused her to jump or run into traffic." And God knows, if she had got killed while I was taking care of her, I would have been in another place [a mental hospital] because I would never be able to handle it. So I said, "You need to stop snowing people by just trying to pretend you are doing your job by bringing kids and placing them in situations and not telling anyone information. . . . It is not right for the foster mothers." (Beatrice Rollins, a single African American woman in her late fifties)

What made these interactions feel especially like violations was that foster children were injured as a result of social workers' misconceptions of the fostering relationship. Since most women saw protecting children as an important part of fostering and identified strongly with children's pain, injuries they could not prevent were experienced with helplessness and anger.

I sit and watch the visits [between natural parents and their children]. You get a sense of who really loves their kids and who doesn't. Workers don't want to hear it. I've got a worker right now who's the pits and her supervisor is even worse. It's like, "It's none of your business. It's our decision to make." That's it. It alienates me and my feelings because there are certain things that we see and we feel and its like, this worker says, well, "That's our decision and it's got nothing to do with you." And it does have something to do with us. We're the ones who love these kids and deal with them twenty-four hours a day, and we're the ones who have the instinct to protect them. That worker doesn't care for that kid. It's a job. She goes home at 4:30 and forgets about it until Monday morning. [She sees the kid] once in two months. You know, she comes out here, spends ten minutes in your home, shows up late for a visit. . . . You know, they're supposed to be here at 10:00, they show up at 10:30, and they're supposed to be out of your house by 11:00. They spend a half an hour with the kids and they're the great experts on what the kid needs. They're looking at paper. And, heck, they stay on the case for six months and then they're gone and another one comes along. (Lillian Rosebud, a married Native American woman in her mid-forties)

This same mother recounts another experience in which she and her husband had raised a child for three and a half years. The child came to them as a drug-addicted eight-month-old baby. Because they had five children ranging from three years old to teenagers, the family felt they could not financially or emotionally take on another child. Since the foster family would not adopt, the judge ordered that the child should be returned to her natural mother, a course the foster mother had advocated three years earlier, only to be ignored by caseworkers. On the day the child was to leave the foster home permanently, the foster mother bitterly recounted,

She knew she was leaving for good, and she did not want to go. She kept saying, "No, no, no. This is my home, my daddy is here. This is my home. This is my home. I am not going. I am not going. . . ." It was like trying to put a wild cat in water trying to get her in the car, and I kept saying to everyone, I wish I had videotaped *that* for the judge.

As another mother suggested, devalued status and lack of communication had implications for the kind of services children received.

And I kept calling the state to find out where do I take her [for counseling], who do you recommend, who's got Title 19, what do I do, and I was getting nowhere and I was getting really frustrated. So, finally I found, through my associates, resources, and I took her and I put her in therapy. And two weeks after I put her in therapy, they told me it had been recommended six months before. I said, why didn't you tell me. They said, oh, we thought you knew. And I said, and how would I know, did you send me anything, did you give me any documentation whatsoever? I said, I know that I took the child up to a doctor for a family and individual evaluation that you guys never told me anything [about]. And I said, oh, I'm so furious at you, all the things that I've done to try and find a place [that would provide therapy for the child], I said, and this child could have had care long before. (Anne Howell, a married Euro-American woman in her late forties)

All women expressed sympathy with social workers who could not convey information because they did not have it and appreciated it when, upon receiving information about children and their families, social workers called to let them know. However, even in these situations, foster mothers found it frustrating that the agency had no way of preventing so many "emergencies" that necessitated removing children without giving them a chance to gather their possessions and without ascertaining their preferences, needs, or history.

## Managing Social Relations with the State

Women's relationships with state social workers or with the Department of Children and Families were not optional; they could not remove themselves from the relationship without quitting. Many women, like Mrs. McKnight, asked, "Why do I keep doing this?" Their answers lay in a sense of responsibility that made it hard for them not to care for children. Frequently those who raised the question "Why do I do this?" answered it by saying, "If I quit, children would suffer." Thus, to some degree, women's empathy held them hostage.

In response to delegitimating social relations with the state, foster mothers developed three basic ways of interacting with social workers. From most women, I heard evidence of all three responses. First was a discourse of resignation and resolve coupled with techniques for maneuvering past social workers and around agency policy. This response allowed foster mothers to enact fostering in a way that was consistent with their own definition and avoid entanglements with DCF that would ultimately prove futile. The second response was the intentional marginalization of DCF in the daily lives of foster families, so that families had very little daily or weekly contact with social workers. Mothers told social workers, "Bring 'em to me as babies. Come back again when they're grown." When marginalizing DCF, foster mothers requested very little from social workers in the way of financial or material support and tended to rely on friends and family for things they needed. The third response was the active public appropriation of symbols, life patterns, behaviors, names, and rituals culturally associated with "family," i.e., nuclear biologically related family life, in order to actively challenge the state.

In the first response, foster mothers articulated one discourse about the nature of fostering to social workers and shared another among and between themselves or with others perceived as sympathetic. Social workers had to be handled carefully and information about foster children and family relations screened. Policies women felt were antithetical to family health had to be lived with. Most women who adopted this perspective had significant experience trying to be "heard" and had consistently met with defeat. While women expressed some bitterness about their experiences, they adopted the attitude that they would not let DCF policy or social workers' actions impede their work. For the most part, social workers were regarded as people who could potentially make fostering more difficult but not as people who had the power to define and determine what fostering would be.

For example, while at a conference sponsored by the state for foster mothers, Louise Jordan, an African American woman in her early thirties, told me that the caseworker assigned to her two foster children could say nothing good about the children's biological mother. She was deemed irresponsible, uncooperative, and a problem. From the foster mother's perspective, the biological mother had been "written off" and was going to lose her children permanently, something the foster mother felt was unfair. She suspected that the mother's unwillingness to work with the social worker had more to do with the social worker than with the mother's lack of care for her children. The misunderstanding was compounded, in the foster mother's eyes, by the fact that the social worker was a middle-class white woman and the mother a young, poor black woman. While practice often discourages biological mothers and foster mothers from meeting, the foster mother knew of the biological mother through the neighborhood and asked if visits between the mother and her children could take place within the foster mother's home under her supervision. As the foster mother observed the visits, she felt the children's mother was young, scared, and tremendously ill prepared to care for two young children, but not hopeless. As the foster mother explained, the woman needed to be mothered herself, needed to be taken care of, needed to have the chance to grow up. Rather than make her opinions known to the social worker, or attempting to insinuate her assessment into treatment plans, or change agency policy about case procedures—all of which she assessed as futile—the foster mother secretly moved the biological mother into a mother-in-law apartment connected to her own home. There she supervised contact between mother and children, made sure the young mother kept her appointments with the social worker and a community-based therapist, and, most important, showed the girl how to care for her children both through modeling and through overt instruction. Rather than treating the mother like a stranger or a failed woman, she included her in the family and provided her with the care and support offered to all family members.

As this foster mother related her story, several other women standing around expressed shock and fear. Had the social worker found out about the arrangement, the children would have been removed from the foster mother's home, and the foster mother would immediately have lost her license. While Louise Jordan acknowledged that this was possible, and she knew what she was risking, she said she simply had to take the chance. Not to do so would have been to allow, and thus to participate in, a tragedy.

The second response was to marginalize the state as much as possible in daily routines, activities, and thinking. Most women felt competent to be mothers and competent to handle the situations presented to them in fostering. Many talked about being "on their own" anyway, contacting the state only in an emergency or when they needed something the state alone could provide, like a medical card. Foster mothering was predicated on incorporating children into a woman's family, and it was difficult to incorporate a child attached to a social worker. Often, in placements that were working well, the presence of a social worker in a family's life frightened children since it indicated that the foster home was transitory and that children were vulnerable to being moved without their consent or the consent of their foster parents. As a protective measure to both children and their families, many (though not all) foster mothers endeavored to have as few dealings with social workers as possible. These women felt that what occurred in their homes was "their" business and did not rightfully fall under the state's purview, even though they were licensed by the state.

> I know there are some people who rely very much on their social worker. I sort of consider these kids my family and I don't treat them any different than my biological children, so I don't really have the need for a social worker. I take care of my own business as far as their needs and everything else. And I think my kids that have been in other foster homes appreciate that more. That's what makes them feel more like a family, you know. When the social worker's car is in the driveway, [the kids think] it's either good or bad, it's either they've come to take me [the kids] to another place or [else worse]. (Belinda Evans, a married Euro-American woman in her early fifties)

> They either call me or sometime I call them and ask for a medical card, or a child gets sick or something so I'll tell them I need to take them to the hospital or to the doctor. But most of the time not unless there is a problem. Sometimes months pass and I don't hear from nobody. And there was a time when they put them here and you didn't hear from them in years. If nothing went wrong and you was able to take care of it, you didn't hear. (Norma Peel, a married African American woman in her seventies)

The benefit of this perspective was that the delegitimation women experienced at the hands of the state was reduced. They were better able to think about and treat a foster child "as their own" than if the state was consistently reminding them that this child "belonged" to someone else. One inherent problem, however, was that foster mothers often did not receive resources they were entitled to from the state such as clothing vouchers, money for camp, or extra money at Christmastime for gifts. In some cases they did not even receive monthly reimbursements. Rather than contacting the state and asking about the money, or fighting for the reimbursements they were entitled to, several women in the study simply let it go. Some found the state a confusing bureaucratic tangle; others did not want the attention such a battle would bring to them.[3] Therefore, many foster children were limited to what a woman could provide materially, and women assumed much more of the burden of children's care than may have been necessary.

Another problem for foster mothers who adopted this perspective was one of intensified grief when a child left. Systemic overload, in which careful tracking of children was difficult or impossible, often meant that foster mothers could care for children with little or no contact with the state for several years. During that time they simply began to believe the child would always remain.[4] Often, unbeknownst to foster mothers, social workers were working with the biological family toward "family reunification."

> They mostly tell me short term, maybe looks like six months sometimes. Sometimes it's three. But it usually last a year, two years, three. I have had Matt and Crystal, let's see, I took Matthew when he was not quite a year old and Crystal, they about a year apart, and they was gonna be six months. And here they are Matthew's seven and Crystal is eight. But they don't tell you much else. (Norma Peel, a married African American woman in her seventies)

Additionally, foster mothers whose parenting style required little of the social worker often had minimal contact with the social worker on any regular basis. This often meant that the decision to remove a child from a foster home came as a complete surprise and often as a tremendous shock to foster mothers. As this same mother reflected,

> It's hard. I felt like a person, I guess like if you lost a child that died. Nothing you can do about it, you see, but there is nothing you can do about it and you just have a void. I had two, Clifton and Tonya, the little children, I had him about a month old. I took him and his sister and I kept them, and all of a sudden without warning the state was to call me one day and wanted to pick them up the next day. That almost killed me.

The third response, the appropriation of family life signs and symbols that critiqued DCF's version of fostering, was both articulated in discourse and exhibited in women's public and private behavior toward children. While it was a coping response that resembled an attempt to "pass for a real family," it was different because it contained elements of direct confrontation. It was a conscious and concerted redefinition of the state's view of foster mothers. Perhaps more than any of the other responses, it was consistently paired with the others. Confrontation involved an ebb and flow in which women asserted themselves and their view of mothering and then backed off. They resisted and then intentionally acquiesced. Most saw that to offer only resistance meant to burn out and to leave fostering frustrated and angry or to have their license revoked.

Asserting a strong sense of themselves as mothers and fathers in relation to their foster children and developing enduring emotional bonds with foster children helped women negotiate relations with the state that contested their own view of mothering. But it also generated significant tension between social workers and foster mothers, both because social workers saw foster mothers as misinterpreting their "job" as temporary caretakers, and because foster mothers saw their family-making actions misinterpreted.

Some women responded by returning their licenses and leaving fostering. Like women who left the system,[5] those who continued to foster spoke vehemently about the tension between themselves and DCF. Louise Montaro, a married Euro-American woman in her middle forties, fostered a young child for over a year. During an interview, Mrs. Montaro described the day her foster daughter left her home. She was asked if the social worker had ever followed up the departure with a progress report about how the girl was doing in her new setting. Mrs. Montaro wryly commented:

No. But we didn't expect any. You know, we are a facility. You've got to keep that in mind, because they're going to keep reminding you. You're not a human being, you are a facility. . . . [They say] those exact words. They remind you [by saying,] "Hey, look, you know, you're getting too involved, you're a facility. . . ." They tell you what your limits are. I mean you just can't go around for a kid acting like its parent. You're not the parent. You think you're the parent, but you're not the parent. You are a facility. You can't go to the school and tell them to do something; the school doesn't have to listen to you. . . . In the meantime you can have a kid six months in school who needs reading—who needs reading help, who's not been getting it, or hearing help, or speech help. . . .

[Q.: Do you see yourself as a facility?] Of course not! I never stop being a parent. I like to fly into the face of, you know, people anyway. . . . Sometimes it just gives you a bigger challenge. . . . It bothers you sometimes. Like when . . . she broke her finger [referring to a foster child], it took us over a week to get someone who would set it.

As this mother noted, she learned to "fly in the face" of DCF during her training from another foster mother.

I met this wonderful woman. We were near the second to the end of class. They [the state social workers running the foster parent training class] would bring people who were . . . foster parent[s] and there was this—a black woman, Natasha. She's gone through like forty or sixty kids. A single woman living in South Norwalk who had her own home and she—boy, she flew in the face of all their rules and she just said it, you know, "Hey, look, they come into my house, they're going to live under my rules [as opposed to state rules]." And she wasn't taking anything [flack] from those ladies and they knew it. . . . But she, it worked for her, and she did a good job, and she had kids and she said, "When they . . . dump those kids on my door and they expect me to do something with them—I do. . . ." I thought that was pretty amazing.

Finally, another way in which direct confrontation manifested itself was when women arrived at the painful point of having to choose between maintaining their own integrity or continuing a submissive relationship with DCF. Many felt they were held hostage by their desire to keep their foster children and resented threats from social workers. Ultimately, however, many women decided to risk losing their children and stand up to the agency, since, as they suggested, losing themselves meant they could no longer foster. As one mother sadly concluded at the end of a focus group in which women had been talking about their relationships with DCF, "I'm not afraid of DCF anymore. They want you to be afraid. And I love my two children. I am going to adopt them. But if they come around and threaten me, I say, you know what? Take them. Go ahead. And find someone else to have them."

# 6

# Mothering Work and the Art of Fostering

Now when we started, fifteen years ago, the babies weren't sick like we're getting now. They were just basically, [their parents] didn't want them, the grandparents couldn't help out, whatever. Well, from like probably ten years and on they've all been drug exposed, fetal alcohol, premature babies. I mean my first ones were basically full term, now you're dealing with all the medical problems. Tube feedings, oxygen. I had two kids on oxygen.

—Linda Vanderbrink, a married Euro-American woman
in her late forties

In spite of painful interactions with the state, women established daily routines that defined what fostering was and what a foster mother should be. There was significant agreement about the definition of fostering and the nature and range of work that was "normal." Fostering included routine caregiving tasks familiar to women through biological mothering and a host of tasks, behaviors, and thoughts they experienced only through fostering. For example, foster mothers spoke of tasks like meal preparation, helping with homework, or taking children to the doctor juxtaposed with tasks peculiar to fostering like swaddling cocaine-addicted infants, helping children who had been physically battered feel safe, changing the bandages of children who had been burned, helping children to stay in touch with their biological families, or helping children find alternatives to self-destructive behavior. These mothering tasks were integrated into women's daily routines and were seldom commented on. Women approached the relationship with the understanding that they would and could meet children's needs. As long as women were successful, they seldom commented on the sometimes extraordinary lengths to which they went in order to meet those needs. The only exception to this was the pride with which women spoke of being able to acquire new skills in order to increase their mothering competence.

What a foster mother *was* was defined by what a foster mother *did*. Women consistently spoke of the following tasks: (1) knowing, loving, and making sacrifices for children; (2) instilling in children a sense of belonging (3) adding them to the foster family; (4) offering or facilitating healing, and (5) advocacy. Each of these aspects of foster mothering was facilitated or impeded systematically through the procedures and practices of the Department of Children and Families.

### The Work of Knowing and Loving Foster Children

Loving children was most often described as an intrinsic component of mothering work and was referred to as a "natural" consequence of the mothering relationship. Through a relationship, a child's personality, needs, and history could be known and experienced. Without love, there was little chance of adequately caring for children.

Most women were extremely modest in their descriptions of their own mothering. When asked what was the most important thing a foster mother provided for children, most women talked about providing a safe environment in which family and mothering relationships could grow and develop.

> I guess the one thing that I *know* I can do for these children is to provide a safe place while they're here. I can't necessarily say that while they're with their mom or dad things are going to be safe, because if the law says they have to visit, then they have to visit. But while they're here, in my home, they'll be safe. There will be plenty to eat. Their home will be clean. They will be warm. Their things, their physical needs will be met, as many of their emotional needs as I can. They won't have to be afraid of any male figures that are going to harm them nor will I harm them. And I just, while you're here, I'm the mommy in the house, and I will do the best job that I know how to do as a mom, and that's all I can say. But I think that's the most important thing I can do.
>
> If they're only here for a little while, they see what's reasonably normal. God knows our house isn't normal. Early in the morning and late in the evening it does not look normal. I mean maybe that's what normal is, everybody running around. But a touch of what seems to be normal, a mom and a dad figure, other brothers and sisters, with people sharing.

Maybe it's laughing or maybe sometimes maybe it's crying or even getting angry, but it's emotions and that's what goes on here a lot, emotion. And seeing an interaction with people loving and touching each other in a good, healthy way. And if they only get it for a very short time, they know it exists because they saw it themselves. And I think that's probably, if I can say we ever did anything really good, that would be it. (Celestine Gordon, a married Euro-American woman in her late forties)

The most important I think is preventative maintenance, to make sure that nothing happens to them here that will traumatize or affect their life like it did in their birth placement. I think that's the main thing, safety. And they need to know that they're loved. They need to know they're safe. And when they do, and it may take a while, we find a difference in a child. . . . [You] have to bring the best out of that child through love, structure, and consistency in a family setting. (Sylvia Pollins, a married Euro-American woman in her early fifties)

A foster mother—ooh boy—is there to love, because some of these kids come into my home and they don't hug. You know . . . I'm there to support these kids. (Jerry-Ann Matthew, a married African American woman in her late thirties)

The most important thing I do? Gee. I think everything I do for these kids is important, like showing them love, you know, feeding them, or clothing them, or washing them. The normal things I would do for my own children. So everything I do for them I think is important. You know. Mothering, the way I always do it. (Fredrica DaSilva, a married Euro-American woman in her late fifties)

My role is to do the very best I can for the child, get them what they need in school, medically, whatever. I also hope I can make some kind of [an emotional] difference in their lives. I think I do. In some small way. Even if it's a small way, it's something. (Emma Woodhouse, a married Euro-American woman in her mid-forties)

The meaning of love and the importance of sacrifice have long been associated with raising or caring for one's own children. In fact, as Daniel Miller notes, both are a signifier of American kinship: "By the time Schneider (1980) surveys American kinship, love becomes the almost sole legitimatory principle behind any kind of relationship outside of the functionalism thought appropriate to work relationships" (1998:118). When asked about their motivation for becoming a foster mother, almost all women included in their answer "because I love children." Even those foster mothers who defined fostering as a time-limited experience, who saw themselves as "helping hands," or their foster home as a "stepping stone" to a more permanent living situation, also spoke of their love and devotion to children in general and the children in their care specifically. Since foster mothers have been largely constructed as women raising "other people's children" or as temporary childcare *workers*, their ability and desire to sacrifice for children, and the meaning of sacrifice as a significator of kinship, have been either overlooked or actively contested. As this mother related,

> Once I was at the hospital with a sick baby. He was going to be in the hospital for three weeks. It was really hard on me to get there every day, I had a four-year-old at home and everything. But that little baby didn't know anyone at the hospital. He didn't know anybody. When I came early in the morning, he would brighten up. . . . I got him to eat.
>
> I was talking to a nurse, and she said, "If it's so hard for you to get here, you don't have to come. You're *only* the foster mother." I left the room crying, and my pediatrician who knew me asked me what's wrong. I told him that she had said I was *only* the foster mother. . . . Only foster mother? Can you believe that? These kids are part of my *family*. I make arrangements to be there [for them]. (Linda Vanderbrink, a married Euro-American woman in her late forties)

Sacrifice was consistently linked with providing for children's material needs no matter how difficult. Within this context, as Miller suggests, provisioning "transcends any immediate utility and is best understood as cosmological in that it takes the form of neither subject nor object but of the values to which people wish to dedicate themselves" (1998:12). For foster mothers, this sacrifice entailed the transformation of "any" child into "my" child.

> I don't care who pays the bills. It doesn't matter to me. They send [the bills] to me and I put them in the garbage, because the [children] will be taken care of as long as they're here. I'm not going to allow them to be here and something is going wrong, and then ten years down the line we have a murderer or a rapist or something and it could have been prevented. . . . I just have a love for children and I look at these children as my kids. (Mrs. Hansen, a married African American woman in her late fifties)

Loving children with significant behavioral or emotional problems was not always an easy process. Many mothers talked about learning to love children apart from their behaviors while simultaneously contextualizing children's behaviors as a part of their traumatic life history. This necessitated an integrated approach to who the child was and what the child had been through. Consequently, a component of loving foster children was to see them as the sum of their experiences while seeing the potential for growth, healing, and change. Many concluded that while loving children was critical to being a good foster mother, it was not enough *only* to love children.

> I thought it was going to be more like the older ones, I thought that no matter—all you had to do was love them and give them what they needed, that everything was going to be better. But that's not how it is. I thought that, you know, if you took care of them and you showed them things were different, that everything was going to go away, but it doesn't work that way, because they've been through so much. Even—I could not believe that a three-year-old could have so much excess baggage. I mean, Larry broke things, he punched the screens out, he tried to push the air-conditioner out the window. He'd throw things out the window, run across the dressers. [I'd say,] "I don't know how many times I've explained you do not run on the dressers because you can get very badly hurt, they can tip over and I wouldn't be able to pick up the dressers." It just never sank in. Do you know what I mean? Tony rips the wallpaper off the wall. You know, they do things that you don't expect a three-year-old to do? Alex knew things that, because he use to watch [pornographic] movies with the mother, and God only knows what he saw her doing. And then, you know, I'd have to watch Tony with Alex because Tony was the perfect victim, very passive. (Emma Woodhouse, a married Euro-American woman in her mid-forties.)

While many foster parents saw foster children's extraordinary needs as making them more difficult to love, just as many said that foster children were easier to love than other children since their needs could be easily recognized and met. This ease was inherently gratifying for people whose lives revolved around building relationships with children and offering them care and many parents described it as a "fit": foster children needed what foster parents had to offer. Through this fit, family was created.

> They need all the love they can get. They're—I don't know. I don't know how to explain it. I feel that foster kids are a lot closer than my own kids were because they had it made. Well, my own kids, they have a home. They have school. They had this. They had anything. You know? Foster kids come in here. They come with nothing. So you try to get them—give

them as much love as you can and all. Because I think love is the best medicine you can give kids. . . . And it works. It works. If they want to be helpful, let them be helpful. Let them be part of you, part of your family. It gives them a place to be. (Betty Hobbs, a married Euro-American woman in her late fifties)

While love was consistently posited as a gift women gave and received from children, it was also understood as a burden unique to fostering. All women conceded that love had to be given to foster children with the knowledge that children would eventually physically leave the household and that women would eventually feel the sting of losing a part of themselves. No woman looked forward to or necessarily *wanted* to relinquish children she had fallen in love with. Yet most women saw little alternative. As one foster mother conceded, loving children was simply a part of foster mothering. While the end point might be painful, it was something one simply had to bear.

Well, I try to say, this child is going to be different. I want to feed this child, clothe this child, give this child a bath, and don't put out too much love because you'll have to cry again. It don't work. It just don't work and it starts all over. When I know that they're getting ready to leave, it just automatically—I feel my heart break—it's just—I can't help it. I say, now, you know that I'll always love you and you'll always have a space in my heart and you can always come back to visit me. And you know that your mom is welcome too. (Monica Stevenson, a single African American woman in her late sixties)

## Not Loving Children

Some women spoke of the crisis of not loving children. Sometimes this happened because of a personality clash or mismatched temperament between foster parents and children. More often, however, foster parents received inadequate information about the child and were unable to prepare for the kind of care a child would need or unable to make an informed decision about whether or not to accept the placement. Evident in this mother's story is her sense of failure at not having provided this child with the right type of care. Also there is the sense that she was "dumped on," manipulated into taking a child who compromised her and her other children's safety.

That's another one that they brought out and they dumped him on me. I had [a ten-year-old boy] forty-eight hours and I called them, "I want him out of my house now." They just brought him out. It was like—I think they gave me, what, a couple of hours' notice or something like that. They brought him out. The most she told me about the kid was that he was hyperactive, he was on medication. And I said, "Fine. No problem." I took the kid. The first night he cried a little bit. I got him to school the next day. I went to work. My daughter called me on the job about 9:00 and asked me if I gave the kid money. I said no. And I have a big jar that I dump the money in [in my bedroom]. So I said no. So she said, "I think he took your money." So I came home. My jar was sitting in the corner. I said, "Michael, did you take money out of the jar?" And as soon as I walked in [the door at home], the school called and they asked me did I give him money. I said no. I had old, old money like two-dollar bills and half-dollars and stuff like that. Mike took all of the two-dollar bills and whatever to school. And the big showdown came when I came home. He flipped. The kid flipped on me. Then when I called the supervisor to try to get the worker, the first question she asked me was, "Didn't the worker tell you about his problem?" I'm like, "What problem?" You know? I didn't know. The worker didn't tell me anything. You know? That really kind of upset me because you gave me a kid, you knew he had all these—you know. Someone could have gotten hurt. The kid totally went off in my house. You know? He wanted to destroy things. Then when the worker did get to my house, she then said to me, "Well, he just came out of the [psychiatric] hospital." "You didn't tell me all this when you brought me this child. You said he was hyperactive. Now you're going to tell me he's been hospitalized for his problems?" I was really—and then the same day this happened, she's going to tell me, "Oh, his brother is the one that just raped the little five-year-old kid." And I'm like, "Get him out now. I have kids in my house. You know? Get him out." And I had to think of my other kids. (Clara White, a single African American woman in her late fifties)

Other children stayed in their foster homes for such short periods of time that women said it was impossible to get to know them or love them. For example, it was not uncommon for foster parents to report that some of their children stayed only one or two nights if it was an "emergency" placement. Many parents reported discomfort with short-term placements, especially as their frequency increased, because they could not form familial relationships with children. Many parents bitterly remarked that they were being turned into a hotel or an institution.

And as one mother who had just relinquished her license stated, it undermined her sense of self as a mother.

> One of the reasons we've left it, one of the many reasons, is that you cease to be, it ceases to be your home. You become part of that big picture, that big system, that big bank, data bank, whatever. And you don't function as normal people after a while. . . . And when it ceases to be that—and it had become less of a home and more of an institution, where you've got, you begin to feel like you're stacking kids up against the wall, just stacking them, stabling that's the term that I used. And I'm not a stable, this isn't a stable, this is a home. (Celestine Gordon, a married Euro-American woman in her late forties)

## Instilling a Sense of Belonging

> I have always felt like she was mine. . . . [And] it was like she needed to know she had a home—a permanent place that she sort of like—her behaviors fell away. She latched onto my son like he was a life preserver. Every time we pulled into the driveway, she kept saying, "We're home!" It was like she was looking for a place. (Michelle Frost, a single Euro-American woman in her forties)

Once children were placed, foster mothers began to instill in them a sense of belonging and to let them know that they now had a home. All women spoke about the empathy required to begin a familial relationship with children whose reasons to trust adults had been shattered. Some foster parents, seeing children's obvious distress and confusion, joked with children when they first arrived or hugged them. If children were old enough, foster parents explained to them what foster care was and what it would be like in their home. Some went over house rules, carefully laying out the family's expectations for their newest members. All parents talked about assuring children that they were safe and would be well cared for. When asked what they told children upon arrival about themselves or about foster care, foster parents offered these comments.

> We would tell them that this was going to be their home until they could go back to their home and just explain how we did things here and that we had some simple rules and we would always listen to what they had to say and that they would have to listen to what we had to say—that it

was going to be a partnership and that we were going to be a family. And that while they weren't really our children, they were going to be our children for a while. (Sandy Pescatori, a married Euro-American woman in her late thirties)

Well, I tell them as honest as I possibly can, I am the foster parent, I'm your friend. I will be your friend if you let me be it. I said, but you know, I think we're going to be very good friends. Sometimes they withdraw and sometimes they don't. But no matter where they go, they are in a strange place at first. And they don't know what's going to happen when night falls. It's dark and they're not used to their surroundings. Even though they left a house that is so bad that they can't stay in it, they may not have no food in two days, they want their house, they want their mother, they love those places. So you've got to sort of, sometimes you can get them to come to you, and then again, sometimes you have to wait. (Monica Stevenson, a single African American woman in her early sixties)

We let the children [referring to two particular children] know we're not your mother and we're not your daddy, we love you very much, and we'll keep you—stay on as grandparents. (Martha Conrad, a married Euro-American woman in her late fifties)

Foster parents also tried to normalize the situation for children by stressing to them, the social worker, and those with whom the family had contact that foster children, like all other children, needed food, clothing, love, security, and routine. And with good care, they would be "all right." They thereby suggested that while the situation (a child being taken out of his home) might be unusual, the child was not. In this way they converted the stigma of foster childhood to the usual patterns of childhood.

Part of instilling a sense of belonging was taking care of physical needs. When children arrived, most women talked about bathing them, washing their hair, combing and styling it, and either washing children's clothes or discarding them and providing new ones. Sometimes children were delivered to foster care with no clothes (several mothers spoke of receiving infants wrapped only in blankets, or of children being delivered in their pajamas); sometimes, the clothes were in disrepair. "All the clothes that they came here with to this day are in boxes in my basement. [And] that's where I want them to stay. They weren't fit to be worn."

Making foster children into children who belonged to the family, and to their foster mothers in particular, was followed by overt and subtle cues about family-appropriate behavior, mannerisms, values, and beliefs. Foster children were incorporated into the family and transformed into "new children," "my children," children who resembled to some extent their foster families and bore the marks of their foster mothers (clean and newly styled hair, a washed body, new clothes). As Russell Belk suggests, "the idea that we make things part of self by creating or altering them appears to be a universal human belief" (1988:144–50). Changing them is part of the way in which the self is extended both into possessions and arguably into people whom we identify as belonging to us.

Of concern to many foster parents was the fact that when children were placed in care, they arrived with little attention given to their belongings. For foster mothers, this signified the foster child's devalued status and the stripping of the child's individuality. That is, as wards of the state, children became dispossessed of their rights or privileges within a consumer society to own, possess, or retain objects. Instead they became owned objects. As these foster parents suggested,

> There's something else I'd like to say. And if they'll consider doing this, is when the child is taken, no matter what the circumstances, get a hold of his blanket or get a hold of his pillow or get a hold of mother's sweater— something to put in the crib with the baby. And that way he hasn't lost everything and it's something to cuddle. Because he didn't have *anything*. He didn't have *anything* when he came. (Al Hobbs, a married Euro-American man in his late fifties)

> I always try with the first contact that we have with the parents to work out to get some of the kid's belongings are brought here, like a stuffed animal. Because usually when they take them they just sweep through and you're gone. Most of the time when they get here they don't have hardly anything clotheswise. Cory got dropped off in a pair of pajamas and that's it. I still have the pajamas, I saved them. I don't know. It's like I try to put myself in their place, how I would feel if somebody took me away? And they have to be terrified. (Karen Smith, a married Euro-American woman in her late thirties)

Another way in which women instilled a sense of belonging was through the use of discipline. I often observed women shouting orders or commands at foster children, such as "Harry, you get down here now and pick up these socks! I'm not going to tell you again," or "Jaquisha, don't even think of going outside without that jacket! And where are your glasses?" Or threatening children who did not do their chores or follow through on something their foster mother had requested, as in "Don't let me catch you all going outside before your chores are done!" or "I said put that down and I meant it. If I have to get up, you are going to be in some serious trouble. Don't make me have to get up!" When talking with women about discipline and about the meaning of their behavior, I learned that far from being hostile or rejecting, shouting was often an indicator that the foster child had become "part of the family." Foster children had to meet the same expectations as other family members with respect to chores, duties, and responsibilities and suffered the same consequences as other same-age children within that kin group. They had moved from "outsider" status to "insider" in women's minds and were no longer treated "like guests." In this respect, abrasive shouting signaled a degree of warmth and familial affiliation. My observation of foster children's reactions and responses to their foster mothers' shouting (other than seeing them scurry) indicated that children understood this. Rather than acting dejected or offended, many seemed to respond positively, completing the task and then seeking the foster mother's approval or affection.

This was also true of corporal punishment. The state of Connecticut has strict policies against using corporal punishment with foster children. Women can have their licenses immediately revoked for using physical discipline or for admitting that they did. During interviews, I routinely asked women how they disciplined children. Most said they used time out or withheld privileges. However, many women used words similar to the following: "I treat my foster kids exactly like my own. If mine get something, my foster kids get the same thing. If mine get beat, they get beat. No differences." Women took this risk because it was very important to treat children "just like their own" and to incorporate them into their family. This was the criterion by which "good" mothering was defined.

> Well, I do her the same way I do with my children. If they get discipline, she gets discipline. I don't go beating on her just to beat on her, but when she does things she gets a spanking. If they get hit, she gets hit. . . . But she is good. She does everything, you know. She is very good. (Tanya Collins, a married African American woman in her late thirties)

## Adding Children to the Family

As women's relationships with children progressed, foster parents communicated to children that regardless of their problems, disabilities, or kin affiliations, they were valued family members. As one foster father asserted, whether a child is present for a week or for several years, foster children are family.

> We feel when they come in that they're going to be a part of the family.
> . . . Any time they want to come here, they can, regardless of whether the agency is involved or not. They're actually members of our family. You know? They have curfews and they have chores and an allowance. So it's not just "You don't have to do that because you're only going to be here for a week or so." So that's just the way it is. We've had foster kids from three years ago come by or call or stay. . . . We're just parents who are extending our family. (Tom Gordon, a married Euro-American man in his early forties)

Belonging to the foster family was permanent even though it was often at a significant cost. As one mother stated,

> I got her when she was thirteen, and we had just moved into an all-white neighborhood. And you know how it is when you move into an all white neighborhood. You've got to be cool. Don't make a lot of waves, 'cause people are watching you all the time, seeing how you are, what you like. And I got my last one when she was thirteen, and we had just moved in, and she had seven foster homes before coming to me, they saying she was all out of control and all. And don't you know the first week we was there, she stole $500 from a neighbor. And she says to me, "So, I guess now you gonna have me moved, huh?" And I said, "No, baby. You mine now. You one of my children. You gonna stay here. You gonna turn that money back, you gonna go to court. You gonna suffer. But I'm gonna suffer with you. And you *never* gonna do that again. (Delia Johnson, a single African American woman in her early thirties)

For Belinda Evans, a married Euro-American woman in her fifties, fully incorporating children into her family was an imperative that defined foster care.

> [T]he social worker wanted a home that was nurturing for these—there were two boys whose mother was dying of cancer and had no family to take them. At the same time, we had absolutely no room to take them, but situations worked out differently and we took them. The foster fam-

ily before me was going on, quote, a "family vacation" and needed a place to place the boys while they were on their family vacation, which I think is awful. Because when there's children in the family, biological children, and they're going on a family vacation, and you tell somebody, "We'll see you when we get back," it does not make them feel part of the family. . . . So we took them, and it was time for our family vacation, and we took them to Vermont with us. But they never wanted to go back to the first home. And they said that, you know, the other home gave them a meal and a clean bed, but period. They felt like they were in a family here. So that was really good, so we ended up keeping them. . . . And my feelings on foster care—my children come and they're no longer in a *foster* family, they're . . . *home.*

Often a foster mother's extended family and social network affirmed and supported the foster children's membership, most often by offering emotional or material support for the foster children or by acknowledging their emotional importance in the foster mother's life. This broadened the familial context the child entered and supported both the child's place in the family and the mother's efforts for a kinship relationship. Through shared recognition of a child's membership, extended family supported a foster mother's identity as a mother and assisted in "mothering" tasks. For example, one mother talked about the support she received from her family and neighbors as she began to add her foster son to her family. Their support acted to welcome him into a larger kin network and offered his foster mother support in her caregiving role.

Well, they would come over and would hold the baby and play with the baby, help me do different things. But we are family like this—fourteen kids. We used to laugh at my mom, she used to take people's kids off the streets. And she just loved kids. And when Christmastime came and that's how I really supported my first kid, because when Christmas came he had everything. Everything. I didn't have to worry about that. Any clothes. I called the people that I knew and they had smaller kids, smaller grandkids. They brought stuff over, even for the baby that I had for twenty days. I had more stuff. See, because my niece sent me . . . she called up friends of hers that had babies, they brought all kind of clothes and stuff, oh yeah. . . . Even my neighbor down here, he, when Christmas came, he'd come over with a big shopping bag full of stuff. It's been great. Oh, yes [he is a part of the family]. (Racine White, a single African American woman in her late fifties)

Most women were close to at least one other woman who also fostered. These friends were called on in times of crisis or hardship and were considered a part of women's kin network. As Ellen McKnight, a Euro-American woman, said, "My family and I have a very good friend who has done foster care for years and years and years, so that's who I turn to when I need the answers. It seems to work best that way."

## Mothering Knowledge/Skill and Healing Transformations

Mothering work also included technical skill. Women described in detail the expertise they needed to care for foster children. Many described participating in training classes as well as forming collateral relationships with community social services workers to learn new skills. For example, women who fostered cocaine-addicted babies often worked with the Visiting Nurse Association to learn how to swaddle and hold the babies and help an addicted baby eat. Women who fostered children diagnosed with ADHD (attention deficit hyperactive disorder) were well informed about the virtues and drawbacks of medication, and many offered their opinions about whether or not their children should receive medication and even what the optimum dose should be.

None of the formal training replaced or displaced intuitive knowledge. When asked how they knew when to intervene with their foster children or how they selected certain responses, most women simply said, "It felt right," or "I just knew." Women also spoke about the intimate knowledge they had gained of individual foster children. Such knowledge often revolved around the ability to understand a child's emotional or psychic pain and find the remedy or simply keep watch while the emotional storm raged.

Sarah Perkins, a married Euro-American foster mother in her late forties, described what it was like when her four-year-old foster daughter, the second child she fostered, arrived. She spoke on the one hand about knowledge of her child's trauma and on the other of the knowledge of how to keep watch while delicate bonds of trust were being established. This mother became a part of the child's life as the child permitted it and slowly established a relationship through which healing began.

I was well aware of the physical and sexual abuse and the abandonment and the beatings. . . . Her room was over a porch that had no heat and only would fit her crib, and her hands were blue and her diapers were three days dirty, and she didn't have three squares and she had a bottle until she was four. . . . And I found that knowing all of that as she screamed around here [made it easier to understand her]. She screamed from the time she came in, she screamed. If you walked by her, she would fold up and scream, like, "Don't touch me, don't touch me." And if you tried to bathe her, somebody would think that there was some horror show going on in this house. And at night she would just stay up. If you tried to put her to bed, she would scream and scream and scream. And that went on for over a month easily.

When I asked how she managed a child who screamed and could not comply with daily living tasks, Sarah replied:

Well, she could do what she could do. She didn't go to bed. I would try rocking her, but she was stiff. She wasn't a child that molded to you. She just— didn't want to be held. And then finally it reached a point where . . . [I had] to draw some lines, and so I told her, even if she stayed awake, we had to stay up in her bedroom. And we sat there, and I closed the door, and she would play for a while, and then she might scream. But I would just sit there with her. You couldn't hold her. She wouldn't let you. And then gradually [she began to heal]. Now . . . I say, "Sandra, it's bedtime." And in she goes and that's the end of it. . . . It seems to me that if a child is frightened about where she is and is frightened about going to bed, and is scared to death of a bath, I mean, she was more than traumatized, and would ball up when I walked by her as though I was going to kick her or beat her [then you give her time to heal. You don't push her]. . . . I don't know. It just seemed right.

Many women spoke of teaching foster children behaviors they had always taken for granted in family life like not hiding food, changing their clothes, going to the bathroom, or not lying or stealing money. The failure to conform to such simple expectations had to be understood in the context of the child's trauma. Such behaviors were part of a complicated pattern of unlearning, relearning, or healing. For example, many women spoke of the difficulty they experienced toileting children who had been raped. These children often wet or soiled themselves rather than use the bathroom and often refused to change their clothes. Getting them to do both meant understanding the trauma, and engaging them in a complicated healing process.

Women conceptualized healing in very particular ways. Rather than a mental or biophysical condition, healing was almost always defined by the "improvement" or the "changes" children experienced. Healing was a transformation from one state of being to another. Almost always included in this transformation was an improved ability to form or sustain a trusting relationship with an adult.[1] One mother, Abigail Mackey, a married African American woman in her early thirties, offered an experience with healing and transformation common to many foster mothers. She took three siblings, the oldest of whom was a six-year-old girl. She described her experiences integrating the oldest child into her family and helping the child learn for the first time to be a child.

> Well, the oldest one I have, she was seven, her brother was five. [When she came,] her brother was four and she was six and her sister was a baby. When she came here she was like, "I know how to cook, clean, wash dishes." So I even told them that experience at school. And they were like, "Well, most of the kids usually don't know when they say that." And I says, "Well, she knew because she had been taking care of those children while her mother was out doing drugs, so she knew." But those are the things I had to try to break her out of. Because I was like, "You're too young to be cooking, cleaning, and all that other stuff, you know, you're just too young for that, and that's not your responsibility. That is mine. I am the mother." But she did all those things. . . . Well, I just weaned her less and less and less. It's like, who told you how to do all those things? [She would say,] "Well, that's what I used to do at the other foster home, and that's what I used to do home when my mother lived there."
>
> Wow, I was like, "But you don't have to do that here." She didn't even know how to ride a bike. She didn't know how to read. So those are things I told her [to do]. I said you go sit down and read a book or you go outside and play, because you don't know how to ride bikes and you don't know how to read a book. She still has a lot of, she has a hard time in school. I guess when she was younger they never really taught her anything. But yeah, those are some things that I have to break her of. . . . It was hard. . . . We were persistent. She's calmed down a lot. We've [got] the teachers involved. We've got the social workers involved in school . . . and she has calmed down quite a bit.

Foster mothers defined their mothering interventions with children as important, immediate, necessary, and ultimately ensuring children's survival and protecting their quality of life. Women saw this survival both metaphorically and literally. Many children entering care have been physically battered or neglected to such an extent that their health and potential survival are compromised. It was not uncommon for women to receive children who required extensive, acute medical intervention as well as long-term medical care.

> And this was a messed up kid when I got him. Oh, God. He was—first of all, he would take his head and like bang it on a wood table if you said no to him. Then he would like beat himself upside the head. He would like throw tantrums. He will bite. If you walk in, he might grab you by the leg or arm and bite you. You know? And I have to say, when he first came to me, I saw him fall. I watched him fall. He was bleeding so bad. He felt no pain. You know? He felt no pain. And every week I'm taking him to a psychiatrist. You know? Finally, he began to come around a little bit. Now he will let me know when he gets hurt or he's hurt or whatever. Oh, he was a messed up little child. A messed up child. (Clara White, a single African American woman in her late fifties)

Women as family healers is not an uncommon cross-cultural theme. For example, McClain (1995) shows how complex and nuanced images of women as community and family healers emerge when gender is used as a salient variable. (For additional perspectives, see Spector, 1979; Cheney and Adams, 1978; Manzanedo, Walter, and Lorig, 1980; Clark, 1970; Kleinman, 1980; Herrick, 1983; Young, Wolkowitz, and McCullagh, 1981; Helman, 1984; Martinez and Martin, 1979; Litman, 1979). But in the United States healing has not commonly been associated with foster mothering, or, for that matter, with mothering. Yet clearly foster mothers saw themselves as both mothers and healers, not only for individual children but through children for society as a whole.

> You're with your child from day one and you know that you sort of gradually, like a graph every day, you know, you're getting—and that child is reflecting from you. So, it's become a very easy thing, like your—like a clock that winds, you know, and it all goes in rhythm, as long as you keep your own life balanced. But when you have a foster child coming in, usually he's coming in because his whole life is all mixed up. I've had these girls that have been sexually molested since they were ten years old, by the mother's boyfriend. And you can imagine what that's done to their lives and their minds. They've lost their innocence. And you get these girls that are just—in fact their whole world is shattered, and they don't know where they're going or what they're doing or—and the thing they think about is, you don't really care about me, you know. And you

don't win any trust with them for a long time. Years, if they're lucky enough to stay with you. Yeah. It takes a long relationship in order to get—to win a child who's over ten. (Beatrice Rollins, a single African American woman in her late fifties)

## Advocacy

Because I feel Tony has been with me for a year now and I know the mother's background. I have dealt with his mother. I had to go to court with this child. And the mother hasn't done anything to get herself together. They have offered her all kinds of programs. And now this social worker here, she's doing all she can to take this child back with the mother. The mother hasn't gotten any kind of help yet. Okay? And the psychiatrist—this boy is seen by psychiatrists and everything. Why should you give him back to the condition that he was in? It's going to set him back even further. And this time he might not ever come out of the situation. And this was a messed up kid when I got him. . . . Well, they know how I feel. We had a meeting with the psychiatrist, his teacher, his worker, the speech therapist. We had a meeting about a month ago with the worker because she was going to take him up to the prison to see his dad he doesn't even know. He hasn't seen him since he was two months old. And we was against it because he acts out when he gets around people he don't know. He begins to act back to the way he was when he came. It takes an effect on him. And we didn't want that. So they know how I feel on that. [But] like I said, this worker he got now, she's all for putting him back in the home. And that's going to really totally set him back. I'm all for the mom into getting him back. Don't get me wrong. But she will have to prove herself. Okay? (Clara White, a single African American woman in her late fifties)

He's a good boy, but he is—when I got him he was on the borderline of retarded. And I had a hard time keeping him in school. I didn't have no hard time sending him to school, but I had a hard time—the teachers calling me and telling me he wouldn't behave himself. So the state decided that he needed to be put in a special school. And we fell in love with him so much when they said they was going to take him from me and I didn't want them to take him. So they sent him away to a special school. But he was treated—really if you could see—when he came home for Christmas, I went to go pick him up. And it was an all-white school in Georgia, and this teacher or whoever it was over him, you should see how he had beat him. (Norma Peel, a married African American woman in her seventies)

Finally, another aspect of mothering work that women identified was to advocate for children and to protect their rights as women defined them. These were frequently seen as children's rights to return to their family, to remain in the foster home, or to be provided with various community or state social services. Unfortunately, this was perhaps one of the most painful tasks women engaged in, since overwhelmingly women spoke of being discounted, ignored, or reminded of their "place." While some DCF offices attempted to include foster mothers in the child's treatment plans and actually invited foster parents to a child's formal treatment plan reviews, most offices, according to foster mothers, did not. Most women felt intentionally excluded if they knew of the meetings at all. One dilemma of advocacy work was as follows. What do you do with a child with whom you have established an intimate kinship-based relationship, and for whom who feel you know what is best, when there is no way in which your knowledge will be officially recognized?

In response, generally either women fought DCF actively and aggressively, seeking out social work supervisors or contesting policies they felt were harmful to children, or they resigned themselves to their lack of control over the child and simply accepted their powerlessness. In some cases they did both simultaneously, negotiating a relationship where they alternately pushed for their perspective, acquiesced to the state, and pushed again. Confronted with their helplessness, many women harbored a deep-seated resentment toward DCF and bitterness at seeing children placed in situations that compromised their health or survival.

One mother, Ellen McKnight, related a story that illustrates one of foster mothers' greatest fears and worst experiences. She had been fostering a child she received as an infant for two and a half years. The little boy's parents had been in prison, or their whereabouts had been unknown to the state. Since his parents had been absent from his life for long periods of time, he did not recognize his biological mother or father. Mrs. McKnight wanted to adopt him. She felt this was the best thing for him. But by virtue of DCF policy, the child had to continue seeing his biological mother. Mrs. McKnight's story is marked by helplessness and despair. The parents' legal and blood relationship to the boy took precedence over his foster family's claims to him and his claims of belonging to his foster family. Mrs. McKnight's expertise regarding the child's needs were not seen or heard, and she felt she had to be careful in asserting them. On a regular basis, the child was picked up by DCF social workers and taken to a women's prison to visit his mother. Prior to the inception of these visits, he had not seen his mother in fourteen months. The child had what Ellen described as stranger anxiety and cried wildly when he was taken from day care by different social workers. Ellen was not allowed to accompany him on the visits, even though she felt this would make him feel less frightened.

> I understand that we can't ever say to them we want to adopt him, because then that could be interfering with the reunification process. So that's where we stand. They know if they terminate, we'll definitely be interested. [In] this particular case, they've never had a clearer case of terminating. Both parents were in jail . . . shortly after the baby was born. Baby has never lived with either parent. Mom gave him up for adoption at birth. When she got arrested when he was six weeks old, she changed her mind and canceled the adoption, so he went into a foster home. She went to jail. Dad's still in jail at that point. [Baby] is four months old and the foster mom that had him couldn't care for him anymore. I think she got a job in the evening, so we got him from there.
>
> [Baby] used to do once-a-month visits with mom in prison, and he used to do once-a-week visits with grandma, and the reunification [plan] at that time was mom living at grandma's house [and both] jointly have custody of the baby. Mom got out of jail and disappeared. And we did not hear from her for fourteen months. Mind you, the child is just now two. Grandma at that point said, if she's not doing it, I'm not doing it, I've got five kids of my own. So we heard nothing. So there was no more talk of reunification with mom at all, that was it. Fourteen months [go by and] we haven't heard from her. So dad, in the meantime, is in jail. We're doing once-a-month visits with dad. Dad gets out and says he wants him. So they give dad twice-a-week visitations. They give him a treatment plan that says we need you to get a job, you need to have a stable place to live, you need to keep up with your visits, and at some point, we need to get you some parenting classes. Twice-a-week visits ended up to be, this year, January 3 and April 5. In the meantime, mom's back in jail. Now mom wants her visits back. We haven't heard from her in fourteen months. Mom's had another baby. We want our visits back, because we're in jail, so we get out of our jail cell for an hour, so we want to see the child.
>
> So we take the child to the jail to visit. The first visit went okay. The second visit, he wouldn't go to her. He does not know her. He's literally seen her six times in his life. And up until this time, they were all before he was six months old. So mom gets very upset. "I don't like the system,

he doesn't know me, I don't ever want to see him again." They leave the visit. Now mom writes a letter and apologizes and says she's sorry for her behavior. And so they've postponed the termination, and we're going to give her another eighteen months to try to reunify. This is a very clear case [for terminating the parental rights].[2]

They can't reach dad. Dad hasn't had any contact since April. They don't even know how to find dad. And now we're going to do another eighteen months here. And this is a baby who never lived with his parents. *We* are his parents, as far as he knows. He is part of *our family*, that's all he knows. That's all he knows.

[Q.: Who takes the baby to the prison visits?] A DCF worker does. Well, this is what I just mentioned to him the last time, because [the baby] was so distraught when they picked him up. I've always asked them to please send the same person. They can't always do it. But it wasn't till the last four months that he had this real stranger anxiety. So, I have a brand new social worker, which is our third one or fourth one, maybe, for this child. . . . And we have a young man, very young man, and he's very nice. But they don't quite understand. And he says, "Well, I'll tell you what, I'll do better than that, I'll take him myself." I said, "Rex, he doesn't *know you,* that's not solving my problem." So I did make the offer [to take him to prison myself]. Now, I work full-time, so this is difficult. So I said, look, if you're going to do once-a-month [visits] and he's going to get this upset, if you can plan it ahead of time, I will take a half day off a month, and I will take him down to the jail. They said, "That's not going to help. If he won't go to his mother now, he's certainly not going to go while you're there." I don't know. I don't—how could you judge that? When she's only seen him, you know, in one-hour time slots, in jail, since he has been born. But even if they—even if I could wait out in the waiting room, it would be better for the baby.

You know, this child has no rights at all. [Her voice broke and she paused for a moment as she tried not to cry.] They will take him screaming out of the day care and put him screaming in the car, and they'll take him there where he'll probably scream half the time, and he'll come back to the day care, and he'll be hitting and he'll be biting. And I'll pick him up and I will not be able to leave the room for the rest of the night, because he will attach himself to me and I won't be able to move.

And that's really sad that these kids have no rights at all. . . . That is what makes me more angry than anything in this entire system, is that these children, who have done nothing to deserve anything, have no rights whatsoever. Why should this baby have to do that? There are solutions to this. We have mom's past history. When mom gets out of jail, if she wants to do a visit, let the mom come to the baby. End of story.

You know, we've given mom plenty of chances here. There's no reason that they needed to take this kid out. We've got—what could be a healthy emotional child here, because I've had him since he was four months old. We spend an extra eighteen months sending a stranger to pick him up to take him to a stranger, we're going to be causing lots of problems that could be avoided. And it makes me very angry.

In another example Mrs. Peel an African American woman in her seventies, advocated for her foster daughter to be removed from special education and placed in a residential setting where both her emotional and her educational needs could be aggressively addressed. Mrs. Peel realized that no one at DCF or the school felt her daughter could succeed—that is, remain in school—and they did not want to allocate funding for her care. But Mrs. Peel defined the situation quite differently and felt that part of her mothering work was to fight for her child. Mrs. Peel called numerous department administrators repeatedly, documenting each call and each response.[3] She refused to be discouraged when DCF told her several times they had "lost all of Anne's paperwork" and would have to begin again. While caring for many young children, she traveled long distances to DCF offices to attend case hearings and advocate for Anne. Finally, she was able to convince Anne's attorney to take DCF to court and force them to place the girl in a treatment center. As Mrs. Peel said, once in court,

> They admitted it [that DCF had intentionally stalled Anne's placement in a residential treatment center] because they felt like somebody else had better intentions than Anne. They felt that they would help other kids. They felt like Anne wasn't going to make it. In other words, they put her on the bottom of the list. It's no good to waste this money on her. She's not going to improve.
>
> [But] she has improved a lot. She's not ready to come home yet. But we see a difference.

Women's belief that children could and should succeed compelled them to pursue their mothering work with tenacity and commitment. This often, as in Mrs. Peel's case, meant procuring necessary services. In other cases, it meant constructing a vision of foster children based on hope and healing, and maintaining that vision in the face of professional opinion and state pressure to the contrary. In still other cases, advocacy meant *not* calling DCF to have a disturbed child removed and instead finding ways to weather a child's emotional and behavioral problems. Of his foster children, Roger Samuels, a married Euro-American man in his mid-thirties, said,

> Some children with real problems, [the state] had a hard time placing them or keeping them placed. And we would give it our best shot. But we would never give up. I mean, unless it was actually a danger to the other kids, that's the only time that we would give them back, because we would always hope that we could do it. We didn't give up. . . .
>
> They [DCF] will like label and give up, and we know that's not true because we have three kids born under different labels [all of which imply a degree of hopelessness or chronicity], and we know it's not true. They can be helped.

# 7

# Familial Changes
## Integrating Foster Children into the Foster Family

Our family situation almost fell apart. We went though an investigation [because] I hit one of my kids out of frustration and, you know, it was just a very bad time in our lives and so frustrating for us being in the middle, because the department wanted us to adopt this child and we kept saying no, no, no, but you know emotionally after three and a half years of having a child in your home you are emotionally tied and yet you know that with already four kids in the home and the family situation is not in the child's best interest. But the department kept saying oh, but you have done such a good job, and you are such good parents. But let me tell you something. No parents are gods. There is a limit. I don't care whether you adopted four kids and you have done a good job. There is a limit.

—Lillian Rosebud, a married Native American woman in her mid-forties

Once women became licensed, foster children, foster children's biological families, and the state had to be integrated into the rhythms and routines of everyday life. This was a complex process and required enormous personal, familial, and sometimes marital sacrifice. There were few if any support services available to foster families. Most women asked their children and spouses to make a personal commitment to fostering and to assume a portion of the caregiving responsibilities. Jerry-Ann Matthews, a married African American woman in her late thirties, described how a dedication to foster was woven into the fabric of her family as a commitment that each family member had to make.

Oh yeah, it definitely had to be, you know, both of us. The kids that come into my home, definitely, [I] couldn't do it by myself. I wouldn't even try, you know. But my kids, they, they are a tremendous help, and my husband is tremendous. He's right there. If the children had to go to the doctor, he's right there you know. And I wouldn't have it no other way. If it wasn't this way, I wouldn't take them in. Everybody pitches in, yeah. Because that's the only way it could be for me. Everybody has to say, you know, yes, this is what we want. You know, it couldn't be just me, because then I'm going to have trouble, you know?

Each woman spoke of her expectations prior to fostering and the needs foster children presented relative to those expectations. Most expectations were premised on women's experiences as biological mothers. But most women also said this premise was erroneous. While foster parents stressed foster children's similarity to nonfoster children as a way to mark them as social children, they also talked about their differences. For the most part, foster children's behaviors and needs were markedly different from those of children who had not undergone traumas associated with physical, sexual, or emotional abuse or abandonment.

I don't think anybody, doesn't matter what they tell you during your classes, can understand what it's really like. I mean . . . when they called me about Arabelle, she was just about six. She had already been in placement with her brother for about four months. They kept the brother, but they couldn't handle Arabelle. What am I doing? I've never done this before. But I'm thinking to myself, how is it that somebody could not handle a five-year-old child? What could be so difficult about this? Well, let me tell you. I do know now! At first there was a honeymoon. And then the bottom fell out. And she's a very defiant, very, very defiant little girl. She's belligerent. I mean, she just—she's tough. She's tough. And I know that she's giving her grandmother a really rough time right now. . . . I didn't realize how—it's not really a good word, but for lack of something better, damaged, they are. I didn't realize how damaged they are. And each one has—I mean, their needs are so great. . . . And sometimes you feel like peanut butter on a piece of bread, you know, I mean just all over the place. . . . I don't think I really understood the commitment you make when you open the door. (Sarah Perkins, a married Euro-American woman in her late forties)

While women spoke with concern of the demands on their time and energy or the sometimes thankless struggles to raise children with significant emotional or physical challenges, no one in the study spoke of leaving fostering because of the impact it had on her or her family.[1] Fostering was something each woman was committed to. One example of the adjustments and sacrifice that went into integrating both foster children and the state into a family was the family of Deleah Smith, a married African American woman in her late forties who had four biological children. Her situation, decisions, and perspectives exemplify the way in which the women who participated in this study approached foster mothering and the hardships that came with it. Deleah married her husband when he proved that he no longer used drugs. She had just gotten married when the Department of Children and Families removed her sister's four children. Her sister was a crack-cocaine addict, and the children had been seriously neglected. Deleah agreed to take them because she saw it as her family and community responsibility. She, like the other women in the study, defined herself as having always been a mother to any child who needed mothering. These children, like any other in need, became her own.

> My husband has been clean three and a half years now. I have been married to him for two and a half years. Same amount of time I've had the kids. So it's like, as soon as I get him straight, I take on these kids with some *serious* problems. So I got used to it. I guess I'm a sucker! Just the way I look at it. I guess I'm just a sucker that can't help myself 'cause I like kids. I tell all these little crumb snatchers around here, "Why do you come to my house?" They won't leave. They keep coming back. This one over here [a mother in the neighborhood] says to me last night, "Could you buy her [daughter] a pair of shoes?" I don't have *enough* kids that I got to buy shoes for? Now you want me to buy your kid a pair of shoes?
>
> Today, I'm gonna go to the store and buy the kid a pair of shoes. I can't let the kid go around barefooted. I watched her for two weeks barefooted. I can't do that no more. So it's like, you know, you do what you gotta do. What is the total number of years you been a foster parent? I'm not a foster mother. I'm just a mother because I've got my own children and I'm their mother. They're mine.

Of the adjustments that her family went through when her sister's children came to live with her, she said,

> We went through a lot of changes. We went through some *serious* changes in this house! Some *serious* changes! Everyone in this house. My kids, these guys [foster children], my husband. It was wicked. [Like what? she was asked.] Well, "that's my bed." Nobody wants to give up their rooms. Now you're talking five bedrooms, everybody has their own

room. Everybody has their own space. My room was over this room. My daughter's room was down there. My littlest daughter's room was upstairs. My father had his room down there. Everybody had their own space. Now you're taking everybody's space, but you're talking about taking everybody's space as far as time [too]. As far as love! Now you're talking about, it's got to be divided now. I want you over here. This one wants you over there. This one wants you over here—it was crazy. It was hell [on my marriage]. It was tough, really tough. There was no time. Like our bedroom was a community bedroom. 'Cause all the kids come in. The first place they go is the bedroom. And they sit. They don't move. Don't matter if you're laying in the bed. They don't move. That means if you don't have any clothes on, you can't get up to piss. They're not moving! . . . I've never had so much turmoil in my life. Teachers calling me every day. Every day there's something. [But] I deal with it.

Deleah's decision to care for her nieces and nephews entailed considerable emotional and financial hardship. The oldest child had a number of alienating emotional problems. He wet the bed every night; he lied to and stole from Deleah and her husband; he frustrated Deleah by refusing to wear the nice clothes she provided and instead chose to wear clothes that were old, torn, dirty, or mismatched. This often provoked sympathy from adults around him and simultaneously incurred scorn for Deleah when people assumed she was not providing adequately for this child. The child also had considerable difficulty in school, and Deleah was frequently called by his teachers with complaints about his behavior and concerns about his ability to do his work. He was often sullen and uncommunicative when confronted with his behavior, or he lied. Deleah was not allowed to beat (or as she noted, "What you white people call spank") her nieces and nephews, even though this was the method of discipline she used with her own children, and had to sign a paper before the children were placed with her, stating that she would not use corporal punishment.

In addition, DCF placed the four children with Deleah but refused to pay her any support for their care, saying that since the children were relatives, they were not required to pay her as a foster mother.[2] At the same time, they licensed her as a relative foster mother and insisted that she add a dormer to the back bedroom of her house and install fire alarms in order to bring her house up to fire safety code. Because her family was suddenly so large, Deleah was faced with the fact that everyone could no longer ride in the same car. Going to school, church, and the supermarket now required two trips. While she could not easily afford it, she was forced to purchase a new and much larger car.

Her nieces and nephews also needed new clothes. While she was entitled to a clothing voucher as a foster mother, she received no assistance from the state in buying clothes since the state's contention was that she was *not* a foster mother. Because her nieces and nephews were emotionally traumatized from their experiences with their mother, DCF required Deleah to place them in therapy. Since she, her own children, and her husband were all facing the sudden stress of four additional children, all with considerable emotional needs, they decided to enter therapy together. The department initially said they would pay for therapy. However, Deleah and her children were terminated at the family counseling center when it was discovered that DCF would not pay for therapy, and the children were not covered under Title XIX.

Deleah's life, as she said, had been complex enough: she was raising her own children, adjusting to a new marriage, and her father had recently moved in. Then she was faced with raising four extra children, incurring expenses she could not meet, and dealing with a myriad of unhelpful social workers in what she experienced as an unresponsive state bureaucracy. As she pointed out, DCF told her how to care for the children and insisted she meet certain fire and health standards but was not helping with their financial or emotional care.

Finally, one year after the children had been placed with her, faced with enormous expenses, considerable emotional strain, and no support, she called DCF with an ultimatum her husband did not support: either remove the children or help financially with their care. After considerable negotiation with different social workers and supervisors, she was finally offered the standard fostering reimbursement rate. However, as she noted, she was not compensated for the year she cared for the children with no support, nor was any help offered her for the expense of putting a dormer on her house or buying a new car. She noted that they still needed counseling, but they were unable to resume with the clinic, since that bill had not yet been paid and the clinic was seeking payment from her.

Deleah agreed to take her sister's children for the same reason she agreed to buy the neighbor's child shoes. She could not *not* do it and she was proud of her decision and the caregiving abilities that allowed her to care for them. When reflecting on her decision to take them, she thought immediately about the positive changes she had seen in the children.

The best experience I've had is watching them smile. Watching them getting to play and be kids. Just watching them being able to be normal kids again. The oldest one didn't go to school because he wanted to make sure that the [youngest] one went to school. So he would go to school when she went to school in the afternoon and asked the teachers if they would let him in. And because of the situation they would let him come in. Because he would walk [his younger sister to kindergarten and then walk himself to school] . . . over forty blocks. In dirty pissy clothes he would walk. So it's a thrill to me because if you [could] see them when they came here everybody was withdrawn.

During a follow-up visit several months after the initial one, she lamented to me and the social worker who unexpectedly arrived that she was not sure she could continue providing care for her oldest nephew since his behavior had become so disruptive. But her doubts, her regrets, and the pain caused by her decision did not in any way alter the fact that she knew she had done, as she herself said, what she had to do. Nor did they change the way in which she defined her relationship to the members of her family or the vehemence and tenacity she brought to her mothering work.

Yeah, I ain't giving up. If they're here until they're eighteen, then they're here until they're eighteen. Toni tells me, auntie, I'm gonna be a lawyer. And when I become a lawyer, I'm gonna buy you a big house. And I tell him no. When you become a lawyer, buy yourself a big house.

## Foster Mothers' Biological Children

For most women, one of the most significant problems they dealt with was balancing foster children's needs for emotional and physical care with their own concerns about how fostering affected the emotional health of their biological children. Many women were concerned about the impression foster children's behavior made on their biological children.

I think a lot of people think of this as a full-time baby-sitting job. And that's not what it is by any means. It's an addition to your family, and a troubled addition to your family. . . . [I]t affects every aspect of your life. . . . It's not just one thing, you know, it affects everything, you know?

There's been [both a positive and a detrimental] effect on my children. Of course you have to decide what's detrimental. Is it detrimental to my children to know that these things go on in life? They have to know that at some point, you know. But is it detrimental at this point to know? . . . It's certainly not hurting them to know not everybody has everything they can have. [T]he benefits—my eleven-year-old daughter is the most giving child in the world, and I think it's because of foster care. She's very caring, you know, and she has no problem with that. . . .

I mean there are certainly some things that have been said to my children by other foster children that I never wanted them to know—especially the sexual abuse. You don't discuss sexual abuse with a ten-year-old. But when another nine-year-old tells her this is what happened to her, that's detrimental. Luckily, she [her daughter] is real levelheaded and real strong. So we just had a talk about it straight out, and [I said] this is sometimes what happens and that's not what's supposed to happen. And that's why she can't live there anymore. She [her daughter] did okay. She did okay. She didn't ask a lot of details. You can only give them what they want to know. And so to her, sexual abuse is somebody touching her where her bathing suit covers, and that's not what's supposed to happen. And that's all she could handle at that point, so that's OK. (Ellen McKnight, a married Euro-American woman in her mid-thirties)

Women with biological children also spoke with concern about the impact foster children's comings and goings had on their biological children. When foster children left a home, women watched as their children suffered from feelings of loss and bereavement. Many women concluded that they were not sure what the impact of these experiences would be. In response, foster mothers closely monitored their children's emotional responses to fostering, watching for signs of emotional stress, and, when it was apparent, moved quickly to help their children deal with it.

I don't think anybody can ever prepare you for everything. I never expected to get so attached to the children. I thought it would be more like a full-time baby-sitting job; it's not. It's not at all.

I was not prepared for the impact that it would have on my own children and extended family, for that matter. You have to do a lot of adjusting. You have to do a lot of, lot of adjusting.

When you get a child into your home that is very disturbed, and you don't have a—you have to go real slow on the discipline and you have to teach them right from the start. You're not ever prepared for your kid to say, "If I ever did that, I'd be in big trouble. Why do you let her get away with that?" You know. I mean, something as simple as children not liking vegetables. Now, you get kids that have never had any good eating habits. To start with, you can't force too many vegetables on them, they physically get sick. Whereas, you know, your own child would say, "Well, how come you make me eat that and she doesn't have to?" So you can never prepare for every little tiny thing that happens all along that way. So I wasn't prepared for the impact it had on the entire family. And the worst part was, I don't think I was prepared enough for the emotions when they leave. And after our first child left, we almost stopped, because my father-in-law was devastated. *I* wasn't [prepared]—well, we were prepared for her leaving. We weren't prepared for the emptiness it left us. And we weren't prepared for how that would affect our children, especially, you know, the younger ones. [My son] cried for three days. He was five years—he was six when she left, and he cried for three days. I didn't sleep for two nights. I was so worried about her. We had more children. By the time she left, we had our own three and four foster children. And so you'd think that would take up the slack. But you just worry so much, you know. [T]here's just some times when you're not prepared for the emptiness it leaves you, you know. . . .

You know, and I had said to somebody at one point, they need to have services available for our children. I mean, they do a good job with that for the foster kids, but nobody prepares our own children for that. (Ellen McKnight, a married Euro-American woman in her mid-thirties)

As Mrs. McKnight pointed out, there are no services for a foster parent's biological children and few services to prepare families for the impact foster children's comings and goings will have. As she attested, the impact ranges from adjustments of minor house rules to feelings of devastation and bereavement. Many women saw their family size double, their expenses quadruple, and the demands on their time expand exponentially. As the family adjusted to an increase in size and new demands for household resources, it could either expand again as new children were placed or dramatically shrink as children left to return home or be adopted. The nature and daily rhythms of one's family were constantly *altering*.

Women's concerns about incorporating foster children into their families were juxtaposed with the benefits they felt they and their biological children reaped. Fostering was a way to inculcate in their own children caregiving values. It provided an opportunity to teach empathy and to impart a concept of family as an extended caregiving unit based on an ability to recognize and respond to human need. Sarah Perkins, a married Euro-American woman in her late forties, spoke both of her decision to foster and of the impact fostering had on her son, Joseph. To Mrs. Perkins, the benefits of fostering outweighed the risks to her son. Joseph encountered problems like jealousy resulting from competition with his emotionally needy foster sister and had to work on resolving his negative feelings. Once he had done so, he came through the experience in his mother's eyes as a stronger child with enhanced coping skills.

My sister had done foster care for a couple of years. And I had only one biological child [Joseph]. He was about eleven at the time. And I don't think it's really healthy for a child to grow up all alone. Not that he wasn't happy. He certainly was. He was eager to do this too. Then we had a child [Arabelle] that came in who was just six years old. She was just turning six years old, and that was a nightmare. . . . Oh, she was so difficult. She was a survivor. She had all of the [survival] skills Joseph didn't have. Yet, she was also so needy. She needed everybody's attention. She had to be [the] center of everything. And she just came in and he felt displaced. And of course I'm thinking he's a secure little boy and fairly well adjusted for a kid his age. And I think my expectations for him were more than he could give. . . . And there were several times [during the two years she was here] I spoke with the worker, and I said, "I don't think I'm going to be able to make it here." Because it really was not good. Joseph would stomp up to his room. He did not want to be in the same room with this child.

And then she went home to her grandparents, not to her mother, two weeks ago. And Joseph had to write something in school in the eighth grade. And it had to be a paper on what was very meaningful to him, something that happened that had a lot of meaning. He chose on his own to write about foster care. And of course the topic for him was this little girl. And of course this dissension between them went on for two years. And then you could see something [a relationship] was building. And he wrote this paper and he talked about how he [had] hated her and how [sad] he felt when she left. And he was [she struggled to retain control over her emotions and not to cry]—he knew he'd miss her very much, and she was a best friend of his. In fact he was talking to her [on the telephone] last night.

And I'll tell you something. My son, I think he learned a lot. I think all of this has been a good experience for him. And I didn't always think that. I had my doubts. I had my doubts about what I did, you know. During the early part of fostering, I thought, oh my gosh, is he going to be OK? But he's fine. He has his head screwed on pretty tight for a fourteen-year-old.

## Foster Mothers' Partners

No woman spoke of her foster mothering in isolation from her family or life partner. Women's husbands were vitally important both in making the decision to become foster parents and in developing and maintaining kinship relationships. Thomas Simmons, an African American man in his late thirties, spoke about how the initial decision to foster was made primarily by his wife. As he experienced his children and foster children needing him, and recognized in himself needs he had for a close parental relationship, he developed a foster parent identity based, much like his wife's, on his ability to recognize and meet children's needs. He also recognized his importance in children's lives and their importance in his.

My wife had been after me for years to become a foster parent. To tell you the truth, I never even gave it any thought. We always have kids in the house anyway. Since we've been together for about eighteen years, we've always taken more kids with us on vacation with our kids. So eventually it was just a natural step. . . . I really just did it for her, to make her happy. But once I got into it, I thought I knew something too about kids and stuff like that. There's a serious need out there, serious need. When I got into it, I realized I didn't know anything about what was going on out there. It's tough. . . .

I was born and raised in the projects myself. I've seen hard times, you know. I mean I lived in projects in three states, right? . . . But these kids out there, there's a lot of need there, man, you wouldn't believe. The kids out there are getting brutalized each and every day. You know? I was shocked.

[When asked about his role as a foster father, he said,] Basically just to be a father because, well, I grew up without a father myself, you know. My mother was very strong, of course, right, and growing up without a father to me was really no big deal. I mean, I don't really feel like I missed anything in my life, you know. But I'm like, now that I'm older I've met people that grew up without fathers and they're still scarred from it. Emotionally, they're wrecks, you know, just without having a father. These kids we get, I mean, the way they be bonding to me, is like every kid we get the way they bond to me, is like [an] awakening, you know. We used to live in another house right across town, right. I was the only black father living at home on the street. I was the *only* black father on the street that lived at home, that lived as a family. It's like being the male figure of the house, being like an authority, supporting your wife, being there for the kids, helping the kids.

All my life, right, whenever I had a problem, I took care of it myself, right. And sometimes it still like amazed me like how my kids come to me even today with their problems, you know, especially my daughter, right. Even the foster kids, like late at night they come in my room, they knock on my door, and they say, "Dad. I've got to talk to you." Whenever that happens, it kind of like catches me by surprise because all my life I never ever talked to anybody about my problems, you know. I took care of my own problems.

Couples shared a very similar understanding of what fostering meant, why they were doing it, and where children fit into their lives and family. A couple's shared beliefs and actions helped define their familial relationships and situate the couple within a larger social network. It also allowed them to incorporate numerous and often challenging children into their family and to integrate repetitive familial changes into a familial identity. The process of sharing and negotiating a familial and parental identity also allowed couples to maintain their particular sense of family in the face of social relations in which their definitions were challenged.

[I]f you go by the training, right, you would take being a foster parent as a type of business thing, you know. I mean, this training would make you an artificial parent, you know. I personally think that these kids need to be incorporated into your family as a family member. The last training session, I had a serious problem with it, you know. Everybody was just taking things as a business. . . . I mean like for the money, not for the love and affection.

[Was DCF encouraging this attitude?] In fact, almost mandating it, you know. We was told that, to not even touch these kids, and this was like the older ones. Okay, what it is, is abuse allegations, you know. Basically you could sum it up by saying that class was basically about how not to get an allegation. . . . To me, my kids to me are our family. To me, we are a family here, right. We took these kids, we took them on vacation with us. Last year we took them to Jamaica. That cost me over eleven grand. Most of these people that they go on vacation, they find places to drop off the foster kids. I couldn't even comprehend that. To me, these kids are part of my family. They will be for as long as they're here. (Thomas Simmons, an African American man in his late thirties)

Husbands and wives spoke about the importance of supporting each other in the face of invalidation. In this respect, couples created protective boundaries between themselves and those who did not share their views of fostering. These boundaries sustained couples by insulating them from attack and pressure. The ability to share a view of fostering also reduced a couple's sense of dissonance when they felt that others were viewing them in ways that were inconsistent with their own perceptions. Unfortunately, the protective barrier sometimes became a sign of difference between foster and nonfoster families that ultimately isolated foster parents from those who did not foster.

## Foster Children's Biological Mothers

Part of including foster children in one's family necessarily meant incorporating children's biological families. This was perhaps one of the most complex elements of fostering. While the word "kinship" connotes a relationship that is well-defined, to some extent codified, and "family" conjures comforting images of stability and uniformity, the relationships that foster mothers experienced with foster children's biological kin were not any of those things. In most cases they were tremendously difficult, tension-ridden, and prone to failure and then renegotiation. While women were clear that biological mothers were a part of their kin group, *how* they were added or what that meant was always predicated on negotiations with people who were in a very fragile period of their lives.

The ease or difficulty with which women integrated members of a child's biological family was highly contingent on variables such as why the children were removed, the biological mother's ability or desire to have them returned to her, and her feelings about the placement. It was also contingent on foster mothers' ability to see biological mothers as real human beings instead of as objectified and dehumanized "bad mothers" and to resist ideology contained in DCF policies and practices that regarded children as a kind of *private property* and as objects that *belonged to* the family in which they were born. When foster parents were able to establish positive working and kinship relations with biological mothers, it was because DCF was so marginal to their experiences that they were able to successfully ignore these images.

There was another variable that conditioned foster mothers' relationships with biological mothers. When children arrived, most women looked for signs that the previous family or mother valued the child, and when this was the case often (though not always) looked for ways to establish some kind of relationship with the former family. If evidence of the child's inalienable status was lacking, foster mothers tended to be critical of the former family and less likely to form a relationship. This was especially true of children who came from their biological homes. When the biological mother appeared to love the child and regard the child as an inalienable possession, she was regarded with sympathy and her trials with the state and her failure to keep her child were looked at with understanding. This often led to a supportive or amiable relationship between foster mother and biological mother. When evidence of the child's inalienability was lacking, foster mothers appeared not to want a relationship with the biological mother and felt that the child should not be returned to her.

Martha Jones, an older divorced African American woman, who had been fostering for about three years when she was interviewed, lived with her children and grandchildren in a home she owned in a severely depressed urban neighborhood. She worked full-time at the bus station from 1:00 A.M. until 9:00 A.M. and shared parenting responsibilities for foster and grandchildren with her oldest daughter. She began fostering when she found a small boy abandoned at the bus station where she worked. In her view, the foster parent did not exclude or replace a child's biological mother but shared a concurrent relationship to a child with those who could see and meet his needs.

> Every time this department goes in and gets these kids, they take them . . . they don't explain to them. I had one case where the man actually, when they brought the boy here, they were actually yanking on him and trying to get him out of the car. The boy didn't want to get out of the car. They were sitting there yanking on him, yanking on him, yanking on him. And I stood it as long as I could. And I went out and I talked to the kid, for like ten minutes, but eventually I got him out of the car. You know? They were trying to force him, pulling on him. You know? I don't know what they told him, but I explained to him that, "Hey, you know, your mommy is not feeling good. And I'm not your mother, but I will love you and take care of you until your mommy is able to take care of you. You know?" I said, "Come on in the house with me. We'll have a good time." (Clara White, a single African American woman in her late fifties)

Most women spoke about the child's biological family in terms that indicated the child's simultaneous membership in both kin groups and a recognition of the importance of the biological relationship to the child. Tanya Collins, a married African American woman in her late thirties, recognized her foster daughter's need for a mother and a family and responded to the need. She also recognized the child's need for a relationship with her mother:

> My husband is her father—it's not "aunt" and "uncle." It's "mommy" and "daddy." Sometime, you know, like my son [would say], "That's not you mother and father." She would say, "Mommy, aren't you my mother?" You know, I would say, "Yeah, I'm your mother," you know, something like this. 'Cause I feel all children should have somebody that they could call as a parent. So yeah, we are your mother and father. But she knows I'm her aunt and my husband is her uncle, but its still "mommy" and "daddy." . . .
>
> I had her sit down and I had her write her mother a couple of times. She's like, I don't know what to say, you know. Her mother call here every other Sunday or something like that. Her mother also has two other kids now. Sometime, I think it was like hard for her [the child]. 'Cause I sit down and I tell myself, how would I feel at eleven if my mother was in another state—why hasn't she come and got her? You know? Why hasn't she came here to see her? You know? So, I know she has these questions in her mind, and I tell her, "Ask your mother. You ought to know her. You gotta, she's your mother." Things happen in life. I'm pretty sure her mother loves her but she's not here, you know.

In general, foster mothers tended to see their foster children's mothers as neither good nor evil women, but as complex, conflicted human beings. In most cases, children's biological mothers were women with whom foster mothers could empathize. Losing their children did not mean they were less than human or were no longer mothers and should forfeit a relationship with their children. Often foster mothers attempted to form co-parenting relationships with children's biological mothers. When this was possible, foster mothers reported that both women and children seemed to benefit. Other times, women allied themselves with their foster children's biological mother and worked with her for the return of her children. Emma Woodhouse, a married Euro-American woman in her late forties who worked part-time in her husband's construction business, had these comments about the mother of her foster son Larry.

> Drugs and dependency on a man. That's what her problem is. She's very smart. She was in the army. And I think what happened is when her

[own] mother died, the whole family just fell apart. So it's very sad, because you see the potential. . . . I mean here I am sitting with somebody that robbed a store or that drugged [and] I'm thinking how did these women get in this position? Because basically they weren't bad.

Kareena Smith, a divorced Euro-American mother of six in her late sixties who owned and operated a dairy farm with her oldest daughter, spoke of her foster son's mother this way:

He has emotional problems. And it's not his mother's fault. She was an unwed mother, you know, trying to raise four boys on her own. She works nights, and she was exhausted and slept during the day. . . . They [the children] all took care of themselves. And I guess it got real bad 'cause even she was telling me. We get along with her, you know. I understand her situation, I really do. I don't know how I would have done it myself without a husband or a father. You know, you have to have a father, especially when you got boys.

Celestine Gordon, a married Euro-American woman in her late forties living in a rural part of the state, maintained regular contact with her adopted son's mother. Mrs. Gordon had been a licensed foster mother for five years during which time she cared for more than forty-five children. At the time of the interview, she had just returned her fostering license to the state. The open adoption with her youngest and last foster child had just been finalized. She had one biological son in his early twenties. Of her foster/adoptive son, she commented,

He came to us. He was very depressed. He was eleven months old and he was like a little lump when they brought him in. They set him in the middle of our kitchen floor and he was just like this for days. Very despondent. He needed contact, physical contact, desperately. Well, his mom had disassociated herself from him, and she says this herself, even before he was born. So he was very, very unwanted from that point of view. And then . . . his mom just doesn't have it to give anyhow, even at her best there just wouldn't have been enough. . . . She is a nice girl, she just isn't capable of raising five children, and she's only twenty-four and she has got kids all over the place.

Some women within the sample did not have, or did not want, a relationship with their foster children's biological mother. This sentiment was generally conditioned by two things: the biological mother's personality and legal history (often foster mothers feared that a mother's involvement in drugs or crime would endanger her family), and the difficulty foster mothers experienced integrating the biological mother into their lives. An additional factor was how regularly the biological mother visited her children and fulfilled her promises to them. A few women in the sample shared Mrs. Peel's sentiments.

> Well, I had trouble with people visiting my home. We have no visitations at home. You pick up the children and take them to visit the parents, because I can deal with the children, not parents. See, to me, I can't see no reason to let your child go. I don't understand that. Not at all. But the children I can do all I can for. The parents, I don't want them prancing through my home looking healthy and rested, and some of them drunk up, and some of them—I don't want that. So we don't have no visitations in our home. They [the state social workers] come and pick the children up. But most of the time the parents don't show up and the child comes back upset, don't understand. Or when they do visit their parents, they fill their heads with we gonna get you this, we gonna get you that. And if they give them a pencil or a cup it means more than my $5.00 or $6.00 or $25.00 gift. 'Cause they treasure it, and you have to know that and you just brag and be happy about it. You have to not let it hurt you. Just know it. (Norma Peel, a married African American woman in her seventies)

Another factor conditioning foster mothers' relationship to children's biological mothers was the potential need to protect children from their biological parents. This task entailed delicate assessments of children's biological families and forced women to make judgments about a parent's ability to care for her children. At times, this job also divided foster mothers' loyalties between the children they were caring for and the children's parent. This was never easy, since all women seemed respectful of a biological parent's relationship with his/her child (at least initially) and expressed discomfort at having to actively impede or prohibit it. This was also difficult since most foster mothers tried to remain nonjudgmental about a parent's circumstances. While foster mothers tried to maintain a balance between protecting the child and not judging the parent's lifestyle or life decisions, women were clear: their first responsibility was to the child in their care. Regarding her son, the father of Margaret-Mary, Mrs. Michaels, a single African American woman in her early sixties, said,

> My son got into some trouble back, oh, quite a few years ago. They say he abused the stepson. Okay. I didn't know anything about it. You know, if it was true, they kept it from me. And like I told them, I said, "I don't care what"—like I told the judge . . . I said, "If my son come to the door

to see her [Margaret-Mary], if he's been drinking," which I know he don't drink, I said, "but if he's been on drugs or anything and start talking junk, I will call the police on him myself and say, Look you cannot come in the house to see her." And I told the mother the same thing. And I told them this in the court, I say, it's one thing, these kids have to be raised the right way, and whether that they're biological parents or not, they cannot come in the house and take over and cause confusion and stuff with the fighting and the fussing and stuff. I say, they will not come in my house. And I say, I'll let you know that, I said I know the police department number, I will get on the phone and call and have the cops come and arrest them, because I will not tolerate child abuse, I say, I will not tolerate it, and I say, I will take—it's my grandchild, it's his daughter, but he will not come in my house.

Protecting children was also difficult because the stakes were extremely high if a woman made a wrong decision. If she unnecessarily impeded a child's relationship with the biological mother, the foster mother held herself responsible for the termination of a beneficial relationship. Women also felt that obstructing the parent/child relationship was harmful to the child's sense of self. On the one hand, women often said, "That is their *family*," and meant, that is a *part of the child*. On the other hand, supporting the parent/child relationship when the parent was unable to care for a child was a mistake few mothers could live with. Women who experienced this mistake never forgot it and lamented the harm done to children as though they themselves had been the abusers.

It should be noted that DCF made the official decisions about when and how often foster children saw their biological parents. These decisions were often court mandated. When this was the case, the decision about when and how often a visitation would take place was simply communicated to foster parents and they were left to comply. Officially DCF bore the responsibility for determining the quality and conditions of the parent/child relationship. However, there were other circumstances in which contact with the biological parents took place and foster parents assumed significant responsibility. These contacts were often unofficial and hidden from administrative view. For example, many foster mothers negotiated relationships with biological parents with or without social worker knowledge or approval. They also decided whether information about the parent was to be communicated to social workers or withheld from them. For example, if a foster parent felt that a biological parent was trying very hard to get her children out of care, she might withhold information from the social worker that would impede that goal. Finally, another way foster parents exerted influence on the parental relationship was through intentional or unintentional sabotage. This took place most frequently when foster parents felt the child was in physical jeopardy when in the presence of his/her biological family. Sabotage was generally a short-term solution when foster parents were trying to protect children, since social workers, once they became aware of the foster parents' action, took countermeasures.

The next example illustrates the effort required to create a kinship relationship with a child's biological mother. Emma Woodhouse was in her mid-forties. She was born in England and lived with her husband, her mother, and her adopted foster daughter Chalisa. She had two sons, both of whom were grown and living on their own. When asked about her work with children's biological mothers, she first told of her relationship with Chalisa's mother, a young, unmarried woman who was addicted to crack-cocaine. In the hospital, just prior to fleeing from state authorities, Chalisa's mother asked Emma to take and raise Chalisa. Chalisa was African American. The Woodhouses were not. After two years, and numerous battles with DCF social workers, Emma and her husband were finally allowed to adopt Chalisa. Emma maintained contact with the biological mother whenever it was possible and stated that she wanted Chalisa to know her biological mother eventually. Emma also fostered a young boy named Larry. His mother was addicted to drugs and incarcerated on a drug-related offense. Emma participated in a prison program for foster mothers, biological mothers, and their children by taking Larry on a regular basis to visit his mother. A short time after her release from prison, the boy's mother was going to enter a drug rehabilitation facility. She asked Emma if she could come and say good-bye to her son, since she was not going to see him for a substantial period of time. Mrs. Woodhouse said,

> If any mother was going to make it, it was going to be her. And truthfully I felt so too. And the day she took him, I was very naive. I was thinking with my heart instead of my head. Because I'm saying, gee, if I was going into a drug rehab program and wasn't going to see my kid for a month or two, I'd want somebody to let me have a few minutes with him too. So she came to the house and she was talking to Larry and telling him, "Mommy is going to write to you. . . ." I felt kind of bad, you know. And

then she went into the bathroom once with him, and then she came back out . . . and I said, "Well, we have to take Larry to school now." And she goes, "Oh, well, can I go with you?" And I said, "Sure, we'll go in my husband's car."

So my husband was taking the dogs out, they were in the house at the time . . . and the baby was young, she was like an infant. So I was giving her to my mom and I said, "Okay, we'll be back in a little while, we're just going to take Larry to school." And she put Larry's coat on and she was walking down the [entrance] hall. And I said, well, you know, I'll give them a couple of minutes, you know. So I was walking this way and I hear a car start and I know it wasn't my husband's, so I ran to the door and she was taking off. I was like—I was so scared, I—you cannot believe how bad I felt because I only had the child for maybe two months.

And I was like, oh, I started crying and screaming for my husband. My husband comes running up and goes out the front door. He gets in the car and starts chasing her. Now she's going faster, so he backed off. He said, something is wrong here. And he said to himself that he had a gut feeling that something was wrong. But he didn't go on it because he felt sorry because she was the mother. And so I was so upset I got—I was getting sick, and I went into the bathroom and there was coke [cocaine] bottles on the floor, and I said, oh, I was like this [shaking]. I called DCF and the police. . . . They did find her a week later in Florida. And then he [Larry] came back.

Ultimately, the child was returned to his foster mother, and the biological mother went to prison for a year. Again, Mrs. Woodhouse took Larry to visit her and participated in the prison's mother/child programs. Through the intervening months, Larry became a part of the Woodhouse family. Mrs. Woodhouse was told by the state that he was going to be returned to his mother. At the end of a year, his mother was released to a halfway house, and Emma Woodhouse took Larry to spend the weekends with her as mandated by DCF. The mother then secured her own apartment, and Larry was sent to live with her. The rest of her story illustrates the complexity of trying to protect a child, trying to be responsible to a biological mother's claims to her child, and trying to follow the state's plan. Mrs. Woodhouse felt her job was to support reuniting Larry with his mother because the state determined that he should be returned. She did not want to impede what she saw as a rightful relationship. But she was also conflicted about letting him go, frightened that he might not be well cared for, and ultimately held herself responsible for the abuse that befell him.

Shortly after Larry went to live with his mother, she again began using drugs. She lost her apartment, got a boyfriend, and the three of them lived in rented rooms in welfare hotels. Often Larry was not fed and was left for long periods of time alone. He did not attend school. He was once again taken from his mother and returned to Mrs. Woodhouse.

When he had to go [for visits with his mother], you know, like I would keep telling—it's very hard. I cried a lot, because Larry would say he wanted to stay with me forever. And I would say, "Larry, you can't, because you have a mommy and she loves you very much, and you have a family and they want you back, and that's where you belong." And then he would say he hated her, you know, after he was taken and then brought back and he didn't see her for a while. . . . [He would say,] "I hate her, I want her to die." I mean you're talking four years old, four. [He was eventually returned full time to his mother]. . . .

When he left, I felt very bad. Larry wasn't the type of child that showed his feelings, like he didn't cry when he left and I didn't expect it. He did all of his acting out before—doing things to himself, doing things on the bus, that kind of stuff. He acted out—he told me he didn't want to go with his mother, but I had no choice. I said, "Mommy has learned to take care of you, and she's going to do all of the things for you and read to you." Because I read to them. I try to read every night and sing songs and things, just so they know, you know, this is the way it's supposed to be, you're supposed to read books, you're supposed to learn things.

The mother had him for a week and he was already off the wall. She lost her apartment. She was on the move with him. He didn't go to school more than two days for three months. Then they [DCF] called me and asked if I knew where Larry was. And I was kind of like—you know, the last thing I knew he was with his mother and everything was hunky-dory, and I was hoping for the best. And then all of a sudden they called and asked me if I would take him back. And I said, what? And then they proceeded to tell me, you know, she's back on drugs, the whole nine yards.

I didn't talk to him [while he was with his mother] . . . because she never let him call in the three months. When he came back to me, it was very difficult for me. I said I was sorry to him. What are you going to say? . . . Even now . . . I was the one that was telling him mommy is trying to help you. [But he kept saying,] "Mommy is not going to blow-dry my hair like you in the morning. Mommy is not going to feed me like you do."

You know, how do you think I felt when . . . after he comes back from her taking him, and he asks me, "Emma, didn't you hear me calling you?" [she began to cry]. . . . I said, "Oh, Larry, I'm sorry, I didn't hear you. Why did you want me?" "I wanted you to feed me." You know, how do you feel when a kid says, "I want to talk to God because I want to be changed." I said, "What do you mean, Larry, you want to change?" "I want him to change me to Larry Woodhouse." And you have no control over that and you can't say, well, I'm going to make everything better for you because you can't.

# 8

## "They Picked Up the Baby and the Baby Was Gone"

### *Mothering and Loss*

Cindy sits at the kitchen table looking at her hands, the three-year-old boy in her lap alternately resting quietly and then fidgeting with her blouse and hair. He is holding a red plastic suitcase. I ask her how it will be when the two brothers she has raised from infancy leave for their adoptive home. She looks away and begins to cry. She strokes the boy's hair. She takes a long time to answer. "I have gotten very attached," she says slowly. "We have all bonded with each other. They are a part of our family."

Cindy Harris is a thirty-seven-year-old housewife. Her husband is an electrician. They have two teenage daughters. They have fostered Sam and Pete for three years. A year after the boys were placed in foster care, their biological mother's parental rights were terminated. Two years later the state asked Cindy and her husband to adopt the children. Prior to this request the Harrises had little contact with the state. The boys have severe emotional and developmental delays. Cindy's adult siblings, their spouses, and her parents all provide some kind of care and support for the two boys and for the Harrises. Sam and Pete also attend a special school and require a myriad of state-provided home-based services. Once the boys are adopted, unless the parents are able to negotiate a subsidized adoption, they will have to provide many of these services, and the board and care payments will end.

Quietly the youngest boy, Pete, slides off Cindy's lap as though no longer able to endure only half of her attention and opens and closes his toy suitcase with a snap. He looks up at his foster mother and initiates a game I think they must have played before. With a smile he says, "Bye-bye, mommy."

"Where are you going?" she asks.

"I'm going," he laughs and backs away from her waving his suitcase.

She reaches for his stomach and tickles him. "You're not going anywhere, bug," she says.

"Yes, I am. I'm going," he repeats, laughing as though this is further enticement for her to play with him. "Bye-bye, mommy," he taunts.

She reaches for him and takes him into her arms. He buries his face under her neck and smiles. "You're not going anywhere, bug," she says. "You're going to stay with me forever." He smiles and reaches his arms around her neck to hug her and asks for lunch. I realize that in this moment I have become invisible to them. He is delighting in her touch, her hug, her smell, their game. She is engrossed in and with him. She does not seem to be aware of what she has just said to him and the apparent contradiction. But as I continue to watch them I begin to suspect what is confirmed for me later through continued research with dozens of other women. She will keep this child with her forever; this and a thousand other memories will become a permanent part of who she is and how she relates to the world. And thus in the face of a relationship that is physically transient, she will maintain a permanent kinship bond. He is and will remain *her* child.

As I get ready to leave, she walks me to the door. Pete sits in the kitchen pulling a diaper out of his suitcase. Again she begins to cry. "I have been getting the boys ready for their new home for a long time now. But now that the time is here, it is really hard. I'm scared of letting them go. I know them so well. I just wish I could put the whole thing on hold and wait for a while and let them stay with me longer." As she talks, she stares through the kitchen window into the backyard. It is littered with children's toys, tricycles, trucks, dolls, puppets, bats and balls. "The adoptive mother," Cindy says, "doesn't want any of these toys to go with them. She wants to buy all new toys." She is silent for a moment, staring, and then asks, "What will I do with all the toys *now?*"

No woman who fostered a child for a period of months or years was cavalier about the possibility of the child's leaving. While children remained an active part of every woman's family, this did not mitigate the raw feelings of loss, sometimes guilt and inadequacy, when the embodied relationship ended. When women spoke of adding children to their families, they spoke of the inevitability of this pain; knowledge of impermanence was consistently woven into stories of familial attachment and belonging. While some foster mothers hoped that a particular child would remain, and others felt that, when possible, foster children should return to their biological mothers, no woman said that children's leaving, no matter how well prepared they were or how right the decision, was anything other than a painful experience.

> [We had her for seven months.] She was only eighteen months old when we got her, and she was very badly burned. So she took a lot of interaction from our family, you know. And she just quickly became part of our family. And when she left [shook her head and paused] and her mother visited twice a week, so it was not something that we didn't know was going to happen. But I don't think you can prepare yourself or your children for that. (Ellen McKnight, a married Euro-American foster mother in her mid-thirties)

Unlike women who had experienced miscarriage, stillbirth, or perinatal death (Lovell, 1983), foster mothers did not feel that their identity as a "mother" was threatened by the loss of a child. According to their concept of "mother" and "foster mother," the relationship endured the loss of a child. They did not cease to be mothers, even though they were no longer mothers to a particular child in the context of an embodied relationship. That is to say, their concept of "mother" endured this loss. Compounding their grief was the invalidation of their mothering and of the foster-mother/foster-child relationship by agency personnel and practices. Since women's motherhood was not acknowledged, neither was their grief. One mother expressed it this way:

> You have the agency on one hand saying, you've got this child coming to your home and you're supposed to love it for however long you have it in your home. Then all of a sudden, a year later, you've got this agency saying, now you've got to stop loving this child because it has to go someplace else, but we've got this other child and now we want you to love it. How do you just say, OK, this one's gone now, so I don't have to love her anymore. Its like—a part of you just dies. And there were certain kids that left, there were this certain few, that when they left . . . they say that when your heart breaks, there's no such thing, but you actually feel like there's this part of you that is just dying. And you can't explain this kind of thing. I always said that it's worse than losing someone to death. Because when someone dies, they're gone. And you know that it's permanent and that wherever they are they're OK, and you don't have to worry about them anymore. But when you lose a foster child, and they go off, either back to their biological parents, which is sometimes worse, or off

to adoption, you're always wondering—I wonder where they are, I wonder if they're OK, I wonder how they're doing, I wonder if their life is OK, and if the parents—if their marriage lasted. . . . You know what I mean? Constantly. You worry about them. But when somebody dies, you don't worry about them anymore. (Sarah Rill, a married Euro-American woman in her late fifties)

When foster mothers spoke about their grief, they used embodied metaphors to locate the emotional wound and to communicate that something monumental, something life altering had happened to them and their families. Most conceded that it was a wound that never healed.

Giving up babies was the hardest part. Every time a baby left, it left quite a hole in our lives and in our family. . . . It was always like handing over a part of your body, like your arm or your leg. Sometimes I couldn't do it. You would have to go down to the state and hand over the baby. Sometimes my husband had to do it. I don't know how he ever did it. It was like losing a part of you. (Sarah Rill, a married Euro-American woman in her late fifties)

Others were not only keenly aware of their grief but simultaneously aware of the lack of services, support, or recognition from the state.

It messes up your whole life. I mean it's hard. It's hard for you to deal with your own emotions. It's hard for your spouse, it's hard for your family because they've grown attached to each other, especially when you've got adopted children, because it reminds them that they're vulnerable. . . . You end up lashing out at everybody, if you're like me. I'm a very emotional person. Little things get to you because your emotions are just flying all over the place. You know what adolescents are like, emotionally? They have a really hard time keeping the lid on their emotions. Well, every single time a child leaves, that is what you go through. You go through the grieving process. Which is like being an adolescent. You get frustrated, you lash out, you'll be busy washing dishes and you'll just stand there and cry. For no reason. Because . . . that's the grieving process. One of the things the department does not do is to do training on grieving. . . . I took a course [on her own] on grieving and loss, and it gave you an insight to your own feelings and how your emotions deal with situations and how you react to those emotions. . . . Your husband may come through the door and you lash out at him, your kids come home from school and its like, ahhhhh. And that's what you go through every time a child leaves, if you're attached to them. And even if you're not attached to the child and even if it's a situation where you want the child to go home, you still go through a grieving, because you know that when that child walks out that door, you're probably never, ever going to see them again. (Lillian Rosebud, a married Native American woman in her mid-forties)

[These workers] say, oh, it's not bad to let a child go, they'll get over it, they'll adjust. They don't think you feel anything. But I've talked to some of 'em after they've had their own kids and haven't wanted to come back to work after six weeks. They didn't want to put their kid in day care. And they've said to me, "boy, it really is hard. How do you do it?" I think maybe a few more of them should start having children. (Linda Vanderbrink, a married Euro-American woman in her late forties)

Consistently, the foster care system privileged biologically based claims to kinship over claims of kinship premised on a caring relationship. This bias was supported in legal rulings where, as Evelyn Nakano Glenn reminds us, "relationships based on seed are given precedence over relationships established through nurturance and commitment" (1994:12). Consequently, foster mothers were left with their grief, their sense of maternal concern, and a sense of impotence as a child entered a situation they felt potentially dangerous or less than nurturing.

Larry was a very sickly child. He was only about two pounds when he came to me. He was just born. He was so sickly, if Larry died during the night, no one would have been surprised. He was that sickly. I talked to my friends. They said, "Well, we'll do what we always do, give 'em lots of food, and warmth, and lotsa love and watch 'em grow." And he grown. Now he's two, and his grandmother wants him. Now that he's well and strong again, she wants him. But Larry had chicken pops last week, and she didn't want him for the visit because he wouldn't be feeling well and so would be cranky. She don't really want him, she wants the child 'cause he's well and 'cause she thinks she should take him.

But I had him for so long now. And I wondered if I should take him and run. I wondered if I should just take him and go. But then I thought, well . . . (Louise Anderson, a married African American mother in her late fifties)

In response to the specter of loss, many foster mothers spoke of adopting children to maintain the physically present relationship. But as discussed in Chapter 4, whether or not a foster mother could adopt was, for most, an uncertainty. Consequently adoption could not eliminate the possibility of loss. As Racine White, a single African American woman in her late fifties, said,

[When he leaves,] oh, I'm just gonna lay down and die. It's gonna be hard. And I know the day may come—but when I spoke with the lawyer, they said that they'd put him up for adoption if the mother don't gonna put her act together. And I said, "Well, if you put him up for adoption, make sure my name go in the pot." Well, the lawyer had told me that my name would be considered, and she said I had one up on a lot of people that might want him, because my daughter is adopted and I've already been approved for adoption once, and they probably since he's been with me so long, that they probably would give me a shot at it.

[Q.: Did you think about adopting children when you went into foster care?] No, because see, no one tells you about all this before you get into it. You don't know—how attached you get. . . . Because when I had that baby for twenty days, the social worker tried to take the baby from me, take the baby out to the car, and I said, "No I'll take him out to the car." And I think I cried for the next two or three days. He was a lot of work, it was a lot of stress, but you have to be less than human not to get attached to a baby. You really have to be coldhearted not to get attached to a baby.

The insensitivity with which partings were handled consistently added to women's sense of injury. The expectation that women should "detach" when they were told to by DCF social workers or judges violated foster mothers' sense of mothering work. Many relationships ended before foster mothers felt it was time. In these situations, endings breached mothers' understanding of a relationship's sequence and caused a sense of helplessness and emotional violation. Compounding the injury was the damage they saw wreaked on the children they impotently sought to protect. Women also bitterly complained about the lack of information they received from social workers about where children were going and how they were fairing once they got there. As mothers, this was simply information they had to have. Its omission gave rise to worry, anxiety, and helplessness.

You hand the baby over and you don't know what's going to happen to it. You're not allowed to know. I had the baby all of its life [when it went to adoption]. I was the one who knew why it woke up in the middle of the night. I knew what made it cry. I knew what to do for it. . . . Social workers came maybe once or twice and then they picked up the baby and the baby was gone. (Sarah Rill, a married Euro-American woman in her late fifties)

When a foster mother had regular contact with the biological mother or grandparents, she was generally able to retain her claim to kinship through an ongoing relationship with both the parents and the child. Since the state discouraged this contact, or simply made it impossible by telling foster mothers little about where a child came from and even less about where a child was going, it happened less often than mothers would have liked. To many women, the lack of information about the child was a disrespectful sign of their devalued status: neither they nor their relationship with children was considered significant enough to warrant any afterthought.

> [When] this little girl left, I have never heard from her. And I was devastated by that. I thought that, you know, I know that everything was for this little girl's family and getting her through this as best we could. And [the social worker and I] both worked towards that. But she left a household that missed her. And I just thought that it was not very—it wasn't a very nice thing to do. I think that we deserve the consideration of the phone call, not that it's going to change anything, but . . . I would like to be able to follow how this child was doing. I know that there are some things that they can't report to me. But certainly I would feel better just having contact with the worker at that point so she could reassure me that all was going well. (Sarah Perkins, a married Euro-American woman in her late forties)

Endings also occurred, as many women complained, without their input regarding future plans for children. Foster mothers felt that their expertise relative to children and their needs were devalued and denigrated.

> I sit and watch the visits [between natural parents and their children]. You get a sense of who really loves their kids and who doesn't. Workers don't want to hear it. I've got a worker now who . . . [says,] "It's none of your business. It's our decision to make . . . and it's got nothing to do with you." And it does have something to do with us. We're the ones who love these kids and deal with them twenty-four hours a day, and we're the ones who have the instinct to protect them. That worker doesn't care for that kid. It's a job. (Lillian Rosebud, a married Native American woman in her mid-forties)

Not only did agency personnel and policy reflect a view of foster mothers as nonmothers, but friends and acquaintances also treated foster mothers as nonmothers. One woman described the social isolation she experienced resulting from both loss and being out of sync with her friends from a developmental perspective. When asked if there was anyone she felt she could talk to about her pain, she replied:

> No. I don't think any of our friends had any concept of [why we fostered]. Most people don't . . . understand it to begin with. So it's hard to understand your loss. You know? And just having foster children all these years, my husband and I have almost no friends. Years ago we had friends that we were really close to, that we spent time with and went on vacation with, we were with all the time . . . because our kids were all the same age. Well, all of a sudden, their kids grew up, and we were still playing with babies and doing baby stuff. So we couldn't just spur of the moment go places. . . . We didn't have the freedom they had. (Sarah Rill, a married Euro-American woman in her late fifties)

As a result, feelings of loss and bereavement became private sentiments women carried with them but seldom shared. Many did not feel that anyone other than another foster mother would understand that these feelings even existed. Often foster mothers experienced difficulty finding the emotional space they needed to mourn, since for many mourning was premised on social acknowledgment that an important relationship had existed and was lost. Often a time of mourning for foster mothers was obfuscated when social workers requested that mothers receive another child. Such requests also acted to reinforce the construction of foster mothers as emotionally distanced workers. They were not given a time to mourn, because none was thought necessary.

Sarah Rill, a married Euro-American woman in her late fifties, told a story that illustrates the sensitivity with which the death of a biologically related family member, a stillborn infant, was handled by hospital personnel. The act of saying good-bye was ritualized and the mother's and grandmother's feelings of loss legitimized. It is interesting to note that there is a ritual for saying good-bye to a child who is a blood relative but, as this mother observed, no ritual to say good-bye to foster children, even though the sense of loss is in some ways greater.

> Several years ago . . . my first grandchild . . . was stillborn. As much as that hurt, and to this day I still miss this baby, it's still [not the same as losing a foster child]. I got to hold her. She wasn't alive, but I got to hold her and I loved her . . . but it's not the same, because I didn't spend time

with this person, you know? Even though [the children she fostered] are babies, they are little people that you become attached to, and as much as you love a child, even your own if you're pregnant, as much as you say you love it, you have to get to know it before you can love it. . . . There are times when losing some of my foster children was even more difficult than losing my own grandchild through death. Because I never really got to know her as a person.

## Giving while Keeping: Rituals of Remembrance

In the face of imminent loss, women still considered their relationships with children permanent. But how permanence was enacted varied. Some women who were not able to maintain physical contact with children, or who thought it best not to, maintained the memory of the child and of the relationship through pictures or mementos. Others maintained the relationship through letters, notes, or small gifts. Many, especially those who parented older children or adolescents, maintained daily or weekly telephone contact. When talking about children's goings, many women talked with great pride of the things they were able to send with foster children, like bags of clothing and toys, possessions that bore the individual mark of the sending family. To foster mothers these items indicated that this child was a well-cared-for family member and an owner of possessions rather than a possession himself. They were also a sign of transformation, an outward sign that his/her life had improved.

And naturally, he came with nothing and he went back with a great big bag full of clothes and—so he has something when he goes into that other home now. He has something to associate with us . . . you know,

I did get a voucher for, you know, $100 to buy him some clothing. I go up to the Goodwill up here in Monroe. And the lady that runs it used to be a foster mom. She was a foster mom fifteen, twenty years. And she knows I'm a foster mom. So, you know, I get clothes and things practically for nothing. So I didn't even use—I didn't use the $100 voucher I had, because I had gotten him shorts and T-shirts and shirts and long pants and three pairs of shoes. So I just gave the vouchers to the worker who picked him up. And if they want to—you know, I says, "He doesn't have a jacket." So if they want to use the vouchers to get him a jacket or whatever, they can. (Betty Hobbs, a married Euro-American foster mother in her late fifties)

Mothers also talked about the importance of giving foster children something of theirs to take to their next home. In most cases, these were "special" gifts separate from those commodities that signified the child's well-cared-for status. Not only did these items indelibly mark the foster child as part of the foster mother, but they insinuated the presence of the foster mother into the child's next family.

> I always buy them something, something they are going to be able to keep, so they will know that we were there. And it is usually in the form of jewelry most of the time. So something, you know, that they can [keep]. Some of them I buy crosses, necklaces, some I buy a ring for, some I have given my mother's rings to—the one's I am real, real close to. You know, something, you know, it is a part of me, for them. And almost always they want pictures of us, so we have pictures and we just give it to them. (Linda Snell, a married Euro-American woman in her late forties)

Most women told stories of their attempts to stay in touch with foster children in spite of the state and to convey to the next family their kinship claims to the child. Women sent their telephone numbers with children. Most sent pictures of the foster family that included the child, others sent their address with the child. When it was possible to know the address of the next home, and once a relationship had been established, many women sent packages of small gifts to the child or sent gifts at holidays or birthdays as a way of maintaining an active relationship. These gifts were clearly equated with kinship and reproduced, on a smaller scale, foster mothers' obligations to provide for their children. For example, one woman whose foster daughter left after two years to join her grandparents stated, "I just called her. I was at the mall and got her a pair of earrings."

When women were allowed no contact with children after their departure, when they were not able to ascertain children's destination, or when biological or adoptive mothers felt threatened by foster mothers' claims of family membership and refused contact, most foster mothers still included children as active members in the family household but held their ability to act on their claim in abeyance. In these cases, which were perhaps more frequent than those in which they were able to maintain contact, women held the hope that in some way, at some time, children would remember their life in foster care and would find their way back to the family. Since such renewals of contact were enacted at all stages of the life cycle, even after several years of absence, this hope was not unreasonable. As one mother suggested, the idea that children are permanent family members is often a mutual understanding.

> One little girl lived with us for four months the first time and then a year and a half the second time. She was like ten or eleven when she was with us the second time. She's twenty-six now. I heard from her for a while after she left, then I hadn't heard from her for a while. And then this past Christmas, we got a card from her with a picture of her and her two children, and you know . . . its just kind of neat. Here she is an adult and we got a card, saying, "Dear Mom and Dad". . . . You know she still considers us mom and dad. (Sarah Rill, a married Euro-American woman in her late fifties)

When an embodied relationship was not possible, the preservation and curation of commodities associated with individual children, along with shared reminiscing, were one way foster mothers retained children who had been given-away. Rituals of remembrance legitimated foster parents' bereavement and created an enduring place in their family for the given away or loaned member. Through objects associated with particular children, or with children's place in the family, foster parents were able to tangibly mark the child's existence, to affirm the kinship relationship, and to retain their identities as mothers to particular children.

For example, the Samuelses, a Euro-American couple in their middle forties who had adopted four children and had three biological children, maintained the active presence of foster children who were no longer physically present by creating a Christmas tree ornament for each child. The tradition was started when the Samuelses were grieving over the loss of their first foster child, Amy, who lived with them for over three years and then suddenly died. Their pain at this loss was compounded when they were not allowed to attend the funeral for the baby or to purchase a headstone since they were not the child's biological family. Each Christmas tree ornament was fashioned in the likeness of something that reminded the family of that child. Christmas was a time for reminiscing and for sharing with new children the presence of former children. In essence, remembering was a way of educating present members about the extended kin group and sharing the kinship relationship. Through reminiscing, the Samuelses in some respects held their ever-changing family constant. Since the tree was public, this was also a way in which nonfamily members were educated about these kinship relations. As Mrs. Samuels said,

> Our Christmas tree. We have, for every child we had, we have a gold or-
> nament with their name on it. And the year that they were here with us.
> When we're doing the Christmas tree, I'll say, "Oh, remember him?" and
> then we'll tell little stories and remember.
>
> My Christmas tree is a memory tree. You know, there's ornaments on
> the tree that my twenty-one-year-old son made when he was in kinder-
> garten. And each year we bring them out. . . . And we clean them off and
> they'll [the children] say, "Well, tell us about this one," you know. And
> "Why is this one [ornament] a football player?" And we would tell sto-
> ries about how he liked football, or "Why is this one a fire truck?" Or
> you know, "Tell us about the angel, mommy. Tell us again about the
> angel," which is Amy. Amy was our angel and you know [her voice
> trailed off and she paused].
>
> We would sit for days and talk. . . . And people come over and say,
> what a beautiful tree, you know. And we'll say, this is our memory tree.

Many foster mothers also spoke about the importance of photographs. Most photographs depicted typical scenes of family life, and
most featured several members interacting. Portrait-style photos were
consistently displayed next to other photographs of family members.
Through the dialectics of present and absent images, women preserved
children's active presence and membership while also creating a space
for bereavement. As one mother suggested, the hope that the loaned
child will return or that an embodied relationship will continue does
not exclude mourning or the creation of a permanent place in the family for absent children.

> Well, we keep memories of the person that's left by pictures in a photo
> album and by contact. We talk about it. It's not a hidden thing. Elisha is
> six, she's my daughter, and Dawn is thirteen. Elisha was nine weeks old
> when she came here, Dawn was five, and they've seen it, they've seen the
> children come in crying, they've seen children who leave crying, and
> they've made best friends, you know, with a lot of the children that were
> here, especially the ones that were close to their age when they came or
> that were here the longest. And that's what you do, you keep their mem-
> ory there. We always [also] give them our phone number, we always give
> them a notebook with our names and addresses in it. And we always
> keep their photos in our photo album. (Marcia Granholm, a married
> Euro-American foster mother in her forties)

In addition to photographs, foster parents often retained a child's
toy, an outgrown article of clothing such as a favorite dress or baby

shoes, or items the child made, as tangible symbols of a particular child's presence and concomitantly of foster parents' parenthood. These items were often curated in a special place within the home. This accords with Linda Layne's findings about objects preserved after later-term miscarriages:

> Through the use of both physical and evocative homologies bereaved parents use objects to construct the "real babyhood" of their embryos/fetuses/neonates. They use the culturally prescribed, appealing qualities of baby things (smallness, softness, naturalness, sweetness, cuteness, preciousness) to normalize their child. These things assert not only that a baby existed but that this baby (even if born dead and/or malformed) possessed many of the shared qualities of babyhood which are so culturally valued. (2000:339)

### Compounding Bereavement: Problematic Kinship Relations

While the state consistently missed women's kinship claims to foster children and their rights to simultaneously maintain a relationship and to grieve over the given-away child, biological or adoptive mothers did recognize foster mothers' claims and were often threatened by them. Toys, gifts, photographs given to the child within the context of foster family life often became problematic for adoptive (and less often biological) mothers. According to foster mothers, adoptive mothers asked that these items not accompany children and refused to allow children to have those that were sent. When a child went from foster care to adoption or returned to the biological mother, signs that the child was a part of another family or had another mother were problematic since they signified ownership outside of the context of a legal relationship. These "new" parents were anxious to "redeem" children, make them their exclusive property, and erase all signs of contagion from their last family. Items used and favored by children and imbued with the contagion of "real" children in "real" families were rejected because they signified that the child "belonged" to someone else and might not completely belong to them.

As Annette Weiner suggests, "[H]uman beings "live in memory and by memory. . . . The basis of social life [is] 'the effort of our memory to persist . . . to transform itself into our future'" (1992:7). But the process of family making through foster care and the desire of memory to persist are themselves problematic, since culturally children are viewed as the exclusive possessions of their biological or legally related families. Foster mothers recognized multiple kinship categories and communal or shared ownership as a condition of their motherhood. They recognized children's previous "ownership" and incorporated children as inalienable possessions into their family. In so doing, they created kin networks. Adoptive and biological mothers, however, because their rights were defined and conferred by law, did not *have* to see possession as communal and therefore rejected these claims.

When foster parents' attempts to maintain contact with their foster children's families were rebuffed, many felt betrayed and once again demeaned. In spite of these feelings, most carefully curated items associated with a child until the time when they might see their foster child again. But with the curated objects, they were left with an unremitting a sense of loss. As one parent, Betty Hobbs, suggested,

> I don't think we really got into that [telling their child about her leaving]. I mean we didn't say anything about it—well, the lady promised she would keep in touch. So we really didn't say too much about—you know, she says we were such a valuable part of her life that she was going to make sure we kept in touch and all this and that, and she was going to have Christina christened such and such a time and we were invited up for the christening and all this. And then nothing. And then I sent her a package. [The adoptive mother] didn't even let her have a picture, have the package. And I thought, well, maybe—you know, maybe working so much, she probably couldn't get to the post office or whatever. You know? So I re-sent it out. And it was sent back. It says "Not Wanted" or something like that. So I said, "Okay. I guess she doesn't want to [stay in touch]." I've asked [the social worker] how [Christina] is doing. And all I get is, "Yes. Everything is going fine." But I figure, well, we'll probably see her someday, hopefully. . . . So I put the box in the attic. It's got pictures and a pair of her bronzed baby shoes and some real cute little dresses. You know, maybe she will want them for her own child, you know?
>
> [But] we'll never be over it. You know, I mean the lady who took her, if she said, "I don't want you to have anything to do with her. I want her for myself. And, you know, you were just her foster parents and now you're out of the picture," I may not have liked it, but we would have accepted it. But don't give us false hopes that everything will be fine, we could see her in a couple of months or whatever and we're going to come for her christening and to keep in touch. And like I say, even if she sent us a picture once a year—I mean that would be fine. Oh, it would be fine.

We got our first picture of Samantha at Christmastime, and with Phoebe every year for Christmastime we get a picture and all. And I mean it's— you know, your heart just swells. You know that the people who adopted them give a damn about them. It really makes you feel good. . . .

And if she still maintains the smartness that she had, you know, like I say—well, hopefully someday we'll see her. I mean I would like to get someone to tell me how she's really doing. I know she was supposed to be—you know, she's five, just turned five May 7. So she's got to be in kindergarten. How is she doing in school? Is she taking dancing? Is she taking music? What is she doing? Anything? You know? Any kind of anything from her.

# 9

# Portrait of a Foster Mother (2)
## Motherhood, Loss, and Social Action

*Field Notes, September 22, 1996*

I went to Lillith's house for dinner last night. She showed me pictures of her daughter Arielle when I asked if a picture hanging on the refrigerator was her. Lillith went to her bedroom and came back with a large manila envelope of photographs. She laid a black and white portrait of Arielle on the kitchen table. In the picture Arielle sat near a window, staring straight at the camera. Her dark hair was done in braids that curved around her head.

After looking at it with me for a moment, Lillith turned away and began to make dinner for us. As I thought about how she had killed herself, it was hard for me to take my eyes off the picture.

Lillith asks me if I have been upstairs in her house. It is where Arielle lived. I do not want to see it. The sadness that clings to Lillith is visible and I see it as a gray film that coats her and everything she says and does. She does not always talk about Arielle, but even when she does not, Arielle's presence and absence hang on Lillith like a tormented spirit that has not yet ascended. I am afraid of what I will see if we go to Arielle's room. But we go. Together.

Most of the furniture has been cleared out. I am impressed by the emptiness and only vaguely hear Lillith say that Arielle's relatives came and took most of her possessions. Against one wall is a stuffed animal collection. It was Arielle's. Lillith says she really did not know what to do with it. So she just left it. Arielle's sisters came and each took a teddy bear. The rest stand against the wall, their bright colors and goofy expressions no longer impressing anyone with their silliness or their homeliness or their softness.

At the end of the motionless parade of stuffed animals, in a corner under the eaves of the sloping roof, is a wicker laundry basket painted white. There, nestled amid the blankets, is a life-sized infant doll. She looks so much like a sleeping baby that I am startled. She wears a white lace cap, and wisps of brown hair show from underneath it. Her eyes are closed, and her head is turned slightly toward the wall as though she were really asleep. Lillith says Arielle always wanted a doll. A friend of Lillith's made porcelain dolls, and Arielle asked her to make one. Lillith and Arielle's therapist encouraged her to get it. Lillith says, "That comes right out of the inner child movement—but we didn't know that then; Arielle didn't know that. But we encouraged her to get the doll if she wanted it." Lillith says Arielle was looking for something to put the baby in when she found the basket: an apt symbol for foundlings.

I stand next to Lillith as she stares at the doll, and I realize how much of our friendship is based on a mutual understanding of loss and the ability to see in each other the pain we keep hidden. Her arms are folded in front of her, and one hand rests on her mouth. She stands absolutely still. The sleeping baby in her daughter's empty room is a symbol of her pain, and so it remains, undisturbed, often unobserved by others.

How much a metaphor for Arielle's life this sleeping doll is. Arielle purchased the doll in the hopes of symbolically nurturing that part of herself that needed a mother. But it was not enough. Nothing that was tried was enough. And the doll's significance changed from hope to futility. Through death, the doll in her basket became frozen in time, or perhaps moved beyond time. Sunlight enters and leaves the room every day but no longer signifies what has passed and what is to come, since the attic itself has become a realm frozen in liminality.

It occurs to me that it has been a year since Arielle's death. The doll has not been moved. She is exactly as Arielle left her, as though this could preserve the last remnants of care and tenderness Arielle expressed. I wondered if Arielle too is frozen in time in Lillith's life, always twenty-two, always lost in madness, always unreachable and forever asleep, the way my own foster daughter is forever almost eleven.

Lillith shows me an easel she has set up in one corner of the room, facing away from the odd parade of toys. She says she has vainly tried to paint here since Arielle's death, but cannot, and has finally abandoned her efforts. Slowly, she turns her back on the sleeping doll, on the row of stuffed animals, on the half-painted canvas and tubes of dried paint. She looks at her feet, her arms folded firmly in front of her, her eyebrows pointed toward each other in a pained grimace. She does not speak. Nor do I. Instead we walk slowly toward the stairs and do not look back as we leave the attic.[1]

Arielle had a history of psychiatric institutionalization when she came to live with Lillith. She was one of triplets who had overwhelmed her young mother and so had been rejected and ultimately abandoned, although she did not enter foster care until she was sixteen. She was always very shy, sometimes withdrawn. When she was eighteen she suffered a major debilitating depression and psychotic episode. Lillith had her hospitalized and drove the long round trip every day to see her. Lillith kept notes on Arielle's progress. She chased down doctors and therapists to hear about and supervise her treatment. She attended hospital case reviews and team meetings and kept the DCF social worker apprised of her progress. When Arielle's depression did not respond to medication, Lillith advocated for the electroconvulsive therapy that ultimately proved successful—for a while.

Arielle was diagnosed with depression, and Lillith admitted she did not want to see the schizophrenia that was also present. After six months, Arielle was released from the hospital and was able to go back to her job as a kennel nurse in a veterinarian's office, where she was well liked. That six months of caring firmly bonded the two women, and both agreed that it was probably Lillith's involvement that made it possible for Arielle to get out of the institution. Over the next four years, there were other bouts with depression. Each time Arielle became more withdrawn. During these periods, her normally fastidious room turned into a disorganized mess, an external reflection of internal chaos. Toward the end it was hard for her to go to work, hard to do her household chores, hard to carry on a conversation.

Lillith liked living with Arielle, enjoying her company in the good times, trying to be a stable presence during the bad. I heard about these times when Lillith and I went to an Indian restaurant and she said, "Arielle liked their chicken curry; it was the only exotic food she would eat," or when we talked about some aspect of Lillith's life and she mentioned having shared it first with Arielle or told me Arielle's preferences in books and hobbies. These stories contained the routine normalcy of late adolescence. They were temporarily free of the debilitating illness that forced Lillith to stand on the outside looking in, helpless to reach her daughter's pain.

After four years Arielle was hospitalized again for two weeks. They gave her ECT right away. However, the schizophrenia was becoming more evident and she was steadily deteriorating. She could not go out of the house anymore; sometimes she could not even leave her room.

The drugs were not working; shock therapy had worked only for a little while; she was actively psychotic at times. Lillith said it was almost as if her brain were deteriorating and wondered whether the antidepressant/antipsychotic medication she was taking gave her the energy to carry out what she had often spoken to others of doing: committing suicide. Two weeks later, she was dead. It was two weeks after her last hospitalization, four years after Lillith adopted Arielle, six years after they first met and began living with each other.

Lillith began to think about adoption during Arielle's transition from adolescence to adulthood. She wanted a more permanent connection between them, even if Arielle were to move away. *Socially* the connotation of "foster daughter" excluded the enduring relationship women developed with children and instead signified something temporary. Lillith was clear that her relationship with Arielle was a permanent one. One afternoon, Lillith asked Arielle if she wanted to be adopted, and Arielle said yes almost immediately. When Lillith reflected on the adoption, she said, "[I am eternally grateful I adopted her] because it made me realize the depth to which I am capable of giving," and, through giving, the depth to which she was capable of receiving. Lillith experienced not only the intimacy and power that come through caregiving, but renewed meaning and direction in her life.

But enduring relationships through fosterage are almost always constructed in the context of physical impermanence. Not all foster mothers I interviewed had Lillith's experience with death, but the symbolic deaths marked by children's leavings characterized almost every woman's experience with fostering. It was common to hear women talk about losses that had happened not once but repeatedly. Grief, and the personal memorials erected in and through women's lives, were a part of the story, part of what it meant to be a foster mother. Hearing the stories meant paying attention to the pain and bearing witness with the storyteller to the markers of personal loss. Within women's lives, loss ultimately created space for new beginnings, but new beginnings signaled the potential for new loss. While it was the child that was lost and necessarily mourned, it was the value placed on the relationship—on the ability to give something of one's self—that allowed women to love in the face of certain loss, made them continue in the face of failure, and made these acts make sense.

Emily Jean McFadden and Patricia Ryan (1991:209–31) argue that "chronic grief" impels foster mothers to quickly replace children they "lost" with other children. This was not my understanding or experience. On the contrary, continued fostering in the context of certain loss pointed to what these women most keenly valued, i.e., intimacy and the ability emotionally to form close, caregiving relationships. The cycle I observed was not one of unresolved grief, but one of unending commitment to the possibilities found within new relationships and the ability to hold onto those who left through an active memory. New relationships became a part of the rituals of remembrance to commemorate the dead, the lost, and the absent. Thus continuing, remembering, and hoping were synonymous.

For Lillith, as for many women, fostering emerged from the intersection and balance of oppositions like loss and holding on, like life and death. These oppositions could not be resolved through social or emotional mediators, but resolution was beside the point. Each opposition referred to a challenge or task, such as loving, or caring, or healing. Women risked loving children whom they saw as precariously unable to respond emotionally, or unable to remain physically in the relationship. They applied healing knowledge and skills to wounds they had already assessed as potentially irreparable.

What defined fostering was the ability to accept the challenge and to face the task. Participation did not nullify or ameliorate failure, loss, or estrangement. It simply made it bearable. In some respects, the experience typified the Sartrean vision of human nature as Sisyphus-like women attempted to do what they knew they could not do but always hoped they might. And they valued their ability to try. In part, each woman's narrative was a story about her experience of the human condition, about how she gathered hope in the face of enormous and threatening odds against hope, about how and why she loved in the face of certain or potential loss. Like Lillith, women continued to foster, continued to build their memorials, continued to remember.

## The Room to Foster: Social Action and Caregiving Relationships

It is a warm evening in June over a year after I wrote those field notes. I am waiting to interview Lillith "officially"—that is, with a tape recorder and a set of questions. The week before this interview, I was on my way to see her when I wrecked my car. When she found out, she offered to pick me up from the hospital emergency room and take me home. Now she has offered to come to my apartment so we can talk.

We have known each other for several years through our involvement in foster parenting associations. I met her shortly after Arielle committed suicide, shortly after the foster daughter I was adopting left for good in search of her family and an angry DCF social worker forbade our communication. It was through the shared sense and understanding of each other's loss that we became friends. She has always been very active in various foster parent associations, often taking on enormous amounts of work, diligently applying herself to each task. My involvement in these organizations has always reflected ambivalence about the appropriateness of my participation. I am a former foster mother, a former social worker, and currently a researcher taking notes on all I observe and hear.

She does not question the legitimacy of my presence, nor does she feel it intrusive. More than once she has said simply, "We could use your help." She has never gotten angry or frustrated at the ebb and flow of my participation, at the ambivalence that undercuts my ability to be consistent and responsible. On the contrary, she has shown both patience and friendship, inviting me out to dinner, calling me when there is a movie we might both want to see, reminding me when there is a foster parent meeting I might want to attend. At other times, she has listened to and commented on my research findings, made suggestions, read drafts, arranged for me to talk to other foster mothers. All of this she does with enthusiasm and what seems like boundless energy. There is no idea I have ever shared with her that she has not quickly responded to and thought how it could, and should, be implemented. She is forceful in her words and actions; she is always thinking. We have agreed in the past that tact wastes time in a relationship. She has said that she appreciates a relationship where she can be frank and open without worrying about being too direct or offensive.

We have dinner before our "interview" and talk about her current foster daughter, Theresa, and a new foster daughter, Marybeth. Marybeth has recently come to live with Lillith, and, unlike Theresa, she will probably leave at the end of the summer and enter an independent living program while she finishes high school. Marybeth entered foster care as a young child after being physically abused by her mother and stepfather. She lived for eleven years with an older Portuguese woman named Mrs.

DaSilva, a widow who was raising her granddaughter, a girl slightly older than Marybeth. After living with Mrs. DaSilva for two years, Marybeth was sent by DCF, against her will, back to live with her mother. Recently she told Lillith about large burn scars on her stomach incurred during her few months' stay at home. She was returned to Mrs. DaSilva. When her foster mother was hospitalized because of abdominal pains, Marybeth was placed with Lillith. She did not know that Mrs. DaSilva had been diagnosed with pancreatic cancer and was dying. On the day Marybeth arrived, the social worker asked to see Lillith privately. She handed Lillith $175 and told her that Mrs. DaSilva had asked that the new foster mother be given the money so she could buy something nice for Marybeth. Mrs. DaSilva wanted the gift to come from the new foster mother, so Marybeth would feel at home and wanted. Within a month Mrs. DaSilva was dead. Marybeth and Lillith and Mrs. DaSilva's granddaughter went to the funeral together.

Theresa has lived with Lillith for over a year. She is the first child Lillith has fostered after Arielle's death. Theresa is a seventeen-year-old Hispanic girl with long black hair, stunning good looks, and a raspy voice. She has been in foster care since she was ten years old. During most of Theresa's childhood, her mother was addicted to drugs and often abandoned Theresa and her baby brother for long periods of time without food. Theresa and her brother were placed in foster care when their mother was arrested and sent to prison. Theresa has been in at least twelve or thirteen foster homes and youth shelters. Most of her homes were overcrowded with numerous foster children; in one she was sexually molested by the foster father. She ran away from several of her homes, once going to New York City at the age of twelve to find her father; other times she simply lived on the street. She was on "runaway status" when Lillith read a story about Theresa in the newspaper and said to herself, "That girl needs me."

[L]ast October . . . I read a series of articles in the *Hartford Courant* about a girl whose mother was HIV positive, whose younger sister had died of AIDS, who had gone alone through an operation for scoliosis, who had been in several different foster homes. I later found out she was sexually assaulted in one of those homes. She was on runaway status, and I said, that girl needs to be in my upper room with her privacy and her own bathroom and with me as her foster parent. So I actually aggressively went about finding her. I called up people in the DCF office, and then a couple of months later I did get a call back, telling me she was on runaway status, but her mother convinced her to get back to foster care. So her mother and Theresa and her social worker all came to my house for dinner. The social worker said, "My God, I've never been to dinner at a foster parent's home." And we all agreed that Theresa would come and live with me, and she is living with me.

[Privacy] was no small part of what I had to give her. Let's not forget that there are virtually no homes for teenagers. The few there are, if they can pack them in they can have five other girls. I can also give her—I wasn't frightened of the fact that her mother had AIDS, because one of my oldest friends, who did the gay rights lobby with me back in the seventies, was one of the very early deaths from AIDS. And I'm just not afraid of it. That's what I could give her. I could give her an adult who knows and likes teenagers. My very conscious thought is, I'm willing to give you a safe place to live where you can learn to be an adult and from which you can fly. I want you to become independent. I hope we will have a relationship after that.

Tonight, as she talks about Theresa, Lillith's face is tense. Theresa has been acting out at home, talking back, shouting, refusing to do her household chores, breaking curfews, challenging Lillith's few house rules. She is rude and sullen. Lillith is emotionally exhausted and confused, but feels most of Theresa's behavior has been instigated by Marybeth's presence and Theresa's fears that she may have to share Lillith. She says she does not always know what to do or how to interpret Theresa's behavior. I know she hopes their relationship will continue. This evening, it is clear that she fears this may be in jeopardy. She says, "When Theresa does this acting out, people like you and her therapist say, that probably comes about because of her fear about getting attached to me. . . ." I tell Lillith this because I have spoken with Theresa and know how frightened she is about a relationship where she might again be abandoned or disappointed. Theresa says she does not know why she is so mean to Lillith, or why she can not just tell Lillith how she feels. Lillith says much the same thing. "[Y]ou see, I myself was raised in a family where we didn't talk about emotion. . . . I never learned to articulate love." Both struggle through their own needs to maintain the commitment, and affection, that gird their relationship; both struggle to build a kinship relationship where none previously existed.

After dinner, Lillith says, "Come on. Let's sit down and talk," and heads into my living room. She sits back on the couch, makes herself comfortable, and, before I can ask her any questions, says, "Where do I begin? Shall I identify myself for the tape? My name is Lillith K. Anderson." When I look alarmed and tell her that the transcriptionist has been instructed to take all identifying names out of the tape and that I change all names when I write, she smiles boldly and slaps her hands on her knees. There is nothing she could say tonight that she has not already said publicly. She has no problem with my using her real name. I ask her to back up and tell me how it was that she began to foster.

I never wanted to be a mother and I never wanted to marry either. I mean, I've known my sexual orientation for a long time, although I did not come out sexually until I was twenty-nine. . . . Because before that I never knew another lesbian. There wasn't an option for me. And I was in misery and agony, and I think a lot of us who spent miserable, painful adolescences are the people who then want to work with adolescents.

I got into foster parenting about nine years ago. It was in the spring of '87, which I remember quite vividly, because I got a call from a woman who was part of a lesbian couple, a white woman, who was calling everybody they knew. They had a foster daughter, a black girl whom they had gotten two years before when an announcement had been made at a gay rights celebration [that] there was a black girl who was kicked out of her black foster home for being gay, is anyone interested and willing to be a foster parent? And these two women had taken her. The girl is now eighteen or so, and she, the girl, whose name was Louise, had met Susie, who is a white girl . . . who was living in the YMCA shelter, who was a self-identified sixteen-year-old lesbian. And the couple, CeeCee and Anna, just called everybody they knew who had room and who might be a potential foster parent for this girl. And when they called me, I remember saying, "Well, my mother died six months ago, I'm over the initial shock. I'm interested, let me know more." So they had dinner with her, and she came across as very intelligent, and she was saying she had been kicked out of her house for being gay.

I followed through and decided I wanted to meet her. She claimed to have been raped by her father, so, of course, feminist that I am, I believed her, and believed her for a long time. I will tell you, it turned out to be that very unusual case of a girl who lied, and the DCF people right off the bat suspected it. I mean, they deal with sexually abused kids all the time, and she didn't ring true. . . . It turned out she was an extremely bright girl who they now call attachment disordered. . . . So she . . . had called around and found out that when you're under sixteen, DCF can make you go back home or wherever they think you should be, but over sixteen they can't. So a month after her sixteenth birthday, she concocted this story.

I had bought a house about six years before, and it had a totally un-finished attic [and a full basement]. Now I'm a person who likes fixing [things] up, so I put my workshop in the basement, and I finished off the attic. I did all the Sheetrocking, all the framing. I didn't do the plumbing and the electrical and the tiling, but everything else I did, and I put in bookshelves for my fabulous lesbian collection, and I kind of said I don't know what I'm going to do with it, I'll make it my spare bedroom. So I was almost finished with it when I got this phone call. And it was a huge room, it's the whole upstairs of the house with its own bathroom. Well, perfect for a teenager. She has her privacy, I have my privacy. . . . I've al-ways liked teenagers. So what I said was, this feels like it could be right.

For Lillith, the initial decision to foster emerged from an intersection of circumstance and ideology. As she talks about fostering, she talks about a long personal history of commitment to social causes. The de-cision to foster fit within that context. As Lillith hastens to point out, while she became involved in fostering through a lesbian community, all of her subsequent placements have been "straight." Social justice and social action are not limited by sexual criteria.

I have always liked adolescents. I was a biology teacher for five years. I was an early burnout. I learned afterward that people who burn out are the people who cared the most passionately. [T]hat was me. . . . [S]o I went to graduate school and got my masters degree and then a doctorate in public health, and worked for the state, which gave me a nine-to-five job, a good paycheck, and allowed me to do my causes. I mean, I've been active in women's liberation and the tail end of the civil rights move-ment—mostly women's liberation, and then I was very active in gay lib-eration. . . . I have never experienced a problem being gay . . . because my life is really kind of dull and boring and settled in middle-class suburbia. I don't make anybody nervous. As a feminist, yes, I make people nervous. As a lesbian, no. I'm a nice lesbian—a pushy feminist.

The reward for commitment and involvement is knowing that she has irrevocably changed someone's life and through that process has al-lowed herself to be changed. Through participation in social justice movements, she has found an outlet for passions and caring that she had previously experienced as painful and depleting. Lillith also locates herself in relation to other women in terms of ideologies and lifestyles (feminism and lesbianism) and glibly speaks of the relationship be-tween her work and her beliefs. Much like the adolescents she cares for, she locates herself as something of a rebel, a fighter, and an outsider. In that respect there is also a match.

When people express admiration at how much Lillith seems to be giving, she responds, with great feeling, that she gets back far more that she gives. Participation in social causes meets her needs to be needed, to think, to be creative, to solve problems, to effect change. Unlike many foster parents, she immediately involved herself with the organization and planning of a nascent foster parent association. This is consistent with how she sees herself and her skills. She is both a caregiver and an organizer. She flourishes when there are no limits to her participation. A growing foster parent association, like teenagers, needs all that she can give.

> I'm a person who's been a cause person all my life. And as I said, women's movement, gay rights, then . . . just about the time that I . . . started foster care, I got into Habitat for Humanity and got deep into it. When I do things, I do not do them halfway. So I am a person of causes.
>
> I got really involved in the foster parent organization . . . they really needed my skills. I started to draft the bylaws, and then I was the person who found the lawyer who wrote the final bylaws. I also prepared an initial budget for them, the initial grant proposals. I was very involved in that. There's [also] the thrill of involvement with the kids, the feeling that this is a cause where I can make a difference.

## Thinking through Mothering

Like many women, Lillith linked her emotional readiness to begin a relationship with the physical space to accommodate a child. Her home, with boundaries and rules learned from her own mother, was an important feature of fostering relationships, since it was the stage upon which negotiated mother-child intimacy was to be enacted. Without thinking about fostering, Lillith made an extra room in her house. The completion of the room allowed her to make a home in which, like her mother, she could become an emotional nucleus for a child and unite caregiving work and social change. Foster mothering as a "cause" made sense because it was the nexus of valued work and longed-for closeness. She was well aware of how these relationships had given her life direction and meaning.

I have been saying for years it [foster parenting] is my primary emotional relationship. I do not have an adult partner and I don't do one-night stands either. Now thank God I have a rich friendship network, but it's real clear to me that my emotional relationship is with the kid in my house, whenever I take them, one or max two at a time. I have a very real relationship with them. I can't envision what my life would be like without that. I'd be a miserable, lonely person. Having foster kids gives my life meaning. I'm fifty-four years old and I have always had meaning in my life. I couldn't live any other way.

The other event that precipitated Lillith's participation in fostering was the death of her mother, with whom she had been very close. After the initial shock of loss, fostering made sense. Fostering was a cause that connected her at once with the future in terms of hoped-for social changes and with the past through a legacy of caregiving work found in her relationship with her own mother. Fostering mitigated the emotional void left by her mother's death by providing companionship and a chance for Lillith to move from being a daughter and care receiver to being a mother and caregiver. It was a move that began when her mother was still alive and continued after her death.

When my mother was dying of cancer of the pancreas . . . [she] spent three months in a hospice unit, and my sister would come and then she'd go back to [Canada]. And she said to me once, "Gee, Lillith, I really feel sorry that I'm not here more for you." I said, "Margaret, to tell you the honest truth, I would be totally happy if you and Mary and Nicholas never showed up, and I had mom all to myself." That was the honest truth. I mean, I was leaving work Thursday night, driving to New York, spending a long weekend with my mother, coming back Tuesday morning. I mean, it was an incredibly powerful watershed event in my life, my mother's death. And it was after that, I told you, six months after that, this feels right. And I think I didn't consciously articulate it at the time, but what I have realized since is, I really was brought up in a very loving household. No strong emotions were expressed, neither anger nor love. [But] it was there.

As she reflected back on her childhood, she saw that mothering is necessarily hard work that requires strength, consistency, and vigilance from women. Her family showed their love through their actions rather than through words that came hard, if they came at all.

My father had two severe breakdowns and [was treated for] depression. . . . [M]y father was chronically depressed with a biochemical [imbalance].

. . . So, he wasn't loving. My mother . . . came from Germany and worked as a maid for ten years, and then she married my father and didn't have to work outside the home. We never had a lot of money, but we had enough. . . . [My mother] loved kids. She loved us, she loved her grandchildren. She was very much a nucleus and center for her family.

I was raised in a family where we didn't talk about emotion. There were, nobody got angry and yelled and screamed, nobody said, "I love you," and you were surrounded by this cocoon of my mother's love. My father was never abusive, but he was depressive, so he was pretty distant. On the other hand, here is this depressive man, he'd never threaten us. As I look back on it, know from other experience, we were incredibly lucky. He put one foot in front of another, he brought home a paycheck, he took care of the family in the way that men are supposed to do, and never frightened us with threats or attempted suicides. So in that respect we were fortunate. But my mother was the loving one. But it was there; we took it for granted.

For Lillith, the ability to mother stemmed from the mothering one received. She applied this perspective to herself and her foster daughters. Lillith's mother, by single-handedly holding her family together, taught her daughter that women through their relationships to each other gain power and agency (Bassin, 1994:163–64). In this respect, mothering is a part of the "vocabulary of gender" (Stack and Burton, 1994:33–44) passed from mother to daughter through a relationship premised on the ability to recognize and sympathize with the needs of another while simultaneously longing for, and thus working toward, closeness (Bubeck, 1995:87). Lillith thought of herself in relation to her mother, and tried to think of her foster daughters in relation to their mothers. This perspective makes mothers fellow travelers and allows foster children's mothers to be seen as human beings imbued with complexity and contradiction, failure and success.

Thinking through mothering meant that understanding Theresa included a view of Theresa's mother and the mothering Theresa received as a child. While Theresa's mother and Lillith had very different child-rearing styles and sometimes argued with each other, the fact that they were in regular communication signaled the extent to which they co-mothered Theresa and were co-trustees of Theresa's past and future. In this way, even disagreements between the women affirmed the importance of the mother(s)-child relationship.

What I have come to see is, Theresa was her mother's only child for about the first ten years of her life, and she was the apple of her mother's eye. Now the mother wasn't always on drugs, so that Theresa was raised well. Theresa for instance was honest . . . and when she doesn't do her chores, it's a blasting-out kind of thing, and when she does them, she cleans better than I do. She cooks for herself. So you can see the effect of that positive upbringing as a small child. The damage that starts very early you can't overcome, but Theresa, if she can get a handle on her own behavior, which is difficult for her, [can make it]. She never had limits or boundaries put on her, and when I said this to her mother in our last explosive conversation, I said "Well, Theresa didn't have any limits while you were in prison," and the mother said, "Yeah, and she didn't have any before that, either," saying it like this was good. Wrong! I mean, see, the mother is so guilty now that she'd let Theresa have anything, and she yells at me the least minor . . . attempt I make to discipline Theresa. The mother goes around the bend. So why wouldn't Theresa? I mean . . . children need limits.

Through a mother-daughter relationship, Theresa became family to Lillith. Through a relationship in which both Lillith and Theresa's mother cared for Theresa, they all became family to one another. Lillith and Theresa's mother developed a tenuous but sympathetic view of each other and a respect and appreciation for each other's mothering. This was possible because recognition of each other was not dependent on blame as an explanation for current or past events. Instead, Lillith saw Theresa's mother with a degree of sympathy—sometimes empathy—and placed her experiences on a continuum of mothering experiences, like Lillith's own, that included loss, suffering, and failure. In this example, foster mother and mother became uneasy partners as each woman appreciated who the other was and what the other had been through. Each appreciated what the other could offer Theresa and what the other meant to Theresa.

So Theresa is like family to me. But on the other hand, her mother is very much in the picture. Her mother lives at St. Bartholomew [and] talks to Theresa every day, [so] is to an extent part of my household except when she explodes and herself busts up the relationship. . . .

[I]t's important that you do have some relationship with the parent, because the parent is important to the kid, particularly in the case of Theresa. Theresa and her mom are like bonded, and joined at the hip.

[B]ut the mother has said, quite frankly she has to concentrate on herself
. . . let's not forget this mother is a drug addict. She's I believe off it now.
She's in this halfway house. She goes to meetings all the time. But I read
in the newspaper article she was in prison for three years after her fourth
conviction for drugs. So this is a woman who'd been . . . a long-standing
drug user. So the mother's very glad that Theresa's with me.

## Success and Failure

Women often spoke metaphorically and literally of "seeing" their foster children. This refers to women's ability to recognize children's needs
as separate and distinct from, yet intimately connected to, their own.
As Sarah Ruddick echoes, "To be a 'mother' means to 'see' children as
demanding protection, nurturance, and training and then to commit
oneself to the work of trying to meet those demands" (1994:33). But
with adolescents, this giving is not one way from an omnipotent
provider to a needy child, but proceeds in two directions, both participants struggling against their needs and vulnerabilities to sustain an
ongoing dialogue of care and commitment. It is ultimately a process
whereby both individuals "see" each other. Lillith shared with Theresa
insights gained from her own experiences and through the sharing of
both strengths and weaknesses searched for a point at which they could
both connect.

> Much of my years in therapy has been spent getting in contact with my
> feelings, literally. I mean, I would spend time with my therapist [and] I'd
> get a funny body sensation and we would work through what came into
> my mind, what was that connected with. Because being such a head-ori-
> ented person, I often don't know what I am feeling. And I was describing
> this to Theresa. . . . I described how I could understand how she would
> sometimes [be explosive] and not be conscious of where it was coming
> from, but all of a sudden find herself cursing at somebody, and how she
> might not want to do that on a job. And I described how that happened
> to me. For a long time I thought I was doomed to spend the rest of my
> life putting my foot in my mouth, making tactless, hurtful remarks with
> the person I most wanted to communicate with. Until we finally figured
> out it was [an] awkward thing when I was with the person I wanted to
> communicate with and couldn't. So I would say something that was the
> truth [but] that would alienate the person and drive them away. So that
> was, and I was describing that, saying, "Theresa, I think that might be

similar to what happens with you." She's listening, and she's drinking it all in. It clicked or something.

For Lillith, mothering was a dance of independence, dependence, and interdependence that connected her life to those she cared about while preserving her separateness. She studied her foster daughters to know their needs and to know how best to meet those needs. But she carefully balanced her ability to mother against what she needed in order to maintain the relationship.

> [With teenagers] I can be out for a night or two. But when I know something is happening [with one of the kids], I know to be around. . . . I just make sure to connect with them. I mean, they're not like little kids that need your attention right then at that minute when they need it. To a certain extent that happens, but one of the things is as you grow up, you do need to learn to delay a certain amount, so if I'm not going to be there, I say I'm not going to be there tonight, we'll talk tomorrow. But I make sure that I do connect. And I'm pretty good. I get a lot of enjoyment out of figuring the kids out. Like figuring out with Theresa, what's going on with Theresa's disruptions. What's going on with Marybeth when she was as different from Theresa as you can imagine. . . .
>
> It's hard work. You have to have a life of your own, particularly with teenagers. [F]oster parents for teenagers have to have their own lives for their own sanity and for the kids' sanity too. You can't be wound up with their life. You have to be involved and supportive but have your own distance. That's critical.

"Mothering . . . like any kind of caring labor is relational work in which others' responses serve as an intrinsic and primary measure of achievement" (Ruddick, 1994:34). Success, reward, and achievement, very important attainments for Lillith, were measured by the formation of intimate relationships with her foster children that could be sustained through time. Since most of Lillith's foster children had had a tremendously difficult time trusting adults or caring, a relationship was an indicator that the adolescent in her care had grown, and that her mothering had been effective and ultimately healing. It was also an indicator that Lillith had been seen and that the parent-child interaction was a reciprocal relationship.

> [I]f it turns out fine you will know it because they will likely want to get in contact with you. [T]hat was always my goal and still is my goal. I want to have a relationship with the kid afterwards. I've said that from

day one when I first get the kids, that they would stay with me until they
*(a)* get out of the system or leave the system, *(b)* graduate from school or
college or whenever, but then I would want to have a relationship with
her, even when they are no longer my foster daughters. That's what I
would consider a success.

It was this definition that marked the pain Lillith felt in her relationships with foster children. It is also this definition that makes mothering work within the context of fostering so tremendously difficult.

> I don't have relationships with any of my other foster children. I've had
> nine in approximately nine years. A couple, they have called me. They
> don't forget me, but except, well, Arielle died, but until she died, she was
> very much with me. The others, there's always been disruptions where
> they've left, and they haven't worked out. One where there was a disrup-
> tion, she went to live with her boyfriend. She had dropped out of school
> in tenth grade, was bright, wouldn't go back to school, and can't seem to
> get and hold a job. I mean, she's a kid who's been in foster care most of
> her life and is very damaged. I came to the conclusion, and it's not stop-
> ping me from taking kids, teenagers, is that these girls aren't going to
> make it on their own. [Most] find a man to support them, because they
> can't hold a job. They are not competent to handle living an adult life.

While she was committed to a close relationship with each foster
daughter and hoped each relationship would endure time and distance
as adolescents moved to establish their own lives, Lillith also approached each relationship with a logic drawn from experience. One
must be prepared for "failures," that is, relationships that never form,
those that are neither enduring nor based on affection, or those that are
disrupted and end in estrangement. From this perspective, the task of a
foster mother is to be very clear about what she can offer, what can be
received, and what can change. If the relationship is detrimental to either party, then it must be ended. Her matter-of-fact approach did not
mitigate the pain of an ending or a sense of failure but indicated that
the nature of fostering relationships is that they must be good for all
participants.

In part, this perspective was possible because her participation in the
relationship was limited historically. She knew her foster daughters
only as young adults. She accepted them, knowing that each carried
with her psychological and emotional scars that would make forming a
relationship precarious work. Her response was to create a boundary

around their past and offer a relationship that could be a turning point. Her role was to be available and to offer the support, guidance, and skilled caring she knew how to give. If they were able, their task was to enter the relationship and work with her.

> You have to be realistic about the potential. You also have to be prepared [for problems in kids that are beyond your help]. . . . You can set boundaries. You don't have to take just any kind of a kid. If the kid turns out to be significantly a problem, you can get rid of the kid. That may not be the best thing for the kid, but you do have to think of yourself and your [other] children first—and yourself as a resource for future kids. . . . I never stop hoping that I'll get Anne of Green Gables. In fact I go into it assuming that I can. Any increment, at least due to me [is success].
>
> The other thing is, you see, being a foster parent, I don't carry a speck of guilt about the baggage that these kids bring with them because I'm not their family. I didn't cause it. . . . I come to them with a clean slate. I come to them only with something to give. If they are able to use that, partly it's me. But if they can't, frankly, mostly it's them, because of the damage that they've suffered. I mean, I do everything I can. I get all the supports and training that I can get. If they are going to make a success, assuming that there's a certain amount of temperamental match, they are going to make it with me. If they can't make it with me, they probably can't be in a foster family.

## Money and Work

Because women thought about mothering as work and thought of themselves as women who worked at caregiving, the idea that they should be compensated financially was something many thought about. Not all women were comfortable with the idea of "professionalizing" foster motherhood, because their idea of mothering and work did not fit comfortably within a paradigm of professional/nonprofessional or mother/wage laborer commonly articulated to them by social workers. At the same time, women thought about their time, labor, expertise, and expenses as something that should be recognized, valued, appreciated, and financially compensated. Women often looked at the board and care "reimbursements" as a way the state "paid" them and felt justified in using this money for household expenses. Women felt they were entitled to reimbursements because mothering work involved giving something, expending something—themselves and their talents—and what they gave should in some way be paid back. Reimbursement differed from payment, which meant receiving money for a service. Reimbursement meant getting something back for what you had given. This conceptualization of money, work, mothering, and kinship often contradicted DCF policies and practices.

When Arielle was hospitalized, DCF told Lillith that since Arielle was not living in her home, she was not entitled to board and care reimbursements. This was ostensibly because Arielle was not using the material resources Lillith would provide a foster child, such as electricity and groceries. It was also assumed that fostering was a board-and-care arrangement rather than a caring relationship, and if Arielle was not actually living with Lillith, then Lillith's participation in the fostering relationship was optional. Lillith challenged this pronouncement and the logic upon which it was based. In her interpretation, the "work" she did ensuring Arielle's health and recovery was critical to her foster daughter's survival. It was not optional. Nor was their relationship premised solely on Arielle's physical presence in her home. In other words, the decision to foster Arielle created a caregiving relationship with the same responsibilities, duties, and commitments one has toward kin.

According to Lillith, her ongoing participation in the relationship entitled her to the board-and-care reimbursements. She pointed out to DCF that she had expenses—transportation, telephone bills, and incidentals for Arielle's comfort. She also insisted that as a familial relationship, their affiliation with each other was not confined to the physical boundaries of Lillith's home.

> Now Arielle was, she was with me for six years, and I adopted her. You've heard me talk about her before, but I'll quickly summarize for the occasion. She was with me for six years, she was seriously mentally ill. After about three years with me, she had a breakdown and was six months in a mental hospital, and I had a ripping argument with DCF, which I won. They said she's not living with you, we're not going to pay you board and care. And I said I've been visiting that girl every day. I am coordinating her medical care, and you are going to pay my board and care, and they said, well, okay, we'll pay you, but we're going to go to a hearing, and if you end up losing, you'll have to pay us back. I said, I'm not going to lose.

So I went to the hearing, I gave them reams of material, all the letters I had written [to the hospital], and they said well, we'll pay you your transportation back and forth [from the hospital], and I said no. I said if you want to pay me caseworker rates for all the hours I'm spending, that would be okay. And the hearing officer ruled in my favor. And at the time of the hearing, Arielle was out of the hospital, and she was at the hearing. So, also at the hearing was a newspaper reporter, but there was nothing to report because they ruled in my favor.

It would be hard to say that it was need [that prompted my action with DCF]. I had a good job, but I wanted it [the money]. Shoot. I mean, at this point I get about roughly $600, a little more now, it was a little less when I started. I mean, do I spend every penny on the kid? No. But on the other hand, I could rent out that attic room with its own bathroom for as much or almost as much as I get for the kids and a lot less hassle, but I don't want to do that.

By insisting on a public hearing to which she invited a newspaper reporter, Lillith challenged gender and family relations ideologies in which women's domestic work is largely invisible and devalued in relation to "professional" wage labor outside the home (Moore, 1988; Katz Rothman, 1994). Additionally, she asserted that kinship based on blood or legal relations is not the only recognized form of kinship. Her relationship to Arielle was neither "optional" nor dispensable. She demanded that her work be valued and recognized. When her work as a caregiving mother was minimized and she risked losing her payments, she suggested that she be paid caseworker rates, since the duties and tasks performed on Arielle's behalf were arguably the same. The argument over money became a medium for recognition.

Unlike many foster mothers in this study, Lillith challenged DCF and their authority over her with unyielding tenacity. She insisted on legitimation and recognition, and if they were not given, she would extract them. She would not be subservient, as evidenced by her unwillingness to defer to their authority or accept their constructions of foster mothering when they conflicted with her own. Some parents, like Lillith, confronted DCF. But most did not. Many parents also felt that discussing money, their need for money, or their ability to run their households because of the money received for fostering cast them in people's eyes as money-grabbing mercenaries. Paradoxically, through their threat to withdraw board and care payments during Arielle's physical absence from the home, it was DCF that equated fostering with a commercial relationship rather than a familial one.

The debate over money points to an emotional need as significant as the financial need to which Lillith also referred. After fostering Arielle, her financial situation changed. She lost her job and took work that was only part-time. Aware of accusations leveled against foster mothers who foster because of financial need, and thus debase mothering, she referred somewhat defensively to her current economic situation and the board and care payments she received for her foster daughters.

> So, yes. The payments have been important to me as cash, and I'll admit, like with this business of Marybeth staying an extra month. I will admit in all honesty, I mean, I was on a layoff, I had a part-time job, I truly think it is the best thing for Marybeth to stay another month with me [but it helped me too]. . . . I'm putting out money, and I mean, I bought Marybeth not only the cookbook, but I bought her shoes which weren't covered by her clothing voucher, and I don't spend as much on Marybeth as I do on Theresa. I spend a lot on Theresa. So some of the money obviously, when you think it goes to pay the rent, it goes to pay utilities . . . .

## Conclusion

As we end our interview we finish up by talking once more about her foster children. When asked about her ability to relate to teenagers, Lillith says it is her skill with empathy and her ability to talk with foster children that have been her greatest gifts—those that she has been given and those that she gives.

> Marybeth says all the time that she can talk to me. The contrast is probably greatest between me and Mrs. DaSilva. Mrs. DaSilva just used to do, she would tell Marybeth essentially my way or the highway. Marybeth would say I never got to talk to her. Mrs. DaSilva would just say this is the way it is. If you don't like it too bad. Whereas, I'll talk about things. Sometimes I'll end up saying, "But you still have to do it." In moments of frustration I'll say, if you don't like it, too bad. But they can always talk. They can always talk, and they believe they can get me to change a position. I don't believe in, I believe in setting standards and limits and expectations. But there's no need to be rigid. In fact, I mean, there is nothing like the positive way of getting your kid's attention by saying, yeah, I was wrong. Actually I learned that back in college. I was walking down

the street with somebody. We were having this vigorous discussion. . . . I looked at her and I said, you're right. She just kind of stopped dead in the street because people don't do that. I learned, wow. Certainly if somebody is right, you need to say that out loud.

But the conversation quickly shifts away from her foster children and on to her continued work with the Foster Parent Association and DCF, recruiting other parents to foster for teenagers. Then she turns her attention to me. She is pensive for a moment and then, in a way characteristic of a "cause person," says,

I do know that you're concentrating on women and most foster parents are women. Even when they're married couples, the woman takes the primary role. Because there are a significant number of men, and at some point there will probably [need to] be a subsidiary study, and you're a good person to do it because you are heterosexual, is to look at men in foster care. Once you're done with this study on women, then do it on men, and look at what is there about male nurturing.

# 10

## "I Wanna Make It through the Week"

*Field Notes, February 13, 1996: Interview with DCF Worker Antonia Vovnyestevski*

The security guard in the DCF office had me sign in and watched as I told the receptionist behind the bullet-proof glass who I was and who I was there to see. The lobby was small and grimy, with a few officelike couches and a few beat-up magazines. Along the side walls of the lobby were playrooms. I knew from my days as a social worker that these were for parental visits. DCF workers could watch parents' involvement with their children; brothers and sisters could visit each other while social workers assessed familial functioning. These were rooms made to accommodate rituals of rehabilitation as hoped-for reunifications between parents and their children existed beside the realities of failure and distance.

Deep inside one room, surrounded by toys, an African American boy of about ten, maybe eleven, is playing. At first glance, it strikes me that the toys are too young for him. But there is nothing "cool" about him—no foreboding of adolescence and all its turmoil. A young, African American man sits on a stool by the door. There is someone else in the room, but I only occasionally perceive this person's movement out of the corner of my eye. The child is playing frantically. It is not the abandon of a child who forgets himself and really plays—impervious to time or place, or space, or people. It is a kind of forced abandon that, while joyful on the surface, never allows him to relax. While he plays, he always keeps a wary eye trained on his surroundings. He never looks at the man sitting by the door, even though he never turns away from him.

I sit down on a dirty couch in the main lobby to wait for Antonia. The boy throws a blue-green ball up in the air and with a smile plastered on his face asks the man, "Have you gone to court yet?" His voice is strained with joviality.

The man says, shaking his head, looking down at his feet, "Yup. I been to court."

The child asks, "You talked to the judge?"

The man says, still looking at his feet, "Yup, I talked to the judge."

The boy throws the ball into the air again. He watches the man—or perhaps a spot above the man's head. "What did the judge say?" The smile is still on his frozen face.

"The judge say—" He stops. "Well, I don't exactly know what the judge said."

The ball is thrown into the air again, but I don't believe I ever see it come down.

Antonia breezes through the lobby door, smiling. She shakes my hand and says, "Let's see if we can find a room down here to use." Her parents are from Eastern Europe. She is second generation—maybe first, though she does not have any trace of an accent. She is very pretty, with large round blue eyes and long red hair. She moves swiftly, fluidly. While she talks to me, she seems always to be either moving or just about to take flight.

A number of women come bustling in and out of the small lobby while Antonia glances into one room—the one with the boy and the man—and then the other. Some of the women appear to be social workers, recognizable by the comfortably casual dress and a look that pronounces their destination before they arrive. Others could be the mothers they work with. They come and then vanish behind locked doors that are buzzed open by the woman behind the bullet-proof glass.

The walls in the second small room are bright yellow. A young African American girl sits near the door, with her coat on, not moving. Her back is to me. I noted her mentally when I came in but never really noticed her; she sits so still, motionless and emotionless. It is as though she sits there hoping not to be noticed, hoping to be invisible, hoping to blend in with the grimy walls and be missed in the confusion of the office. Antonia breezes into that conference room by leaning into the room, her hand holding the door jamb for balance, her long hair falling to the side. There are no toys, just a desk and two straight chairs. The girl sits facing the empty desk. Antonia leans toward the girl and asks, "Honey, are you using this room?" The child does not speak. Antonia leans further into the room. "Honey, are you having a visit in here?" She has a sympathetic voice.

All of a sudden the little girl's shoulders begin to shake. She has on a faded navy blue down coat that hides much of her form, but now her whole body leans forward and convulses silently. Antonia lets go of the door jamb and in one fluid motion is inside the room kneeling down by the girl's side. "Honey," she says, touching the shapeless girl lightly, "are you all right?" The child is crying so hard she cannot speak. I see her face as she turns to look at Antonia. I see lines of tears, made silver by the bright fluorescent lights, streaming down her face, into her mouth, and off her chin. The child tries to speak but cannot. Tears fall onto Antonia's hands. "Oh, honey. Are you waiting for a visit?" She thinks a minute, perhaps recognizing the child, familiar with the case. "With your sister?" The child convulses harder, still silent. "She'll be here." Antonia's tone is reassuring. "You having a bad day?" she asks. The child's mouth falls open, but she does not answer. Tears mix with a line of spit that runs out of the little girl's mouth. She can only cry.

The activity in the office seems suddenly to intensify as more people come through the door, bringing with them a burst of cold February air. In a second, a small child runs past me and darts into the room. She pushes unapologetically past Antonia and stands with her feet planted firmly on the ground in front of the crying girl. She must be about four. They seem to be sisters.

The little girl stands in front of her sister looking at once doleful, frightened, happy, and confused. For a second the older girl looks at her, motionless, silent, and then a fresh round of tears spill silently out of her eyes as another inaudible sob shakes her shoulders. The younger girl says nothing. She twists on one foot, then the other, then she adjusts her hat, as though, I think, to make herself more recognizable to her own sister. The older girl, who has to be about nine, sticks two bony fingers into her own eyes to try to stop the tears. Finally, she grabs her little sister around the neck and pulls her to her. She sobs harder, this time making long, soft, choking sounds. She buries her face in her sister's hair, knocking askew the red hat that has been tied on against the winter wind.

A frantic-looking young adult is about five paces behind the little girl. Antonia stands up and backs away from the two sisters. "Are you with them?" she says to the breathless woman, who nods. "She," Antonia nods to the older girl, "was crying." The guard, who is about ten feet away, says, "They are not to leave here. They have to stay there. Violette said so." There is more confusion as more people come through the door, taking the guard's attention, distracting Antonia and the woman with whom she has been talking. For a moment, the two sisters, unmoving in their embrace, are unnoticed. Then Antonia, without looking back at them, leaves the room, and I follow her to the lobby door.

We are heading for the elevator in the hallway when a young Hispanic woman breezes through the door. "Are you supervising that visit?" Antonia asks.

"No," she says, "Violette is."

"Well, " Antonia says, "the older one was crying very hard—"

The woman nods, almost uncomprehendingly. She does not stop, and I do not see where she is going. Antonia and I leave the lobby for the elevator. I am silent. I have never seen a more miserable or pitiful child, I think as we get in. "That's so sad," I say to Antonia.

She answers me by saying, "Yeah. Yeah. It is. You never know if they want to tell you something—you know. Like—now maybe there is something she wanted to say." Antonia looks distracted. When we find a conference room we both sit down. She looks straight at me and says, "One of the worst things we do here is separate siblings. I simply won't do it. I won't do that. I am the oldest of seven children. My youngest brother is nineteen years younger than me. I always knew that if something happened to my parents, I would take care of my brothers and sisters, I would take care of my family. But I always wondered—who would fight me for them? Would the state say I could not have them? What would happen if we could not stay together—if I could not keep them together?"

This chapter presents the perspectives and opinions of a small sample of social workers drawn from a statewide convenience sample. There are several things about this portion of the data that require an explanation. First and foremost, every social worker who was interviewed spoke about the human pain and tragedy they faced daily and about the way they felt "the system" failed them, parents, foster parents, and children. Each spoke of the ways system rules, policies, and accepted practices created the pain they experienced and witnessed. All social workers also spoke about being overwhelmed and consistently operating in a crisis mode where they had little time or energy to plan interventions with families. And as will be discussed, almost all felt impotent to make changes. Within this chapter I identify a "social worker discourse" that is at times both classist and racist. I am not necessarily talking about people who in other contexts would exhibit classist or racist beliefs and practices. Instead, I believe that there is something about the way social workers experience their jobs that creates the likelihood of evaluating certain phenomena through class or race biases. That my belief may be erroneous is beside the point. What is significant and what makes it *appear* true are the systemic variables that lead to the creation of this discourse.

Second, I did not have the same kind of access to social workers that I had to foster mothers. I was unable to secure permission to spend time with social workers during the workday, to follow them around, and to participate in and observe what they did and how they felt about what they did. I was told this was because of confidentiality. Therefore, the perspective I can offer of social workers is somewhat less informed and less empathetic than the perspective of foster mothers. My research assistant and I were able to *hear* about social workers' experiences as they were described to us, but we were unable to see for ourselves. Most of what we did hear was from social workers who were concerned enough about the state of foster care to risk talking with me, since I was unable to secure "official" permission even to interview social workers. Third, the social workers who participated in this study were informed that their answers and comments would be shared with the Legislative Program Review and Investigations Committee as well as used in my book. And they were told that both the LPRIC and I were looking at problems in the foster care system. Consequently, I believe that many social workers emphasized *problems* they experienced in the system and deemphasized ways in which they thought the system succeeded, since many hoped that their comments would be used to change foster care.

Fourth, even though there was ultimately little variation in the themes social workers expressed, I tried to include the range of opinions represented in the data. Based on the small sample, it was not possible to know what caused variation; nor was it possible to know how the sample compared with all social workers employed by DCF in terms of age, ethnicity, gender, education, social class, years of experience, or years of employment. I was unable to obtain this information. What these results *do* indicate is that there are patterns that bear further investigation, since they have a direct relationship to how social workers perceive, evaluate, and interact with foster mothers and are potentially indicative of systemic, and social, problems. This is especially important in light of the nationwide shortage of foster parents.

Each social worker articulated beliefs, assumptions, and practices that simultaneously referred to an unspoken image. For example, through their definitions of failure, they defined success. Through their references to "failed" families, they defined what a family is and what it should be. This chapter examines the way social workers talked about and thought about their jobs.

## The State and Foster Mothers

In some respects, social workers' experiences were remarkably similar to those of foster mothers, yet the perspectives and meanings they attributed to their experiences were dramatically different. Like foster mothers, social workers were real human beings struggling against incredible odds, hoping every moment that what they did made some kind of a difference to someone. In general, social workers saw the foster care system as steeped in failure. Children were placed in care when their own families failed to adequately provide for them. Most regarded the act of placing children in foster care as ultimately damaging to them. Most social workers talked about the enormous responsibility they felt with respect to their decision since the damage resulting from placing children had to be weighed against the potential damage resulting from leaving them in their homes. Most of the time, there was no good choice. On a daily basis, social workers entered volatile situations in which they saw the physical manifestations of human degradation, exploitation, and pain imprinted on children who had not been fed, who had been beaten, raped, whose bones had been broken, or whose flesh had been burned. Pain was impressed on parents who could not pay the rent, could not buy food, could not live without the drugs to which they were addicted.

Their job was to deal with the human pain that much of America prefers to ignore and to work with those who in popular political discourses are easily blamed for their own misery. Their fervent hope was to try to make the situation better for someone—mostly, for children. The trick was to avoid making it worse. All of the social workers who participated in this study felt overwhelmed by their jobs. They constantly battled failure and chronic fatigue. Seldom did a social worker report feeling as though her goals for the day or week had been accomplished. Not uncommonly, daily routines were upset by crises that necessitated immediate attention. The demands of each crisis far outweighed the resources social workers had available to meet them. Most tended to think simply in terms of their own emotional and occupational survival and concomitantly the survival of those with whose lives they were entrusted.

While current trends in DCF were to hire people with undergraduate or master's level education, most social workers found little time to think, plan, theorize, or even to problem-solve. Most of their jobs involved reacting and reacting immediately. Social workers' reactions were frequently conditioned by a heightened emphasis within the agency on the child protection policy. This shift had come about after the deaths of several children. They feared that they, too, would be blamed if there were more deaths. There was an awareness among social workers that the need for a scapegoat did not stop with their clients. When asked what he hoped to accomplish in his job, this social worker answered,

> Honestly? Really? I'd just wanna get through this week. Sometimes it's that tough. We're dealing with increasing numbers of, well, you know, a lot of things that have happened—the Baby Emily case last year, which pushed everything into high gear. We've been more aggressive about pursuing kids and removing them. And then they struggle. My goals are on a daily basis to provide a shelter for the kids and to keep sibling groups together. More often than not, we end up splitting them up. We send them to different homes and that's bad. Or there are disruptions. That's the worst." (Rick Thomas, an African American man who had worked for DCF for over seven years)

All social workers stated that their reasons for seeking employment at DCF were to contribute to the improvement of society by helping children. Many, like Mr. Thomas, felt that through their work they could effect critical social change: "This occupation will determine the future and direction of this country. Well, you know, without being cliché, the kids really are our future. They are going to, you know, we are going to pass the right to run the country to them. And it is going to be theirs, and they are going to need to be able to make wise choices and informed decisions."

All social workers reported feeling disappointed at their inability to effect the kinds of changes they had initially hoped for. As impediments to success, many cited volumes of paperwork, high caseloads, an inability to do anything but move from one crisis to the next, or the enormous and complicated problems confronting the parents and children with whom they worked. Few saw any real solutions to the problems they encountered. Most felt the tasks they faced on a daily basis were daunting, often hopeless, and approached each day with anxiety about potential catastrophes. The agency's reaction to mounting social and personal problems among those identified as clients was to remove children from their families and place them in foster care.

This was the only resource that both ensured a child's physical safety and was consistently available to social workers. But it was problematic. Children were damaged by their familial treatment, damaged by the ravages of poverty and the sequelae of inequity. They were damaged when removed from their homes; they were damaged when placed in strange homes with people to whom they were unrelated. They were damaged once again when removed from foster homes and returned home when little had actually changed. As people who saw the pain children experienced, social workers held themselves responsible for children's safety and well-being and for a failed child welfare system.

> I placed kids in a volatile environment where gunshots go off quite often. I can understand not taking the child from the environment,[1] but some of these children need to come out of these dangerous volatile environments and be given a chance with fresh air in an environment surrounded by love where they can sleep at night rather than jump in their beds listening to bullets. I think the system has failed these children. I think the agency is failing these children. I think these kids are damaged . . . in the beginning, and when these children are returned to their families, I think they're far more damaged. (Ann Novak, a Euro-American treatment social worker who had worked for DCF for three and a half years)

DCF specified that the state was responsible for protecting children's safety and charged DCF social workers with enforcing or enacting that policy. The policy also specified that children, when removed from their birth homes, should be placed in an environment that closely resembled their own home in terms of language and location.[2] This was done so that children felt comfortable with the foster family, so that birth parents could easily visit, and so that when the child returned home, trauma resulting from change in social/familial environment was minimized. This policy was consistent with the purpose and nature of foster care: foster care was a temporary experience and used only when a child's physical safety or development was compromised.

For social workers, the policy conflicted with the nature of the problems they experienced within families and with their interpretation of what it is that makes a child safe. Most social workers, when talking about the problems they encountered in "identified" families, spoke first and foremost of drug addiction (primarily citing crack cocaine and heroin), then poverty, and then family and neighborhood violence. Drug addiction was often seen as chronic and insidious. There were few treatment programs available for women who were addicted, and there were often waiting lists to get into programs. Withdrawal and rehabilitation were lengthy processes with potentially high recidivism rates. For social workers who worked with biological families and who saw these problems as potentially chronic, foster care was often not a temporary solution to an intermittent or short-term family crisis; it was potentially long-term. Second, in the mandate to place children in a safe, reliable home, "safe and reliable" was often equated with social class. The knowledge that children might in fact not be in care on a short-term basis made finding a home in which a child could have certain opportunities even more imperative.

### Better Families

Social workers saw themselves as central figures in protecting children's lives. They saw that they alone were shouldering this responsibility, and they carried this burden like an omnipresent weight. Like foster parents, social workers consistently referred to children in possessive terms, such as "these are my children," or "I placed my kids." However, unlike foster mothers, they used this language to connote not kinship but the sense of responsibility and level of trusteeship they felt toward children.

As Mukti Jain Campion notes in her critiques of current child welfare policies, child protection statutes specify that "[c]hildren cannot determine and safeguard their own interests, and since the young are the builders of future society we all share a responsibility to protect them" (1995:9). Social workers took this mandate personally. And the stakes for their decisions were very high, since the type of placements they were able to secure had lifelong implications for children and for society as a whole. If they made a "wrong" placement and something bad happened to the child while in care, *they* were responsible, to the child, to the child's parents, and to society, which demanded accountability.

Social workers also saw foster care as a way to enhance children's upward mobility. While this latter concept is commonly related to fostering cross-culturally (see Bledsoe, 1990; Gordon, 1987; Silk, 1987; Goody, 1975; Castle, 1996), it is not commonly thought to be a function of American foster care as specified in DCF policy or training manuals. In the interviews with social workers, protecting children and effecting upward mobility were commonly entwined, and often inseparable. That is, children could be protected by being placed in a home where the parents had a higher standard of living than that of the children's own parents. For social workers, there was a direct, immediate, and *causal* link between poverty and child abuse.

Since poverty was a causal variable in child abuse, removing the child from poverty eliminated this cause and reduced the chances of further harm while simultaneously exposing the child to greater opportunities. Safety was also often equated with lifestyle patterns. Physically neat, clean, and organized homes, where there were recognizable routines and where children's activities were structured, were considered to be safe. Frequently in interviews, social workers stressed upward mobility over physical safety.

Most workers complained about the lack of agency licensing requirements for foster parents, often citing a lack of educational or economic criteria. Education and income requirements were a way to ensure that the agency could find more middle-class foster parents, parents who could provide class mobility for children.

> I think the stipulations on foster families should be more training. They should definitely check into the background of people they are licensing. They should have a background, the education. You don't [have any educational requirements]. There is no level. So we are placing this kid in a home where this lady is educationally limited and can't help this kid on its homework, from the mom who can help this kid but is a loony. What is the difference? Yeah, she is not beating the crap out of

the kid, but educationally the kid, you know, will be mentally distraught because they are going to go to school, and everybody is going to call him, "You're stupid, you're stupid, you didn't do your homework."

[We need stricter guidelines.] We need to know who our foster parents are. They need to do a better background check. They are licensing, they have to have recommendations and educational background, educational level, something, some type of status quo on where they come from, their beliefs. . . . I don't think we know enough about each foster home to say that we are doing our job. I think we are licensing them too fast. Okay, okay, okay, okay, without getting an extensive background check. (Barbara Allyn, a treatment social worker who had worked for DCF for one year)

Social workers whose jobs entailed going from one life-threatening crisis to another had little time to know or experience the nuances of foster-parent/foster-children relationships. In their harried visits with foster children they saw the outward manifestations of caregiving—nice clothes, combed hair, a pretty bedroom, good food—and often translated these things into variables of social class. So, when children were placed with poor families, it was the foster parents' socioeconomic status that made it impossible to meet children's social and material needs; and it was children's transience within foster care that prevented them from staying long enough to be really loved. While in some respects social workers felt love and nurture could come only from children's biological kin, they maintained the hope that children would be "well cared for" if only the "right" home was found.

Social workers often defined children's needs in terms that equated love with material comfort, and clearly saw the distance between what they hoped for and what they got with economically impoverished families. Since these foster parents could not provide what foster children needed materially (by social workers' standards), they were often regarded with bitter suspicion and hostility. While some social workers viewed foster parents with sympathy or admiration and were aware of the ways in which the agency exploited them as dispensable workers, others regarded them with bitter suspicion and hostility. In general, social workers also felt angry at the agency and felt discouraged about their own abilities either to effect change or survive the pressures of their work. It was a system in which all participants, themselves included, were dispensable and ultimately replaceable. They would burn out, they would be replaced. Nothing would change either with the agency or with society as a whole.

> I think they should be looking for better families. I think that we should be out there trying to recruit better families. I mean, I know we believe that the child should stay in the neighborhood. Well, you know, if we recruited outside of the neighborhood, we could probably have better families. . . . Well, I just think that a better home, whether it's in the neighborhood or it's [not], I don't think we should just license anybody. I think we should really look into these families and see what they're willing to do for these kids. And I think when we suggest this to these families and they go through training, they should be told this is not a paycheck. This is money for the child. Because these people, I mean they can't transport them anywhere, they don't get them into programs like they should. I mean Girl Scouts. How hard is it to get a kid into Girl Scouts, you know, I mean, or Brownies or some free organization or an after-school program or take them places? They don't do it. (Brenda Peters, a married Euro-American treatment social worker in her thirties)

## Good Homes and Bad Homes

Discussions of social mobility were commonly divided into two separate categories. A social worker's job was to take children from "bad" homes and place them in "good" homes. "Bad" homes were those where a child's safety was compromised by physical abuse or neglect but were also homes in urban areas where domestic or neighborhood violence was common, where schools were substandard, where housing was inferior and crowded, and where children's play areas were confined. "Good" homes were those where children would not be physically harmed or physically disciplined, where they would be fed on a regular basis, where the food they would eat would be "American" cuisine, where children would have their own bedrooms or share with only one other child, where the schools a child would attend were "good" based on class size and the amount of equipment available, and where playing spaces were ample, not physically dangerous, and generally included a yard or a park.

Good homes were also defined by what was done in them. Like foster mothers, social workers equated parenting with what parents *do* for children. While foster mothers perceived parenting as a range of child care variables and activities, the bottom line was the relationship they formed with the children. Since social workers' time in foster homes was limited, they seldom saw the range of activities attendant on the relationship, nor did they *see* the relationship being developed or manifested in daily child care routines. Thus social workers tended to equate parental "doing" with overt indicators that could be assessed easily and quickly. One indicator that was frequently mentioned was transportation. Social workers expected foster mothers to transport children to their appointments as well as to enroll them in enrichment activities such as Girl Scouts, ballet, art classes, or choir, many of which require transportation. Whether or not a mother was able and willing to provide transportation (two variables that were seldom distinguished from one another) was, for social workers, a criterion for a "good" home.

Social workers commonly expressed anger at foster parents who did not provide children with transportation. For most social workers, context variables such as the availability of an automobile, or whether a woman worked full-time, never entered the discussion. Failure to provide children with transportation indicated a foster mother's inadequacy. Foster parents who did not transport children to appointments or school were "lazy," or were "not doing their job," or were "not caring for foster children like their own." For social workers, these characteristics went hand in hand with low-social-class status and linked low socioeconomic status with poor motherhood. *Poor mothers* were "bad," "lazy," and those who would not perform routine maternal duties. "Good" mothers were those who had few time constraints, whose primary task was child rearing, who defined their daily chores in terms of their children's needs, and who had access to certain material comforts.

This often meant that maternal adequacy was based primarily on social class. Middle-class mothers tended to be those who did not work outside the home or who worked part-time in their husband's business and were more available to transport children. These women tended to either own or have access to cars. Poorer mothers, or women living in urban settings, often did not have a car or did not have a reliable car available to them on a regular basis. In addition, these were also women who tended to work outside the home and who therefore were not always available to take children to appointments during the day. Some elderly women did not feel comfortable driving long distances.

"Bad" foster mothers were those who could not be counted on to meet children's needs, as they were defined by the social workers and the agency, or to comply with agency treatment plans and goals for children. To social workers, fostering demanded the same level of parental commitment as parenting. But the expected level of parental activity was higher in fostering than in parenting. That is, many foster children don't just have to go to school, but have to go to special schools, to therapy, to special medical appointments, to visits with their parents, and to visits with their siblings in other foster homes. Sometimes these expectations were articulated to foster mothers; at other times, social workers simply assumed foster mothers knew them, cared about them, and were committed to supporting them. They were often disappointed. Social workers assumed that foster parents had received training that informed them of their responsibilities to foster children and the nature of the demands foster children present. They did not have time, nor did they feel it was their job, to teach foster parents about fostering. As this case aide said,

> I think a lot of times we expect too much out of the foster parents. Like I said, we forget that they are human. More support I guess is basically what I'm trying to say. A little more, provide them with a little more training maybe, a little more education, a little more background on the kids they are getting, what to expect. We give them these families' kids that are sexually abused, emotionally abused. We don't know, Lord knows how bad. I think the families need to know to what extent and what to expect because a lot of our families, they aren't psychologists, psychiatrists, whatever. It's all new for them too. . . . It's all new to them. They are, the kids are just given to them and they don't know what to expect. (Mark Gonzalez, a Hispanic social worker assistant in his twenties)

One social worker, a Euro-American woman in her thirties, described a situation where the foster mother asked for the removal of a child who had been in her care for two years. The social worker placed the child in another home and in her description of the new home conceptually linked the fact that the family did not like unannounced social worker visits with economic indicators: no lightbulbs, a poor neighborhood, and the foster mother's inability to provide transportation.

> I have a little kid right now. He's two and a half years old. I had to take him away from the only foster home that he knew because they wanted him out, which is, that's fine, that happens. . . . [He was placed with another foster home] and you go to this house and they like, they don't want you to show up unannounced. That's the first thing. . . . And I've

walked in on a situation where there was an elderly woman [a baby-sitter] taking care of my kid and a little baby. She barely could speak, I mean the crackle in her voice, and her movement was really slow. And there she is in this home with a two-and-a-half-year-old and a baby. It was only for brief times, according to the foster mother. . . . And then, you know, the house is dark [no lights, no lightbulbs], which, you know, that's the way they live, that's the way they live, but I wouldn't want to see a child living in the dark.

. . . The previous foster parent had trouble getting him to Child Developmental Services once a week for one hour. So prior to placing this child in this foster home, I asked the woman, I said he goes to CDS Tuesdays from 3:00 until 4:00 . . . he goes to a play group for socialization . . . his speech is like, he's only been there a couple of times, and his speech is a whole lot better. But once a week, and I asked her if she had a problem with this, and she said, "Well, what's wrong with him?" And I'm like, there's nothing *wrong* with him. He goes there for socialization. He may be a little developmentally delayed and might need a little push to develop properly. And she's like, "Oh, well, I'll see how I can do." And at this time this was the only placement that was available, so I had to place him there. She couldn't get him there the following Tuesday, so I said, okay, fine, try for the next Tuesday. She gets to CDS and she tells them she never knew that he had to come here. Why does he have to come here? It doesn't fit into her schedule. But she said she would try to get him there. We're talking one hour a week and they live approximately 3–4 miles from the place. And she's got a husband, too, on top of it, and she's adopted two of our children through foster care. She lives off of Jackson Street, it's a really, really bad section of town. So he can't go out and play. . . .

I was informed by Yale that this particular foster mother was not being compliant in giving the child the Ensure that was prescribed. And I was also informed by the school that they didn't think that the foster mother was actually taking very good care of the two children or the children that she had in the home. Now here is a mom who has two adopted kids through DCF, three foster kids, two biological kids. So we're talking two, three, seven kids living in the home. (Brenda Peters, a married Euro-American treatment social worker in her thirties)

The social worker's conclusion was that this new home was a bad foster home. She did not consider alternative explanations of this mother's behavior, for example, that the mother was already overburdened with seven children, that she may have had a full-time job, or that her husband may have also worked. This social worker's comments appear to offer insight into an observation that foster mothers often made. Social workers assumed children were being cared for inadequately *unless* a foster mother followed parenting as prescribed by the agency. The social worker's conclusion was that the agency had failed to properly monitor who could be a licensed foster parent and had made a mistake licensing this woman.

## The Intersection of Ethnicity and Class Mobility

Ethnicity in social workers' comments was almost always a part of class mobility. In their reflections, some social workers disparaged ethnic food and referred to "bad" homes by geographic location. The areas cited were commonly urban public housing developments inhabited almost exclusively by African Americans or Hispanics. By contrast, "good" homes were often Euro-American homes, and this, too, was designated by geographic area. Social workers tended to see that Euro-American people had greater access to material resources and if they fostered could share resources with children. According to social workers, Euro-American middle-class families also shared their values, like the work ethic. This could be transmitted to children as a skill or a piece of knowledge that they could take with them when and if they returned home. Euro-American people, who lived middle-class lives, also met the criteria for safety. Their homes were clean and were managed with routines that were predictable. There was not an undifferentiated generalization or belief among social workers that *all* Euro-American people were middle class, and social workers spoke of their disappointment regarding the homes of Euro-American women who failed to meet this standard. However, according to most social workers' discourses, Euro-American people were simply *more likely* to live in the suburbs, *more likely* to live a middle-class life, *more likely* to have an education, *more likely* to have a male breadwinner who provided a steady income, and thus *more likely* to provide a "good" home. Many saw the role of foster parents as so difficult and demeaning that only those people who were in dire financial need would consider it an option.

> I think we should have more Euro-American families taking these children in. I am sure they would love to, but I see a lot of lower-income people being recruited because maybe they will be doing it more for the

money and that they could take just about anything that we dish out. . . . And why not? These people, you wave money in their face, and they will come walking. They will say, okay. Of course I am not saying that for *everybody*, because I don't think everybody is the same. (Tania Louis, a Euro-American social service assistant who had been with DCF for almost two years)

Descriptions of foster parents as "warm," "loving," "nurturing," "attentive," and "available" were commonly used in conjunction with social class variables to describe foster homes. "Good" homes were those in which the people were warm, loving, nurturing, and understanding, *and* middle-class, comfortable, and inhabited by Euro-American people. Few social workers readily linked lower-socioeconomic-class indicators with the characteristics of "warm" or "loving." The exceptions were social workers whose daily activities did not involve working with biological, or foster parents or children on a regular basis—for example, social work supervisors, foster parent support workers, matchers, or case aides. They tended to see foster parents much more sympathetically. One man, a case aide hired primarily to transport children to and from medical/counseling services, responded this way when asked whether or not he had any concerns about the physical condition of the foster homes he visited.

Maybe once or twice. But I felt comfortable with it on the other hand because of the person, of the foster parents, good people. They didn't have a lot of money, so they couldn't afford a lot of things. I'm not going to say there was something that put the kids in danger, but maybe just things were a little raggedy and maybe the house wasn't kept up. But other than that, because of the people I felt okay with it. [I think we should have standards] but to a certain extent. I mean, people that lived in the roughest neighborhood are the nicest, loving people. I'd rather have that than take them somewhere in Greenwich or something like that. The people just don't care. . . . You've got to take all that stuff into consideration and find a level there or a line." (Abigail Johnson, an African American social worker in her early twenties who had worked for DCF for three years)

Social workers directly involved in "treatment"—that is, social workers whose primary tasks dealt specifically with child protection—tended to view foster parents as inadequate, incompetent, and uncaring, and as people who were often apathetic or hostile toward foster children. These social workers also tended to ascribe to foster parents nefarious motives for fostering, limited almost exclusively to fostering as a commercial endeavor. One social worker, whose comments were not unusual, was asked, "What do you think a foster parent should be like?" Her comments about foster parent characteristics quickly turned to comments about class mobility, which she stated was the primary reason for placing children in foster care. Social class mobility and child protection were linked.

> I think foster parents should be nurturing and loving to the child and have a lot of patience with the child, because these children are going through a traumatic experience just leaving their home. Even if it's a bad home, it's still *their* home, it's still their parents. I think a foster home should be a *better* place than where they [children] came from. I don't think you should take a child from a home and still put him in a foster home in a drug-infested area of Bridgeport; you're not changing his life any. I think they should go to a better home in a better neighborhood and get out of the rotten environment that helped make their parents the drug addicts they are or the abusers they are. [There are a lot of foster homes in drug neighborhoods.] I think the agency's policy seems to be they want to keep the child in the same environment that they were in, and I think the child should go to a better environment; otherwise, why remove them? [It is important] to show them [children] there is a better life out there if they can work for it. All they have to do is work for it, and I mean, a lot of children, all they see is the drug dealing and money from the drug dealing, and their aspiration in life is to be like that drug dealer on the corner. Yeah, and that's all they care about. . . . And they know that probably by the time they're fourteen years old, they can have that kind of money if they work for that guy, and they need to be shown there's a different life. (Tamara York, a Euro-American social worker in her mid-forties)

If social workers were unable to place children in a "better" home, then they had *failed* at their job and *failed* the child. One social worker reflected on a family with whom she had recently placed a little boy. The family was Hispanic, as was the child. References to "TPR" in her comments mean that the parent had had her parental rights terminated by the court and her children placed either for adoption or in long-term foster care. To social workers, this indicated that the mother's problems were so severe that they were irremediable within the time frames specified by DCF policy (at the time of these interviews, twelve months).

[It would be better if we had] more middle income and even go extend out into the upper, higher. . . . [Y]ou could give these children better opportunities, and I think that is excellent. You think that, I mean I put myself in a situation if my children, and God forbid and I know that is never going to happen, were taken away from me. I am a middle-class person. If they were to put them with an upper-class person, I would love that. I would have no problem with that because I think those upper-class people could probably give them a better education, a better future, expose them and raise them in a more productive atmosphere than I probably can give them. . . .

I feel like I discriminate. They [this family] are Hispanic just as well as I am, but I feel that those are the bottom of the pit. Those are the worst you can get. If you walk into their home, there is so much stuff that needs to be taken into consideration. I mean I could even *guarantee you* that they are infested with cockroaches. That is how it is so unorganized. I mean one day you will go there and there will be one person living there. Next thing the other one's boyfriend is moving in. The other one's girlfriend is moving out. Last I found out, that foster home had one of our ex-clients that we TPRed living there. But you know what is so funny? It was reported. One of the other workers found out. She reported it to the FITSU workers and you know what they said? We called them up. They said she is not living there. That was the end of that. . . . Yes. And you know what? That's it. Foster mother said she doesn't live there, and as far as they are concerned, if the foster mother says she doesn't live there, that's it. It's gone. (Tania Louis, a social service assistant who had been with DCF for almost two years)

What is clear in this social worker's comments is the mistrust with which she regarded foster parents and the way in which this mistrust was heightened by social class indicators. This foster family was "disorganized," their house was not "clean," and they were not to be trusted. She was alarmed that a breach of the rules had been reported to the agency (Family Treatment and Support Unit), and yet the agency had failed to believe the social worker and instead believed the foster mother. Not only had the agency failed to properly screen this family prior to licensing, but it had failed to properly monitor their daily activities. The child was in potential jeopardy, and the social worker felt angry, unsupported, and invalidated. Since DCF had failed to screen these foster parents adequately, the social worker mistrusted the agency.

To break the cycle of failure they encountered, social workers repeatedly suggested that foster parents be monitored more closely by

DCF and held accountable for their parenting and for the money they were given. Themes of accountability in social workers' interviews suggested the need for a product by which foster parents' success or failure could be measured. The end result of fostering should be a well-fed child; a budget detailing expenditures; children with clean, new clothes; proof that children were engaged in extracurricular activities. It was not sufficient for foster parents, as people hired by the state (as many social workers referred to them), simply to *care* for children. They should have to produce evidence of their work and evidence that they were parenting children according to certain specified standards.

The subtext of this message was that foster parents were not only poor role models and unfeeling parents but also unscrupulous swindlers and could scarcely provide the kind of parenting social workers hoped to encounter.

> [It is a problem if foster parents are on AFDC] because when you are not financially stable, when you can't financially meet your own needs, you shouldn't be expected to take on a foster child because we obviously don't pay enough to solely support—we can't. It is just *extra* money. Is it enough to take somebody who has very little money and make it go? Absolutely not. That's, I had a lot of experiences down in Bridgeport and it was—it did, it caused so many problems. I mean these kids were going from, I mean these people were financially unstable. If you can't support yourself, then. . . .
>
> And I also think that, I don't know how it is accounted for, but these people are receiving assistance and it's really welfare fraud if you are also getting more additional money and you are not accounting for it. And I think that needs to be addressed. Here we are placing kids for role models and who is a role model when you are abusing the system by collecting assistance but then you are taking in foster children and getting money that way. (Alison Boswell, a treatment social worker who had worked for DCF for two and half years)

## *"They're in It for the Money"*

Most social workers dichotomized money and love in their descriptions of foster parents' motives for fostering. This dichotomy was often coupled with beliefs about social class. Poor people fostered in order to make money. While no social worker said poor mothers were incapable of loving a foster child, none said that poor mothers were valued because they could mother, or that foster mothers who could nurture and care for a child were valued regardless of social class.

Social workers based their feelings that poor women were "in it for the money" on the fact that poor mothers talked about money and had inadequate cash flow to comfortably provide for children without DCF assistance. Middle-class people fostered because they loved children. This assumption was supported by the belief that middle-class Euro-American parents were economically comfortable and did not "need" the income from fostering in order to survive. Economic need often implied a lack of parental/affective motivation. Middle-class families also tended to inquire less about money, probably owing to a cushion of income. Social workers often assumed that this unconcern reflected parents' priorities: children came first, the money was irrelevant. Their comments reflected a range of sentiments from being understanding about the lack of adequate reimbursement to being discouraged about foster parents' motives for fostering.

> I think a lot of them get involved thinking that they will have extra money in the long run. However, in the long run it's expensive, it really is, because their payments do not go a long way. I mean, I've sat down and I've divvied it up with foster families before, when I've had real problems with finding out where their clothing money is going if I haven't seen different clothes on [foster children]. (Rick Thomas, an African American social worker matcher who had been with the agency for seven years)

> Well, I would hope they go in for caring and loving of a child, but there are some foster parents out there which I feel are in it just simply for the money. (Maria Albert, a treatment social worker who had worked with DCF for three and a half years)

> Very good intentions. Some of them have very good intentions. It is from the heart. Most of them, it is the money. If I got $597 per kid and that is from age six and over, I believe that's, no it is $567 for age six and $597 for under one. That is over $1,000 a month. With two kids, so it is over $1,000 a month. That is a lot of money. That is a lot of money. Does it go to the kids? Where is the money going? Some parents I can definitely see where the money is going. . . . [The child's] hair is done. He had new shoes. . . . He had new shoes and new pants and it was all nice and jazzed up. Others I have no idea. When a foster parent calls me and tells me she can't get diapers, I am like *h-e-l-l-o*, a voucher doesn't pay for diapers.

How can you not have diapers? Get on the bus and go get some diapers. Use your money. You are supposed to be caring for this child as if it was your own. And then I get [from foster mothers when] the kids are removed, "Am I going to be paid for that week that I had the kids?" It is all money. (Barbara Allyn, a treatment social worker who had worked for DCF for one year)

A dichotomization of love and economic need meant that poor foster parents not only could not provide children with improved social and economic opportunities but could not love, nurture, or form enduring parental relationships with children, since they were fostering exclusively for economic gain. To judge by social workers' descriptions of the foster homes and the parents they encountered, little else but economic status was literally *seen* or valued.

As Linda Gordon points out, historically women who were considered "deviant" or "failed" by social service personnel were often those who mixed mothering and wage labor (1994:23). Interestingly, during the late nineteenth century, mothers (usually widows) received financial support from the state in order to stay home and take care of their children. Like social workers, they were referred to as employees of the state whose first task was the raising and socialization of dependent children. In some respects it would seem plausible for foster mothers to be viewed in this manner. However, when social workers spoke of foster mothers as employees, as some did, the criterion by which their potential for success was measured was their distance from economic necessity. The "product" of their success was a child whose class mobility was enhanced. Therefore, poor women were neither "state employees" nor "mothers."

The mistrust with which foster parents were regarded made social worker interactions with foster parents resemble policing rather than supportive casework services. This attitude was reinforced by two basic assumptions: (1) foster parents were probably not fulfilling their obligations to foster children because most lacked the material resources necessary to do so; and (2) social workers, not foster parents, were ultimately responsible for foster children's well-being. This second assumption was sustained ideologically by statutes that held the state responsible for protecting children's rights. Social workers were agents of the state.

While many social workers stated that foster parents should have more economic and emotional support, there appeared to be a distinction between those who needed support and those who, because they fostered for financial gain, needed to be "weeded out" of the system. The purpose of social worker visits with foster children was to ensure that children were being fed, clothed, housed, and treated "properly." Social workers often reported asking foster mothers to show them the children's bedrooms and to open the refrigerator and cupboards to make sure food was available.

> I think that they should have more resources available to their foster families. I also think that they should investigate their families much more thoroughly before they license them. I think there are too many foster homes that are doing it for the money and not for the children. I don't think that the money that they get goes to the children. I picked up a child from a foster home, and he was always in rags, always in second-hand clothes, and when he lived with his mother, who spent less money, he never was. (Janice Hartman, a treatment social worker who had worked with DCF for six and a half years)

Based on the assumption of failure, social workers were frequently in the position of having to ascertain during visits *how* foster parents were failing, since foster parents' failure indicated that children's needs and social workers' responsibilities were not being met.

Almost all social workers described their efforts to report "bad" homes to the monitoring and licensing division of DCF. They also described their frustration that "bad" foster parents' licenses were not revoked. In this way, social workers attempted to exercise some amount of control over the type and quality of parenting care children received. It is important to note that the primary focus of social workers' interventions was not to control foster parents' activities but to secure a certain experience for foster children.

> I think the majority of the foster families that I have are in it for the money exclusively. I will give you an example. I had a little, beautiful little girl who was in a foster home, that they professed to have loved this little kid, but they had problems letting go of the child, and they knew that eventually it would be reunification. I personally went out of my own pocket on her birthday and bought her a watch. This little girl wanted a little watch. And the day of departure from that foster home, I noticed, after I'd had the child at the, where we brought the child, that she had a, I asked her where her little watch was and she showed me the

shabby little thing that I did not buy. From what I understand is that the woman's daughter got the watch and they replaced it with this piece of crap for this little girl. They sent this kid back with hobo's clothes, where it necessitated I had to fight with the FITSU unit and go to the top . . . and say I want some money for clothing or someone needs to go out and get some money, or get those clothes from that lady's home. Apparently they did negotiate something with it which was minimal. These kind of examples. . . .

Another example . . . I brought three children to a home in Thomasville which I understand is now closed. I left three children there. To date, I never saw what the kitchen looked like because there was heaps of clothing, I guess in the dining room, where you couldn't even see the kitchen. I remember bringing the kids back from a visit, where the little girl ran and picked up some medicine off of the living room table. The place was absolutely filthy. It was despicable. (Ann Novak, a Euro-American treatment social worker who had worked with the agency for three and a half years)

Based on social workers' expectations of foster care, everyone failed. Since "mothering" and "good mothering" were equated with material resources and a middle-class lifestyle, the agency failed since it licensed poor women, social workers failed because they placed children only with licensed foster homes, and foster mothers failed, since they were often poor and could not provide for children adequately or be the type of "mother" children need.

I think it should be more as charity. I don't know if that sounds right but . . . out of love. I think as a kindness, as a deed of kindness. [I think that people] just definitely [go into it for the money]. You know which ones do it out of love and you know which ones do it out of money. . . . Because some parents express it themselves, some, I've heard some foster parents express themselves very badly of their children, of the children that they get. Where I think that if it was their own child, they wouldn't do that. And that's not right. Just because it's somebody else's child doesn't mean you have the right to put them down. . . . I get upset. I get upset. Because I feel that, what if that was my child? And these parents depend on us—well, not depend on us, but if we take them away from them because they're not proper parents, then they trust that we're going to find a good placement for them, and if we don't, then, then you know, then we're not doing our job. (Tania Louis, a Euro-American social service assistant who had been with DCF for almost two years)

# 11

## Conclusion

They do nothing. Do you understand that? They do nothing. They placed them here and that was that. . . . Once they're placed nobody gives a damn. And that's unfair. Because if a kid is coming from a screwed-up home, you put him in a home where he is halfway stabilizing himself now, because you don't like the way things go you're gonna move that kid from this house and put him in that house. You've fucked him up again. What are you doing to the kid? Now this kid is going from this house to that house. What kind of kid is this going to be? What kind of life is it going to have?

—Deleah Smith, a married African American woman
in her late forties

What does this research tell us? What can we learn from the voices of those who talked about their experiences? Perhaps the place to begin is to acknowledge that the current foster care system is in a state of crisis, evidenced, in part, by the pain emanating from those who participate in and construct the discourse. In some respects, Shakespeare could not have constructed a more comprehensive tragedy. While many study participants talked about the joy, hope, and transformations they had experienced through fostering relationships, no one spoke of the "system"—that is, the rules, practices, procedures, and policies that establish the rhythms and nature of daily interactions between social actors—as anything but a failure. And it is this failure, in particular, that is part of the tragedy, since the failure of the child welfare *system* is transcribed through social interactions onto individuals who shamefully or sorrowfully accept the burden of failure as their own. I contend that it is the unexamined assumptions and beliefs upon which many of these policies and practices are based that create a template for social interactions bound for failure. The tension between life realities and obsolete ideologies of social and gendered ideals make a feeling of "success," however it is defined, almost impossible to attain.

Through fostering, women chose to create caregiving relationships premised on a conception of motherhood as an empathic experience. Their work was to discern and meet the needs, wants, and realities of the children in their care. The consequences of caregiving were to heal children's emotional, psychological, and physical afflictions and to enhance children's chances for survival. Fostering was the work of creating families and kinship networks based on affective claims of belonging. Fostering, for mothers, was an "act and an attitude" (Bubeck, 1995:9) that not only occurred within an individual and familial context but had an important social/moral dimension. Through transformative relationships with children, women healed a portion of their community and contributed to social reform. Fostering was an experience that conditioned women's sense of themselves as wives, mothers, professional caregivers, and community healers. It was work that placed the work of mothering simultaneously within a social and familial context.

Contrasting with women's definitions of "motherhood" and "family" were those maintained by the State Department of Children and Family Services. Through state policies and social worker practices, fostering was generally looked at as a temporary board-and-care arrangement; foster parents were temporary child care workers. Women's claims to motherhood were dismissed, ignored, or simply not recognized. This construction of foster motherhood was facilitated by ideologies that separated women's domestic work and wage labor and considered women's domestic labor as an essential component of *all* women's natures. Since work that occurred within the home was defined as "women's work" and was a part of what it was to *be a woman*, it should not be monetarily compensated. This ideology was supported in popular cultural constructions of gender, work, and kinship found in the media and also in human services literature (Wozniak, 1995b:5).

Since the majority of women who fostered for the state of Connecticut lived at or below the poverty level, ideologies that excluded women's caregiving work from monetary compensation disadvantaged women who might have few marketable skills and little education, and whose conceptions of selfhood pivoted around their ability and desire to give care. Women's own ideologies of caregiving, namely, empathy and understanding, unquestionably sustained exploitative social relations with the state, since women were not inclined to put their own needs for compensation or fair treatment above those of sick, abandoned, or homeless children. Those who did were generally weeded from the pool of licensed foster parents by DCF. Child welfare agencies depend on women's "free" domestic labor to care for the increasing number of children entering care. The high percentage of working-class foster mothers suggests that the state has found an easily exploitable and expendable labor pool in women who are dependent upon the reimbursement fee.

Most research relevant to the crisis in the foster care system has decontextualized systemic problems and has disembodied the subjects of investigation.[1] That is to say, most research has examined specific problems within the system without examining the ideologies and assumptions upon which policies and practices are based, and has excluded consideration of the historical, cultural, and political contexts through which problems are created and identified. In addition, most research has looked at the social actors whose lives and actions shape contemporary fostering as objects rather than as flesh-and-blood human beings who, through their participation, actively shape and are shaped by the social relations of fostering.

Interventions have been primarily palliative and limited to specific problems, rather than aimed at needed systemic transformation. An enhanced understanding of the relationship between the construction of foster-parent/foster-child identity and concomitant relationships is essential in light of the staggering national need for foster parents and in particular for foster parents who can care for children within a supportive context. Effective policy changes can be executed only through theoretical revision that incorporates an understanding of the ways in which individual and gender identity intersect sociocultural and sociohistorical categories of "mother," "child," and "family." Policy change is effected through a different way of thinking about the individuals who participate in the discourse. The "noose is loosened by breaking with the type of thinking that has led to its fashioning, and by a mode of political action that dissents from those practices of normalization that have made us all potential victims. A prerequisite for this break is the recognition that human beings and thought inhabit the domain of power-knowledge relations" (Bernauer, 1990:142).

Policies that do not incorporate or are not premised on the life realities, beliefs, and practices of those who are affected by them are ultimately abusive, since they impose foreign or divergent standards of behavior. They also ultimately create arbitrary power relations in which some people, and their work, are elevated and others devalued. Child welfare polices enacted through social worker practices at the present time cannot incorporate foster mothers' definitions of fostering, mothering, and family. Little if any effort has even been made to ascertain what foster mothers' perspective is. The ability to define and impose an ideal on others sustains unequal power relations. Once established, this "right," and the contingencies of policy and practice premised on it, must be vigilantly guarded, since it is ultimately about power *over* others. This is a template in which social workers are placed in opposition to foster and biological mothers and children become commodities of trade. What is missing is systemic dialogue in which ideas and realities are exchanged and through a flow of information the definitions and meanings of "family" "work," "woman," "mother," and "child" are negotiated within particular and specific contexts. Within this construction, power over another is redefined as power to effect change, and the social relations of power shift from those of contradiction to those of mutuality.

What has also been missing is an understanding of the way in which contemporary policies and practices are based on ideologies derived from and through a historically specific time period. For example, the economic and emotional exploitation of foster mothers is nothing new. Viviana Zelizer argues that since the inception of payments to boarder mothers in the late nineteenth century, heavy and continuous social emphasis has been placed on maternal affection rather than on payment (1985:169–201). Within nineteenth-century America, payments were either defined as inconsequential to the true cost of raising an orphan and therefore "tokens" of state appreciation, or denounced as "unfortunate" and the women who accepted them publicly condemned. Board payments represented a commodification of motherhood and thereby threatened the "cult of true womanhood" by imposing commercial relations on the highly sentimentalized role.

The construction of social incongruence between payment and motherhood, therefore, stands within a fairly consistent historical tradition. Payment was acceptable if it had low instrumental value, in other words, if it was a token. The underpayment for fostering was associated, within the dominant social discourse, with positive social value. Since the inception of fosterage, women who mothered other people's children for less than adequate compensation have been good women and received social approbation. Adequate compensation, which carried the additional danger of helping women to be instrumentally self-sufficient, has been equated with bad women, with "true woman" gone astray. What is significant is the way this tradition is woven through what Judith Lorber terms "a cultural unconscious" and therefore creates a particular reality. As she suggests, "symbolic language does not just name in ways that praise or denigrate; symbolic language reflects and creates the culture's unconscious" (1994:100).

Unfortunately, unexamined "processes of normalization" have precluded a reflexivity, that is, a critical self-analysis of the ideologies and assumptions governing foster care and the ways they are imposed on others. These processes have also helped eclipse an awareness of power-knowledge relationships and have silenced or ignored those who have challenged the authoritative knowledge of policy makers and policy enforcers. "Systems of authoritative knowledge are constructed in a kind of group consensus-building. There are known penalties for going against these systems; one may be gossiped about, banished, or excluded. Authoritative knowledge seems reasonable, and people continually participate in these systems. As Brigette Jordan says, 'The power of authoritative knowledge is not that it is correct but that it counts'" (1993:153, in Ward, 1996:194).

Substantive systemic change can best be effected through policies that include both an empathic understanding of the meanings care, labor, gender, and selfhood hold for caregivers, and a reflexive analysis of the ideologies and assumptions upon which they are based. Such policies must take into account the way women's individual and gender identities intersect fostering work, as well as the paradigm of mothering foster mothers are establishing through their work. Policies based on a dialectic of gendered work and an ethic of justice are unlikely to reproduce exploitative labor relations in which women's caregiving is regarded as free domestic labor to be appropriated for the state and women are viewed as objectified and devalued workers. In policies thus constructed, "care could be seen as a paradigm or model of social interaction, and *persona carans* could replace *homo economicus* as the individual theorized in social and political theory" (Bubeck, 1995:12).

Recommendations for policy change must take into account the "processes of normalization" that legitimize ultimately painful and exploitative relations between social actors and the policies through and around which social relations are structured. For example, every woman I spoke with, as well as every social worker, made reference to the "bad" foster mother. When I asked what this meant, I was told that this was someone who fostered *for* money and did not care about children. I actively pursued the bad foster mother but did not find her. I found some homes I preferred to be in over others. I found some women I liked more than others. But this was a matter of personal taste rather than of something faulty in their parenting or evil in their motivations. The image of the "bad" foster mother is not a reality but a cultural archetype that exists to sustain the emotional and economic exploitation of women.

What is needed to achieve this change is a different type of thinking, a thinking that can liberate us from these patterns and processes of normalization rather than simply reproduce ideology. The type of thinking that is required at this time is subversive thinking, thinking that defies the traditional rules, practices, procedure, models. This, I believe, is a two-step process. The first step is to look critically at the ways in which social meanings regarding "the family," "women," "children," and "worker" have been constructed both historically and contemporarily, to whom, when, and why. The second step is to begin to revise policy based simultaneously on a micro- and macro-level perspective. The revised policy must incorporate the individual processes, experiences, and meanings fostering holds for individuals like Mrs. Hansen, Lillith K. Anderson, and Ellen McKnight as well as new sociocultural definitions of kinship and gender. Pain emanates when contemporary experiences are abrogated in favor of historical ideals that are obsolete, and when there is no room for tolerance or encouragement of reflexivity.

Women's kinship and mothering claims through fostering have implications for the politics and theories of motherhood and for the sociocultural associations of motherhood. Foster mothers' representations of fostering include texts of family and identity that claim legitimacy for kinship through belonging rather than through reified and patriarchal notions of biological or legal determinism. The ability to offer care and affection and to create kinship networks defines motherhood. Motherhood is also labor that intersects economic need. It is carried out within an economic context. It is work that should, in accordance with women's sense of justice, be economically compensated.

What these women *do* through fostering changes how we *can* think of "family," "motherhood," and "mothering." Policy must be based, not only on their vision, but on their realities. Information and decision making within the current system is unidirectional. It is a one-way street from DCF to foster mothers. What is needed is a reciprocal system of shared information and decision-making power. Sharing information makes possible the inclusion of an alternative understanding of what foster mothers do based on their self-definitions as mothers who engage in the valuable work of building kinship networks to care for children. What changes is the knowledge on which this understanding is based. Policies based on this understanding can lead to practices that support foster mothers rather than antagonize them, that allow foster mothers to support caseworkers rather than work against them.

Second, I propose that the child welfare "system," through the social actors who compose the "system," build into policy and practice a degree of reflexivity. By this I mean that all participants must *become aware* and *stay aware* of their images of and expectations for one another and of the assumptions, values, ideologies, and beliefs on which these expectations are based. This reflexivity includes knowledge of the ways in which gender categories and gender relations are constructed and intersected by social class and ethnicity both historically and in contemporary social relations. Policies based on reflexive knowledge are dynamic rather than static, are subversive rather than sustaining, and can therefore change with those who participate in the dialogue.

# Appendix
## About This Study

### Study Participants

The foster mothers who participated in this study all fostered for the Department of Children and Families, the state agency responsible for child welfare in Connecticut. I collected most of the data on foster mothers through participant observation and intensive informal and semistructured interviews and focus groups over the course of three years from 1993 to 1996. I got my initial sample from a random sample drawn from the database of 1,990 foster mothers the state maintained, and recruited additional women through a convenience sample. Among the women from whom I collected a significant amount of data, the sample was evenly divided between African American and Euro-American women; a very small portion were Hispanic and "other." The majority of women were married. Women's ages ranged from twenty-eight to seventy-eight years old. The number of children women fostered over their careers ranged from none (there were some women who had not yet received any) to 250; the number they "currently fostered" ranged from 0 to 5. Of the children women currently had in their homes, a small proportion were relatives. Study participants also included women who had adopted up to 8 children and those who had adopted none. The length of time children stayed with foster mothers varied from as short as an overnight stay to as long as eight years. Foster mothers also cared for children from a wide range of ages, from birth to late adolescence.

The majority of women in this study were poor or working class. This was true of African American and Euro-American women, though the former were consistently poor whereas some of the Euro-American women appeared to live a solidly middle-class lifestyle, and a few, drawn from very affluent sections of the state, appeared to be quite wealthy. This is not surprising, since Connecticut demographics reflect significant socioeconomic disparity. For example, Connecticut has the highest per capita income of any state in the nation, and yet the poverty rate for African American children has seen some dramatic increases (see Fein, 1990:42). My contention that the majority of foster mothers were poor or working class is consistent with Fein's findings: she reported that 25 percent of foster families had a yearly income of less than $10,000, which was below the federal poverty level for a family of four and that the average median income ranged from $15,000 to $19,999 provided by working-class and blue collar occupations (22–40).

While my findings for the most part are consistent with Fein's relative to socioeconomic status, I did attempt to procure data about foster parents' financial status from the Department of Children and Families. I and my research assistants had numerous frustrating contacts over a period of three years with DCF. Each time we were referred to a different person and different office, and each time were promised data, but none was ever forthcoming. Finally, I was told that information about foster parents' socioeconomic status simply did not exist. In a comment reflective of foster parents' place within the "system," one social worker said, "We don't have that information. Frankly, we never collected that much information about foster parents. We just didn't feel they were that important." Instead I was offered endless data on foster children.

Interviews took place in women's homes and were tape-recorded. Interviews were then transcribed verbatim and coded on Ethnograph or an Ethnograph-like system. I have presented women's language, words, speech cadences, and vernacular exactly as it was spoken to me and transcribed. I have edited slightly some women's speeches, but most editorial changes have been in terms of deleting extraneous phrases (thoughts begun but never finished) or comments that did not affect the meaning of women's messages or alter their speech patterns. In addition I have changed all participants' names and disguised their personal circumstances or appearance so that they could not be identified. I attempted to choose pseudonyms that were consistent with women's ethnicity or real names.

In addition to participant observation and semistructured interviews, I conducted six life history interviews. Most of these were accomplished either in two meetings or in all-day meetings in which I followed the foster mother through a "typical" day, talking and helping her with child care activities. My decision to include life histories has epistemological and methodological relevance. First, I include Mrs. Hansen's and Lillith's life stories, not because they are *representative* of foster mothers or of "American women," but because both women think about and define foster motherhood and motherhood in a certain way, and thus their stories contribute to the definition of fostering within a particular cultural landscape. The stories Mrs. Hansen and Lillith K. Anderson chose to tell, and the way in which they are recorded, are not so much a depiction of a social reality as a social text (Crapanzano, 1984) that offers the reader an opportunity to look closely at the decisions, events, and relationships that shape and define a portion of fostering discourses.

## Reliability and Validity of Cultural Data

Social and behavioral scientists conventionally judge the reliability, validity, and generalizability of findings by reference to classical statistical theory, which requires case-independent samples drawn from a fixed and infinitely sampleable universe. But what I was looking at was very different; the world and meanings foster mothers construct are not fixed but evolving, and thus are not infinitely sampleable. Because people construct meaning through social interactions, cultural data necessarily exhibit case dependence (Handwerker, Hatcheson, and Herbert, 1997:7–9; Handwerker and Wozniak 1997:869–75).

Research on cultural phenomena therefore must focus on historically and regionally specific social interaction through which we create cultural phenomena rather than on particular characteristics or features of experience. This does not make sampling variability go away, but it means that classical tests will not give us the information we need. Research, theory, and methodology must be reoriented to focus on cultural variability between individuals rather than between reified and essentialized groups. This means that we take seriously questions of who agrees with whom about what and to what degree and search for the variability in experience that might explain cultural differences, if and when we identify them (Keesing, 1994:310–13; Handwerker and Wozniak, 1997:869–75).

To assess life experience differences that may have conditioned women's understanding and perspective of fostering, I designed a sample that encompassed the following markers. Each could potentially account for cultural variability. These are (1) ethnicity; (2) age; (3) length of time fostering; (4) marital status; (5) social class; (6) geographic location; (7) number of children fostered; (8) age of children; (9) length of stay of particular children; (10) number of children adopted or in the process of being adopted. My fieldwork experiences suggested two additional sources of potential cultural variability: (1) whether or not a woman fostered children related to her biologically or legally, or (2) whether or not the children she fostered were unrelated to her through these criteria. I then went out and talked with women whose life stories exhibited significant variation in these experiences.

With a few notable exceptions, which I discuss later, foster mothers expressed a high degree of consensus on the core features of foster mothering: how kinship is established through fostering, the permanence of fostering relationships, and the criteria for motherhood (see Handwerker and Wozniak, 1997:869–75). Consensus analysis (e.g., Weller and Romney, 1988) constitutes an explicit test for agreement among informants by applying minimal residuals factor analysis to sets of cultural data adjusted for random variation—drawn from text collected by various forms of informal or semistructured interviews, or from structured interview formats like pile sorts, triads tests, or ranking scales. When we conduct a factor analysis of similarities among what informants have told us, we ask if the responses of each person constitute just one measurement of an unobserved consensus about meaning. If a large proportion of the variance among individuals is explained by a single factor the eigenvalue of which is three or more times larger than that of any other factor (a dramatic scree fall), that constitutes initial evidence of a cultural consensus. Factor loadings tell us how much each informant agrees with the consensus; their average provides a means of measuring the reliability and validity of the identified consensus. The consensus analysis procedure identifies the existence of significant agreement differences by the presence of more than a single major factor. Property-fitting (PROFIT) analysis confirmed that no life experience marker influenced the ways in which foster mothers experienced and configured kin relations. Applying the Spearmen-Brown Prophesy Formula to cases rather than to variables reveals that my findings exhibit reliability and validity scores well over .90.

It is possible that I missed some significant variable bearing on women's life experiences and so created selection bias. But I looked hard, and I asked foster mothers what they thought might condition fostering experiences, and we could not think of any other variables. I infer that the findings I report are generalizable to foster mothers in the state of Connecticut who share the life experiences of the women I spoke to, that is, African American and Euro-American women, old and young women, rich and poor women, women who fostered their kin or nonkin, women who fostered for short-term and long-term placements, and women who fostered all ages of children.

## Unit of Analysis

I chose to focus, for this study, on foster mothers licensed by the state of Connecticut. This focus was theoretically consistent with the aim of the study, which was to investigate the way in which women thought about and enacted a mothering "identity" through foster care. Thus it is an ethnography that examines the significance of gender as a "basic feature of all social life" and understands that social constructions of gender are a basic feature of women's social realities (Reinharz and Davidman 1992:46). The focus on gender was facilitated by state licensing and record-keeping procedures. Even if a woman is married and shares all fostering duties equally with a partner or spouse, in the state of Connecticut it is the woman in the household who is licensed. If there is no woman present, then the male in the household is licensed. What this means is that, for married couples, both husband and wife are required to go to foster parent training, but the license is issued to the woman. Unless there is no woman present in the home, it is only the woman's name that appears on the state database. According to the state database, almost all of the licensed foster parents in the state of Connecticut (90 percent) are female.

However, none of the women developed a sense of mothering or selfhood in a vacuum. Thus, during interviews, I listened for the key players in the women's lives and tried to determine what social relations had shaped and negotiated a mothering identity. For married women, the person most influential in the negotiation of mothering was their partner; therefore a small sample of husbands was included. The consistency and agreement of responses from husbands indicated that a small sample was sufficient (Weller and Romney, 1988). For single women, the social relations through which a mothering identity was most intensely negotiated was often with their adult children, parents, or siblings. It was not possible, because of time and geographic constraints, to interview any unmarried women's close kin or social supports. Instead, all women were asked to talk about the way in which interaction with key individuals shaped and conditioned their thinking about themselves as mothers and their view of mothering.

Foster fathers were also included in this study. In total, eleven foster fathers participated in the interview process: six participated in interviews with their wives, and five were contacted for intensive individual interviews. Contact was made initially through their wives, who acted as gatekeepers. During interviews, women were routinely asked if their husbands or partners would be willing to be interviewed separately. When they answered affirmatively, their partners were contacted. A young Euro-American male research assistant, himself a father, assisted in gathering information from foster fathers. These interviews were also tape recorded and transcribed. I include foster fathers' perspectives and voices throughout the study (1) when both husband and wife were interviewed together and jointly answered interview questions for a particular topic; (2) when the way in which a topic was being discussed by the couple illustrated the negotiation of marital and parental roles and identities; (3) when foster fathers' perspectives helped in some manner to define "mothering" or "parenting" and thus served as an interpretation of "motherhood" (this sometimes occurred when foster fathers talked about or defined "foster fatherhood" or "fatherhood").

Three foster children also participated in the study. They were identified by their foster mothers. All were young women over the age of eighteen. Two were Hispanic and one was Euro-American. I conducted these interviews. Each interview took place during one meeting lasting at least three hours. The interview was usually combined with some activity like going to a shopping mall or out to eat. While it would have been beneficial to include more foster children in this study, it was also highly problematic. Securing permission from the state for minors to participate in the study would have been time-consuming and probably ultimately unsuccessful. Foster mothers, many of whom wanted me to talk to their foster children, were aware that they could lose their licenses for permitting it.

When interviewing the three young women, I asked each of them to reflect on and talk about her experiences in foster care, when and why she entered care, and what she experienced in her foster homes. I also asked her to think about when and if she ever felt like "family" or if she ever felt a sense of belonging while in foster care. Their answers were frank, shocking, and highly illuminating, especially in contrast to the foster mothers' experiences. Two of the three girls reported not feeling at home or feeling like a part of any foster family they lived with. One young woman responded, "You would have to be crazy to let yourself feel like you could belong when you are only a foster girl." These initial findings appear to support earlier research (Fein, 1990; Berridge and Cleaver, 1987) that foster children's tenuous status or their perception of their status as tenuous and impermanent has a significant negative impact on their ability to grow and develop.

Listening to these young women's stories was a powerful experience. Their accounts were nothing short of gut-wrenching. They told of parental abandonment, of physical hunger, of fear and loneliness, of sexual molestation, of feeling like a commodity, of desperation, and of having to make adult decisions at very young ages. Each girl's story was so emotionally traumatic to tell that I became concerned that recounting them in the format I had selected was ultimately harmful. Thus for this study I did not pursue this line of inquiry. I do, however, integrate their comments and experiences into this book, since their voice is a part of the picture, a part of the puzzle, and should be heard.

This study also includes information collected from approximately twenty DCF social workers from four regional offices (Bridgeport, New Haven, Hartford, and Norwich) selected by foster parent and social worker key informants. The social workers included in this sample all had direct contact with foster parents, biological parents, and foster children. Most were caseworkers whose duties included supporting foster families (family support social workers), planning for the permanent resolution of cases (permanency-planning social workers), investigating complaints of abuse or neglect (investigative social workers), and providing ongoing direct casework services to biological families (treatment social workers). One was a supervisor whose duties included the supervision of caseworkers, liaison with foster parents through foster parent training sessions, and emergency casework services when the assigned social worker was unavailable or when a social worker requested additional intervention. And another was a social services assistant whose primary responsibilities lay in providing transportation and case-aide services to foster children.

# Notes

1. I qualify this statement because while the vast majority of women added the children in their care to their kin group, there were some children whose stay in a foster home was so short as to preclude this (for example an overnight or weekend stay), or there were the times when a foster mother had a very difficult time relating to a child in her home for a wide range of reasons, not the least of which was violent, aggressive, or antisocial behavior, and had to request that the child be removed. In these situations, children were not seen as members of the family. Most foster mothers saw a child's removal as a failure to adequately mother the child and felt tremendously guilty. This latter point speaks to the consistently other-centered perspective with which almost all women initiated mothering relationships.

2. Most women said they had experience fostering children who were of a different ethnicity than they. With the exception of one woman, all foster mothers said it really did not matter if the ethnicity of the child and foster family was the same. What was important was a home in which the child could be loved, respected, and well care for. The exception came from an African American woman in her early thirties who felt it was important for African American girls to be placed with an African American family since she could not imagine a white family would know how to do a girl's hair or teach her when the time came how to cook properly.

Several families had adopted children who were of a different ethnic origin then they and reported that the Department of Children and Families insisted on categorizing them as either a "white" or a "Hispanic" or a "black" home when they considered themselves to be "mixed" or a family that was inclusive of all of the above. These categorizations offended their sense of familial identity, and many refused to declare themselves one or the other. Unfortunately, as one mother told me, their refusals carried little weight, since DCF simply assigned an ethnic identity to them. As one mother told me, "John and I are white, OK? And two of our children are white, but Danielle is part Hispanic and black, Darianna's father is Korean, and Lukas is Hispanic. So tell me how you get the idea that we are a 'white' family out of that? We are not. But according to them we are."

3. This should be qualified somewhat. One foster father talked particularly about his experiences as a black man and his contributions to black children and the African American community. It was not that African American women did not have a keen sense that fostering black children was a gift they gave the African American community, but seldom did women foster only children from their communities, and seldom did women see children as belonging to a particular ethnic group. As I was told over and over, "Children are children," meaning that they belonged to those who claimed and nurtured them.

NOTE TO CHAPTER 2

1. Bertie and Sarah's mother is addicted to crack-cocaine. Sarah was born addicted.

NOTES TO CHAPTER 3

1. While grounded in essentialism, foster mothers' discussions of mothering were perhaps more closely related to a Lockian sense of essence in which "nominal essences are not 'discovered' so much as assigned or produced—produced specifically by language" (Fuss, 1989:5) and ultimately culturally constructed. Women were keenly aware of the social and cultural factors that created what a mother was and could be and that inhibited or facilitated their own mothering work. This makes sense since one aspect of fostering work was to actively assert a definition of mothering that contested images of mothering found in social policy, law, and popular culture.

2. This clothing voucher was a one-time payment. If a child entered another foster home, during another season of the year, there was no second voucher that could be issued. Many women complained about this, since it was not uncommon for children to be in more than one foster home during their stay in care (according to the Legislative Program Review and Investigations Committee study, 58 percent of children were in two or more homes). Since children grew and seasons changed, it was possible and often the case that children arrived in a home with few clothes that fit or that were appropriate to the season. The burden of completely outfitting a child often fell to the receiving foster mother. In addition, reimbursement checks often took several weeks to be issued. For women whose income level allowed them some safety net and thus some additional money, providing for children was not always a grievous hardship. For those with very little disposable income, it was difficult if not impossible to provide new clothes. In response, many women created clothes banks

in their homes where they stored secondhand clothes that had been given to them or that previous foster children had outgrown, developed good working relationships with secondhand store vendors in their areas where they might get a price break or free clothes for foster children, or actively exchanged clothes with other women. Even when the reimbursement checks arrived, the money was to cover so many expenses, and the price of new clothing was so high, that most women contended that there was little extra for a lot of new clothes.

3. I am well aware that, according to DCF policy, foster care reimbursements are not designed to be a "salary" for women. Instead they are simply intended to cover a woman's child-rearing costs. However, foster mothers expressed the view that if you looked at the money as a salary (and clearly some did), then it was insufficient.

4. Mrs. Gordon was referring to the relationship that develops between biological parents and foster parents. In her view of fostering, this relationship is a supportive one and is often lost when a child returns home.

5. Foster mothers were frequently given "administrative exception" to take more children than they were licensed for. This was often done to keep sibling groups together, but meant that foster mothers were operating over capacity.

6. I say theoretically because I encountered several women who had specified short-term or emergency placements, with an understanding that most of the time these placements would be no more than two weeks, and who wound up having a child live with them for over a year. In most cases, short-term or emergency placements happened when a child was removed from his/her family of origin precipitously owing in most cases to an emergency, such as the detection of physical or sexual abuse, the death of a sibling, or abandonment. Short-term placements offered a place to put a child immediately, until a long-term placement, that is, one that could accommodate any of the child's or family's special needs, could be found.

7. According to policy, payments to foster parents in Connecticut are a reimbursement for expenses foster parents would naturally incur while caring for a child. Until very recently, foster parents were reimbursed only about 70 percent of the cost of raising a child. Currently, payments cover 100 percent of the USDA estimates for raising a child.

8. This was a point of contention among many poor foster parents. In terms of actual dollars, the amount of money one receives through AFDC per child is lower than foster care rates. Many relatives wanted to receive the DCF regular foster care rate since this would help their financial situation and were upset to learn that since they received AFDC for some of their children, the foster children would also receive AFDC.

NOTE TO CHAPTER 4

1. While there were definitely biological families who did not want contact with foster families, and foster families who did not want contact with children's biological families, it could be argued that DCF policies and practices, and the constructs of biological mothers and foster mothers upon which they were premised, intentionally created a hostile or competitive relationship between the two. Foster mothers were seldom looked at by DCF as a resource for biological parents. Nor were they incorporated with any regularity that I could discern into case treatment plans.

NOTES TO CHAPTER 5

1. I specify only ethnicity here since my data suggest that socioeconomic status, age, religion, and geographic location in terms of rural, urban, or suburban were not conditioning variables. That is to say, middle-class or wealthy Euro-American foster mothers who lived in the suburbs had the same complaints and experiences as poor Euro-American women living in rural or urban settings.

2. While the majority of women's comments, like these, were negative, there was some variation conditioned by two variables. One was geographic location. Those women in rural locations who dealt with smaller DCF offices generally had somewhat more positive things to say about the agency and its social workers. They tended to see themselves in partnership with DCF and relied on it for material resources. They tended to have positive and frequent communication with the social workers and were informed about the child's case disposition and treatment plans. Generally, those women who lived in urban settings who dealt with large DCF offices tended to have a more negative impression of the agency and have a poorer relationship with DCF personnel than their rural counterparts. These women tended to see social workers as overburdened, inept, or incapable of assisting them in any real way. Communication was infrequent, and several women were not sure who their child's social worker was or how to reach him or her. They expressed frustration at not knowing or not agreeing with the child's treatment plan.

The second factor was ethnicity. Those women dealing with DCF in rural offices were all Euro-American, middle class, with some post-high-school education. In other words, in terms of demographics, they resembled the social workers with whom they worked. Those women who dealt with social workers from urban offices tended to be African American. Social workers tended to be Euro-American. Urban-living African American women tended to see DCF as a hostile and confusing bureaucracy that could not help and social workers as malevolent.

3. This response to DCF, that is, marginalization, in combination with poor foster-mother-DCF communication, often led to women's literally raising children with no DCF support. For example, in my sample, one woman did not know the child had a social worker, another woman did not know that the child had a social worker and did not receive money, a third had a child for seven years without state intervention, and several women fostered children they received as infants and raised until they were two or three years old before they had any contact from the social worker. In several cases women were asked to adopt the children because they had been with the family for so long. Several others had minimal state contact—and did not know that the state was working toward the release of the child to adoption until they were called, by their estimation, "out of the blue," and told to get the child ready to visit its prospective parents.

4. I was aware that agency policies had been amended to require social workers to have weekly or monthly case reviews of children in care and regular contact with foster mothers. However, while this was the policy, I was also aware from social workers how difficult it was to carry out and from foster mothers how frequent was the incidence of noncontact.

5. A small sample of women who had returned their license were contacted over the telephone. Their reasons for leaving the system were most often related to a particular incident. However, the context of their dissatisfaction was the same as for women who maintained their licenses.

NOTES TO CHAPTER 6

1. Data analysis reveals that the theme of transformation is prominent in women's discourses about their foster children (see Wozniak, 1999). This is part of the discourse of inalienability. Through the foster-mother/foster-child relationship, the child is transformed from a state child or a "broken" condition to something else. This something else, in terms of health, behavior, appearance, demeanor, all become a part of what is recognizable as familial and is an important part of adding the child to the family. This is especially so since many of the foster child's outward behaviors or actions and even appearance initially appear foreign or unacceptable within the foster family.

2. This statement is based on the mother's past history of conducting visits only while she is in jail, and the state's long-term plan to terminate her parental rights.

3. This mother had a very limited formal education. Writing was not an easy task for her, and documenting phone calls by hand was laborious. She was also quite poor and had to incur the expense of driving back and forth to DCF offices and paying for toll calls.

NOTES TO CHAPTER 7

1. It should be noted that the study sample may skew this finding. These women were "system survivors." The vast majority of them had fostered for more than two years. Most women who leave fostering do so after the first year. Thus, there was something about these women that made them stay or something about other women that made them leave.

2. Deleah's experiences with foster children and with the Department of Children and Families are not unusual. It should be noted, however, that of those who fostered relatives, two African American and no white women had difficulty getting DCF to pay the reimbursement fee. Deleah attributed this to the fact that she was black. As she noted, the lack of payment, rapport, or emotional support from DCF coupled with her suspicion of racial stigmatization intensified her stress and made fostering that much more difficult.

NOTES TO CHAPTER 9

1. These field notes, written in 1996, were revised at the time I wrote this chapter. I made them considerably shorter by editing out many of the more tangential thoughts and reflections I had included when I initially wrote them. Many of these thoughts were about my own experiences with my foster daughter. In general, I used my field notes as an opportunity to reflect on the things I felt and experienced during my research. Many of the things I witnessed or participated in with women were very moving, and I found it imperative for my own survival to have a way and a place to vent my feelings. Many of these experiences, like those at Lillith's house, reminded me of my own foster daughter and rekindled my sense of loss, and thus these notes, at times, read more like a diary than "typical" field notes. I also took out some thoughts that Lillith did not want to have included in the final version of this text. These were some of my reflections about her and Arielle's relationship. Some things she said I had simply gotten "wrong." Other things she simply did not feel comfortable with and so they were removed.

NOTES TO CHAPTER 10

1. This comment refers to a DCF policy of placing children in a physical environment similar to the one they knew often with respect to social class and until recently to ethnicity. That is, if a child comes from a low-income family, policy states that the child will feel more comfortable in a similar environment. If a child is Hispanic, social workers are to seek a Hispanic home.

2. Until very recently, policy specified that foster parents and children should be of the same ethnicity. This policy changed with a change in law.

NOTES TO CHAPTER 11

1. For examples of this type of portrayal of foster mothers and fostering in the social work literature see Urquart, 1989; Kates et al., 1991; Ryan and Mc-Fadden, 1987; Meadowcraft, Thomlinson, and Chamberlain, 1994; Fein, 1990; Tinney, 1985; Berman, 1986; Dando and Minty, 1987; Burke and Dawson, 1987; Wells and D'Angelo, 1994; Humphrey and Humphrey, 1988; Kaplan, 1988; Pasztor, 1985; Dubowitz, Feigelman, and Zuravin, 1993; Wiehe, 1983; Portz, 1982; Fanshel, 1966; Krause, 1991; Tomlinson, 1991; Benedict and White, 1991; Levine, 1988; Berrick and Barth, 1994; Berrick, Barth, and Needell, 1994; Meezan and Shireman, 1982; Rosenthal, Bombeck, and Schmidt, 1988; Carbino, 1991, 1992; Sprey-Wissing and Portz, 1982; Hampson and Tavormina, 1980; Soliday, McCluskey-Fawcett, and Meck, 1994; Hegar, 1993; Smith and Smith, 1990; Miller, 1998; Smith, 1991; Meyer, 1985; Lie and McMurtry, 1991.

# References

Ardener, S., ed. 1981. Women and space. New York: St. Martin's Press.

Barthes, R. 1978. A lover's discourse: Fragments. Translated by Richard Howard. New York: Hill and Wang.

Bassin, D. 1994. Maternal subjectivity in the culture of nostalgia: Mourning and Memory. *In* Representations of Motherhood, ed. D. Bassin, M. Honey, and M. Kaplan. New Haven: Yale University Press.

Belk, R. 1988. Possessions and the extended self. *Journal of Consumer Research* 15:139–60.

Belk, R., Wallendorf, M., and Sherry, J. 1989. The sacred and the profane in consumer behavior: Theodicy on the Odyssey. *Journal of Consumer Research* 16:1–38.

Belk, R. W., and Coon, G. S. 1993. Gift giving as agapic love: An alternative to the exchange paradigm based on dating experiences. *Journal of Consumer Research* 20:393–417.

Bellingham, B. 1984. Little wanderers: A socio-historical study of the nineteenth-century origins of child fostering and adoption reform, based on early records of the New York Children's Aid Society. Ph.D. diss., University of Pennsylvania.

Benedict, M., and White, R. 1991. Factors associated with foster care length of stay. *Child Welfare* 70, no. 1:45–58.

Berman, L. 1986. Foster parents as a resource in preparing children for placement. *Adoption and Fostering* 10, no. 2:14–24.

Bernauer, J. W. 1990. Michel Foucault's Force of flight: Toward an ethic for thought. Atlantic Highland, N.J.: Humanities Press International.

Berrick, J. D. 1995. Emerging issues in child welfare. *Public Welfare* 53 (fall): 4–11.

Berrick, J. D., and Barth, R. P. 1994. Research on kinship foster care: What do we know? Where do we go from here? *Child and Youth Services Review* 16, nos. 1/2:1–5.

Berrick, J. D., and Barth, R. P., and Needell, B. 1994. A comparison of kinship foster homes and foster family homes: Implications for kinship foster care as family preservation. *Child and Youth Services Review* 16, nos. 1/2: 33–63.

Berridge, D., and Cleaver, H. 1987. Foster home breakdown. Oxford: Basil Blackwell.

Bledsoe, C. 1990. The politics of children: fosterage and the social management of fertility among the Mende of Sierra Leone. *In* Births and power: Social change and the politics of reproduction, ed. W. P. Handwerker. Boulder, Colo.: Westview Press.

Brockman, T. 1987. The Western family and individuation: Convergence with Caribbean patterns. *Journal of Comparative Family Studies* 18, no. 3: 471–80.

Bubeck, D. 1995. Care, gender, and justice. Oxford: Clarendon Press.

Burke, M., and Dawson, T. 1987. Temporary care foster parents: Motives and issues of separation and loss. *Child and Adolescent Social Work* 4, nos. 3 and 4:178–86.

Campion, M. J. 1995. Who's fit to be a parent? New York: Routledge.

Carbino, R. 1991. Advocacy for foster families in the United States facing child abuse allegations: How social agencies and foster parents are responding to the problem. *Child Welfare* 70, no. 2:131–49.

———. 1992. Policy and practice for response to foster families when child abuse or neglect is reported. *Child Welfare* 71, no. 6:497–509.

Carrier, J. 1991. Gifts in a world of commodities: The ideology of the perfect gift in American society. *Social Analysis* 29:19–37.

———. 1993. The rituals of Christmas giving. *In* Unwrapping Christmas, ed. Daniel Miller. Oxford: Clarendon.

Castle, S. 1996. Current intergenerational impact of child fostering on children's nutritional status in rural Mali. *Human Organization* 55, no. 2:193–205.

Cheney, C., and Adams, G. 1978. Lay healing and mental health in the Mexican-American barrio. *In* Modern medicine and medical anthropology in the United States–Mexico border population, ed. B. Velimirovic. Pan-American Health Organization Scientific Publication, no. 359.

Children's Defense Fund. 1992. State of the children. Washington, D.C.: Children's Defense Fund.

Clark, J. 1996. Public nightmares and communitarian dreams: The crisis of the social in social welfare. *In* Consumption matters: The production and experience of consumption, ed. Stephen Edgell, Kevin Hetherington, and Alan Warde. Oxford: Blackwell.

Clark, M. 1970. Health in the Mexican-American culture. Berkeley: University of California Press.

Cohen, A. 1994. Self consciousness: An alternative anthropology of identity. New York: Routledge.

Collins, P. H. 1990. Black feminist thought: Knowledge, consciousness, and the politics of empowerment. New York: Unwin Hyman/Routledge.

———. 1994. Shifting the center: Race, class, and feminist theorizing about motherhood. *In* Mothering: Ideology, experience, and agency, ed. E. N. Glenn, G. Chang, and L. Forcey. New York: Routledge.

Crapanzano, V. 1984. Life-histories. *American Anthropologists* 86:51–74.

Dando, I., and Minty, B. 1987. What makes good foster parents? *British Journal of Social Work* 17, no. 4:383–99.

Dinnage, R., and Pringle, M. 1967. Foster home care: Facts and fallacies. London: Longman.

Douglas, M. 1973. Rules and meanings: The anthropology of everyday knowledge. Harmonsworth, England: Penguin Education.

———. 1975. Implicit meanings: Essays in anthropology. London: Routledge.

Dubowitz, H., Feigelman, S., and Zuravin, S. 1993. A profile of kinship care. *Child Welfare* 72, no. 2:153–69.

Eastman, K. 1979. The foster family in a systems theory perspective. *Child Welfare* 58, no. 9:564–70.

———. 1982. Foster parenthood: A nonnormative parenting arrangement. *Marriage and Family Review* 5, no. 2:95–120.

Edelman, H. 1994. Motherless daughters: The legacy of loss. New York: Delta Books.

Edelstein, S. 1981. When foster children leave: Helping foster parents to grieve. *Child Welfare* 29, no. 7:467–73.

Ellerston, C. 1994. The department of health and human service's foster care review system needs a major overhaul. *Children and Youth Services Review* 16, nos. 5/6:433–44.

Ennew, J. 1982. Family structure, unemployment and child labour in Jamaica. *Development and Change* 13, no. 4:551–63.

Fanshel, D. 1966. Foster parenthood: A role analysis. Minneapolis: University of Minnesota Press.

Fein, E. 1990. No more partings: An examination of long-term foster family care. Washington, D.C.: Child Welfare League of America.

Fuss, D. 1989. Essentially speaking: feminism, nature, and difference. New York: Routledge.

Gailey, C. 1987. Evolutionary perspectives on gender hierarchy. *In* Analyzing Gender, ed. M. Ferree and B. Hess. Newbury Park, Calif.: Sage.

———. 1995. Making kinship in the wake of history: Gendered violence and older children adoption. Paper presented at American Anthropological Association, Washington, D.C.

General Accounting Office. 1995. Foster care: Health needs of many young children are unknown and unmet. Leter Report. Blue Book Report. Washington, D.C.: Hubert H. Humphrey Institute of Public Affairs.

Glenn, E. N. 1994. Social constructions of mothering: A thematic overview. *In* Mothering: Ideology, experience, and agency, ed. E. N. Glenn, G. Chang, and L. Forcey. New York: Routledge.

Goerge, R., Wulczyn, F., and Fanshel, D. 1994. A foster care research agenda for the'90s. *Child Welfare* 73, no. 5:525–49.

Goffman, E. 1986. Stigma: Notes on the management of spoiled identity. New York: Simon and Schuster.

Goldman, R. 1992. Reading ads socially. New York: Routledge.

Goody, E. 1975. Delegation and parental roles in West Africa and the West Indies. *In* Changing social structure in Ghena. London: International African Institute.

Gordon, L. 1982. Why nineteenth-century feminists did not support birth control and twentieth-century feminists do: Feminism, reproduction, and the family. *In* Rethinking the family, ed. B. Thorne and M. Yalom. New York: Longman.

———. 1989. Heros of their own lives: The politics and history of family violence in Boston, 1880–1960. New York: Penguin.

———. 1990. Women and the welfare state. Madison: University of Wisconsin Press.

———. 1994. Pitied but not entitled: Single mothers and the history of welfare. New York: Free Press.

Gordon, S. W. 1987. I go to 'Tanties': The economic significance of child-shifting in Antigua West Indies. *Journal of Comparative Family Studies* 73, no. 3:427–43.

Hampson, R., and Tavormina, J. B. 1980. Special foster care for exceptional children: A review of progress and policies. *Children and Youth Services Review* 10, no. 1:19–41.

Handwerker, W. P., Hatcheson, P., and Herbert, D. 1997. Sampling guidelines for cultural data. *Cultural Anthropology Methods* 8:7–9.

Handwerker, W. P., and Wozniak, D. F. 1997. Sampling strategies fore the collection of cultural data. *Current Anthropology* 38, no. 5:869–75.

Haraway, D. 1989. The biopolitics of postmodern bodies: Determinations of self in immune system discourse. *Differences* 1, no. 1:3–43.

Hegar, R. 1993. Assessing attachment, permanence, and kinship in choosing permanent homes. *Child Welfare* 72, no. 4:367–78.

Helman, C. 1984. Culture, health, and illness: An introduction for health care practitioners. Bristol, England: John Wright.

Herrick, J. 1983. The symbolic roots of three potent Iroquois medicinal plants. *In* The anthropology of medicine, ed. L. Romanucci-Ross, D. E. Moerman, and L. R. Tancredi. New York: Praeger.

Hessle, S. 1989. Families falling apart: A report from social services. *Child Welfare* 68, no. 2:209–13.

Hoecklin, L. 1998. 'Equal but different'? Welfare, gender ideology, and a 'mothers' centre' in southern Germany. *In* The anthropology of welfare, ed. I. Edgar and A. Russell. New York: Routledge.

Holloran, P. C. 1989. Boston's wayward children: Social services for homeless children, 1830–1930. Toronto: Associated University Presses.

Humphrey, M., and Humphrey, H. 1988. Families with a difference: Varieties of surrogate parenthood. London: Routledge.

Jewell, S. K. 1993. From mammy to Miss America and beyond: Cultural images and the shaping of U.S. social policy. New York: Routledge.

Jones, E. 1984. Social stigma: The psychology of marked relationships. New York: W. H. Freeman.

Jordan, B. 1993. Birth in four cultures: A cross-cultural investigation of childbirth in Yucatan, Holland, Sweden, and the United States. 4th ed. Revised and expanded by Robbie-Davis Floyd. Prospect Heights, Ill.: Waveland Press.

Jordan, T. E. 1987. Victorian childhood: Themes and variations. Albany: SUNY Press.

Kaplan, C. P. 1988. The biological children of foster parents in the foster family. *Child and Adolescent Social Work* 5, no. 4:281–99.

Kaplan, B., and Seitz, M. 1980. The practical guide to foster family care. Springfield: Charles C. Thomas.

Kates, W., Johnson, R., Rader, M., and Strieder, F. 1991. Whose child is this? Assessment and treatment of children in foster care. *American Journal of Orthopsychiatry* 61, no. 4:584–91.

Katz Rothman, B. 1994. Beyond mothers and fathers: Ideology in a patriarchal society. *In* Mothering: Ideology, experience, and agency, ed. E. W. Glenn, G. Chang, and L. R. Forcey. New York: Routledge.

Keesing, R. 1994. Theories of culture revisited. *In* Assessing cultural anthropology, ed. R. Borofsky. New York: McGraw Hill.

Kleinman, A. 1980. Patients and healers in the context of culture: An exploration of the borderland between anthropology, medicine, and psychiatry. Berkeley: University of California Press.

Kline, D., and Overstreet, H. 1972. Foster care of children: Nurture and treatment. New York: Columbia University Press.

Kopytoff, I. 1986. The cultural biography of things: Commoditization as process. *In* The social life of things: commodities in cultural perspective, ed. Arjun Appadurai. New York: Cambridge University Press. 64–91.

Krause, C. A. 1991. Grandmothers, mothers, and daughters: Oral histories of three generations of ethnic women in America. Boston: Twayne.

Landsman, G. 1999. Does God give special kids to special parents? Personhood and the child with disabilities as gift and as giver. *In* Transformative motherhood: On giving and getting in a consumer culture, ed. L. Layne. New York: New York University Press.

Lange, G., and Rodman, H. 1990. Family relationships and patterns of childrearing in the Caribbean. *In* Kinship and class in the West Indies: A genealogical study of Jamaica and Guyana, ed. R. Smith. Chicago: University of Chicago Press.

Layne, L., ed. 1999. Transformative motherhood: On giving and getting in a consumer culture. New York: New York University Press.

—. 2000. "He was a real baby with baby things": A material cultural analysis of personhood, parenthood, and pregnancy loss. *Journal of Material Culture 5*, no. 3:321–45.

Leach, E. R. 1967. A runaway world? London: Oxford University Press.

Levine, K. 1988. The placed child examines the quality of parental care. *Child Welfare 67*, no. 4:301–10.

Lewin, E. 1981. Lesbianism and motherhood: Implications for child custody. *Human Organization 40*, no. 1:6–14.

—. 1993. Lesbian mothers: Accounts of gender in American culture. Ithaca: Cornell University Press.

Lie, G., and McMurtry, S. 1991. Foster care for sexually abused children: A comparative study. *Child Abuse and Neglect 15*:111–21.

Litman, T. J. 1979. The family in health and health care: A social-behavioral overview. *In* Patients, Physicians, and Illness, ed. E. G. Jaco. 3d ed. New York: Free Press. 69–110.

Lorber, J. 1994. Paradoxes of gender. New Haven: Yale University Press.

Lovell, A. 1983. Some questions of identity: Late miscarriage, stillbirth, and perinatal loss. *Social Science and Medicine 17*, no. 11:755–62.

LPRIC (Legislative Program Review and Investigations Committee). 1991. Department of children and youth services: Child protective services. Hartford, Conn.

—. 1995. Department of children and families: Foster care. Hartford, Conn.

Maluccio, A. N., Warsh, R., and Pine, B. A. 1993. Family reunification: An overview. *In* Together again: Family reunification in foster care. n.p.: Washington, D.C.: Child Welfare League of America.

Manzanedo, H. G., Walters, E. G., and Lorig, K. R. 1980. Health and illness perceptions of the Chicano. *In* Twice a minority: Mexican-American women, ed. M. B. Melville. St. Louis: C. V. Mosby.

Martinez, C., and Martin, H. 1979. Folk diseases among urban Mexican-Americans: Etiology, symptoms, and treatment. *In* Culture, curers, and contagion, ed. N. Klein. Novato, Cal.: Chandler and Sharp.

McClain, C. S. 1995. Women as healers: Cross-cultural perspectives. New Brunswick, N.J.: Rutgers University Press.

McFadden, E., and Ryan, P. 1991. Maltreatment in family foster homes: Dynamics and dimensions. *Child and Youth Services 5*, no. 2:209–231.

Meadowcraft, P., Thomlinson, B., and Chamberlain, P. 1994. Treatment foster care services: A research agenda for child welfare. *Child Welfare 73*, no. 5:565–81.

Meezan, W., and Shireman, J. 1982. Foster parent adoption: A literature review. *Child Welfare* 61 (Nov./Dec.):525–35.

Meyer, C.1985. A feminist perspective on foster family care: A redefinition of the categories. *Child Welfare* 64, no. 3:249–58.

Meyers, D. 1994. Subjection and subjectivity. New York: Routledge.

Miller, D. 1998. Material cultures: Why some things matter. Chicago: University of Chicago Press.

Miller, J. 1991. Child welfare and the role of women: A feminist perspective. *American Journal of Orthopsychiatry* 61, no. 4:592–98.

Modell, J. 1994. Kinship with strangers: Adoption and interpretations of kinship in American culture. Berkeley: University of California Press.

Moore, H. 1988. Feminism and anthropology. Minneapolis: University of Minnesota Press.

Mullings, L. 1994. On our own terms: Race, class, and gender in the lives of African American women. New York: Routledge.

Papell, C., and Skolnik, L. 1992. The reflective practitioner: A contemporary paradigm's relevance for social work education. *Journal of Social Work Education* 28, no. 1 (winter):18–26.

Pasztor, E. 1985. Permanency planning and foster parenting: Implications for recruitment, selection, training, and retention. *Children and Youth Services Review* 7, nos. 2–3:191–205.

Portz, P. 1982. Some aspects of identity problems in foster families. *Journal of Comparative Family Studies* 13, no. 2 (summer):231–35.

Ragone, H. 1999. The gift of life: Surrogate motherhood, gamete donation, and construction of altruism. *In* Transformative motherhood: On giving and getting in a consumer culture, ed. L. Layne. New York: New York University Press.

Rapp, R. 1982. Family and class in contemporary America: Notes toward and understanding of ideology. *In* Rethinking the family: Some feminist questions, ed. B. Thorne and M. Yalom. New York: Longman. 168–87.

Reinharz, S., and Davidman, L. 1992. Feminist methods in social research. New York: Oxford University Press.

Reiter, R., ed. 1975. Toward an anthropology of women. New York: Monthly Review Press.

Riis, J. 1971. How the other half lives. New York: Dover.

Rosenthal, R., Bombeck, B., and Schmidt, D. 1988. Parents' views of adoption disruption. *Children and Youth Services Review* 10, no. 2:119–30.

Rosenwald, G., and Ochenberg, R., eds. 1992. Storied lives: The cultural politics of self-understanding. New Haven: Yale University Press.

Ruddick, S. 1980. Maternal thinking. *Feminist Studies* 6, no. 3:343–67.

———. 1994. Thinking mothers/conceiving birth. *In* Representations of motherhood, ed. D. Bassin, M. Honey, and M. Kaplan. New Haven: Yale University Press.

Ryan, P., and McFadden, E. J. 1987. The role of foster parents in helping young people develop emancipation skills. *Child Welfare* 67, no. 6:563–72.

Schneider, D. 1980. American kinship: A cultural account. Englewood Cliffs, N. J.: Prentice Hall.

Schon, D. 1983. The reflective practitioner. New York: Basic Books.

Scott, J. C. 1990. Domination and the art of resistance: Hidden transcripts. New Haven: Yale University Press.

Silk, J. 1987. Adoption and fosterage in human societies: Adaptations or enigmas? *Cultural Anthropology* 2, no. 1:39–49.

Smith, B. 1991. Australian women and foster care: A feminist perspective. *Child Welfare* 70, no. 2:175–84.

Smith, B., and Smith, T. 1990. For love and money: Women as foster mothers. *Affilia* 5, no. 1:66–80.

Soliday, E., McCluskey-Fawcett, K., and Meck, N. 1994. Foster mothers' stress, coping, and social support in parenting drug-exposed and other at-risk toddlers. *Children's Health Care* 23, no. 1:14–24.

Spector, R. 1979. Cultural diversity in health and illness. New York: Appleton-Century-Crofts.

Speizman, M. D. 1981. Child care: A mirror of human history. *Children and Youth Services Review* 3:213–32.

Sprey-Wessing, T., and Portz, P. 1982. Some aspects of identity problems in foster families. *Journal of Comparative Family Studies* 13, no. 2:29–37.

Stack, C. 1979. All our kin. New York: Harper and Row.

Stack, C., and Burton, L. 1994. Kinscripts: Reflections on family, generation, and culture. *In* Mothering: Ideology, experience, and agency, ed. E. N. Glenn, G. Chang, and L. Forcey. New York: Routledge.

Steinhauer, P. 1991. The foster care service system. *In* The least detrimental alternative. Toronto: University of Toronto Press.

Tinney, M. 1985. Role perceptions in foster parent associations in British Columbia. *Child Welfare* 64, no. 1:73–79.

Tomlinson, B. 1991. Family continuity and stability of care: Critical elements in treatment foster care programs. *Community Alternatives* 3, no. 2:1–18.

Urquart, L. 1989. Separation and loss: Assessing the impacts on foster parent retention. *Child and Adolescent Social Work* 6, no. 3:193–209.

Ward, M. 1996. A world full of women. Needham Heights, Mass.: Allyn and Bacon.

Weick, A. 1993. Reconstructing social work education. *In* Revisioning social work education: A social constructionist approach, ed. J. Laird. New York: Haworth Press.

Weiner, A. 1992. Inalienable possessions: The paradox of keeping-while-giving. Berkeley: University of California Press.

Weller, S. C., and Romney, R. K. 1988. Systematic data collection. *Qualitative Research Methods,* vol. 10. Newbury Park, Calif.: Sage.

Wells, K., and D'Angelo, L. 1994. Specialized foster care: Voices from the field. *Social Service Review* (March):127–44.

Wiehe, V. 1983. Foster mothers: Are they unique? *Psychological Report* 53, no 3:1215–18.

Wozniak, D. 1995a. Some experiences of loss and bereavement by U.S. foster mothers. Paper presented at the meeting of the Society for Applied Anthropology, Albuquerque.

———. 1995b. Angry candy: Child care, child value, and child fosterage in the United States during the nineteenth century. Unpublished manuscript.

———. 1996. Abused kids need lots of help. Op-ed. *Hartford Courant* 157:130.

———. 1997. Foster mothers in America: Objectification, sexualization, commodification. *Women's History Review* 6, no. 3:357–66.

———. 1999. Gifts and burdens: The social and familial context of foster mothering. *In* Transformative mothering: On giving and getting in a consumer culture, ed. L. Layne. New York: New York University Press.

Young, K., Wolkowitz, C., and McCullagh, R., eds. 1981. Of marriage and the market: Women's subordination internationally and its lessons. Boston: Routledge and Kegan Paul.

Zelizer, V. A. 1985. Pricing the priceless child: The changing social value of children. Princeton: Princeton University Press.

# Index

# About the Author

Danielle F. Wozniak is Assistant Research Professor of Anthropology at the University of Connecticut, where she teaches part-time. She lives with her husband and daughter in Connecticut and is a former foster mother.